Endangered Wildlife and Plants of the World

Volume 12
UMB–ZOR

Marshall Cavendish
New York • London • Toronto • Sydney

Marshall Cavendish Corporation
99 White Plains Road
Tarrytown, NY 10591-9001

Created by Brown Partworks Ltd.
Editor: Anne Hildyard
Associate Editors: Paul Thompson, Amy Prior
Managing Editor: Tim Cooke
Design: Whitelight
Picture Research: Helen Simm
Index Editor: Kay Ollerenshaw
Production Editor: Matt Weyland
Illustrations: Barbara Emmons, Jackie Harland, Tracy Williamson

Library of Congress Cataloging-in-Publication Data

Endangered wildlife and plants of the world
p.cm.
Includes bibliographical references (p.).
ISBN 0-7614-7194-4 (set)
ISBN 0-7614-7206-1 (vol. 12)
1. Endangered species--Encyclopedias. I. Marshall Cavendish Corporation.

QH75.E68 2001
333.95'22'03--dc21
99-086194

Printed in Malaysia
Bound in the United States of America
07 06 05 04 03 02 01 00 7 6 5 4 3 2 1

Photo Credits

Cover: Armagosa Vole: Ardea London Ltd, B. "Moose" Peterson
Title page: Cyclades Blunt-Nosed Viper: Suzanne L. Collins
Contents page: (t) Still Pictures, Michel Gunther, (c) Corbis, Susan Middleton & David Liitschwager, (b) Natural History Photographic Library, Martin Harvey

American Fisheries Society: John N. Rinne/U.S.F.W.S. 1682; Heather Angel: 1594; Peter Arnold Inc.: John Cancalosi 1671; Doug Cheeseman 1640; Tom Mangelsen 1683; Luiz C. Marigo 1596; Steven Morello 1636; C. Allan Morgan 1632, 1642, 1647, Gunter Ziesler 1688; Ardea London Ltd.: B. "Moose" Peterson 1609; Erwin & Peggy Bauer: 1663, 1665, 1670; Cincinatti Zoo: 1695, 1696; Bruce Coleman Inc.: Eric Dragesco 1686; Kenneth W. Fink 1591; C.C. Lockwood 1674; Nancy Simmerman 1634; Suzanne L. Collins: 1599; Corbis: Richard Bickel 1606; Raymond Gehman 1648; Susan Middleton & David Liitschwager 1595; Phil Schermeister 1660; Tom George: 1621; Robert & Linda Mitchell: 1638;

Natural History Photographic Agency: Anthony Bannister 1710; G.I. Bernard 1706; Martin Harvey 1692, 1699, 1722; B. Jones & M. Shimlock 1715, 1716; Stephen J. Krasemann 1716; Kevin Schafer 1713; Lady Philippa Scott 1700; Daniel Zupanc 1703; New Hampshire Fish & Game Dept: John F. Scarola 1655; B. "Moose" Peterson: 1605; Warren D. Thomas: 1668, 1690; VIREO: J.H. Dick 1615; Steven Holt 1603, 1677; G. Lasley 1617; R. Roby/K. Brink 1618; Wildlife Conservation Society (H.Q. at the Bronx Zoo): Bill Meng 1611; Zoological Society of San Diego: 1628, 1652; Ron Garrison 1597, 1598

Cover: Armagosa Vole. Ardea London Ltd, B. "Moose" Peterson
Title Page: Cyclades Blunt-Nosed Viper. Suzanne L. Collin
Contents page: (t) Simien Fox. Still Pictures, Michel Gunther, (c) Large-Fruited Sand Verbena. Corbis, Susan Middleton & David Liitschwager, (b) Angonoka. Natural History Photographic Library, Martin Harvey

TABLE OF CONTENTS/VOLUME 12

ESA and IUCN

In this set of endangered animals and plants, each species, where appropriate, is given an ESA status and an IUCN status. The sources consulted to determine the status of each species are the Endangered Species List maintained by the U.S. Fish and Wildlife Service and the Red Lists compiled by IUCN–The World Conservation Union, which is a worldwide organization based in Switzerland.

ENDANGERED SPECIES ACT

The Endangered Species Act (ESA) was initially passed by the U.S. Congress in 1973, and reauthorized in 1988. The aim of the ESA is to rescue species that are in danger of extinction due to human action and to conserve the species and their ecosystems. Endangered plants and animals are listed by the U.S. Fish and Wildlife Service (USFWS), which is part of the Department of Interior. Once a species is listed, the USFWS is required to develop recovery plans, and ensure that the threatened species is not further harmed by any actions of the U.S. government or U.S. citizens. The act specifically forbids the buying, selling, transporting, importing, or exporting of any listed species. It also bans the taking of any listed species in the U.S. and its territories, on both private and public lands. Violators can face heavy fines or imprisonment. However, the ESA requires that the protection of the species is balanced with economic factors.

The ESA recognizes two categories of risk for species:

Endangered: A species that is in danger of extinction throughout all or a significant part of its range.

Threatened: A species that is likely to become endangered in the foreseeable future.

RECOVERY

Recovery takes place when the decline of the endangered or threatened species is halted or reversed, and the circumstances that caused the threat have been removed. The ultimate aim is the recovery of the species to the point where it no longer requires protection under the act.

Recovery can take a long time. Because the decline of the species may have occurred over centuries, the loss cannot be reversed overnight. There are many factors involved: the number of individuals of the species that remain in the wild, how long it takes the species to mature and reproduce, how much habitat is remaining, and whether the reasons for the decline are clear cut and understood. Recovery plans employ a wide range of strategies that involve the following: reintroduction of species into formerly occupied habitat, land aquisition and management, captive breeding, habitat protection, research, population counts, public education projects, and assistance for private landowners.

SUCCESS STORIES

Despite the difficulties, recovery programs do work, and the joint efforts of the USFWS, other federal and state agencies, tribal governments, and private landowners have not been in vain. Only seven species, less than 1 percent of all the species listed between 1968 and 1993, are now known to be extinct. The other 99 percent of listed species have not been lost to extinction, and this confirms the success of the act.

There are some good examples of successful recovery plans. In 1999, the peregrine falcon, the bald eagle, and the Aleutian goose were removed from the endangered species list. The falcon's numbers have risen dramatically. In 1970, there were only 39 pairs of falcons in the United States. By 1999, the number had risen to 1,650 pairs. The credit for the recovery goes to the late Rachel

Carson, who highlighted the dangers of DDT, and also to the Endangered Species Act, which enabled the federal government to breed falcons in captivity, and took steps to protect their habitat.

Young bald eagles were also successfully translocated into habitat that they formerly occupied, and the Aleutian Canada goose has improved due to restoration of its habitat and reintroduction into former habitat.

IUCN–THE WORLD CONSERVATION UNION

The IUCN (International Union for Conservation of Nature) was established in 1947. It is an alliance of governments, governmental agencies, and nongovernmental agencies. The aim of the IUCN is to help and encourage nations to conserve wildlife and natural resources. Organizations such as the Species Survival Commission is one of several IUCN commissions that assesses the conservation status of species and subspecies globally. Taxa that are threatened with extinction are noted and steps are taken for their conservation by programs designed to save, restore, and manage species and their habitats. The Survival Commission is committed to providing objective information on the status of globally threatened species, and produces two publications: the *IUCN Red List of Threatened Animals*, and the *IUCN Red List of Threatened Plants*. They are compiled from scientific data and provide the status of threatened species, depending on their existence in the wild and threats that undermine that existence. The lists for plants and animals differ slightly.

The categories from the *IUCN Red List of Threatened Animals* used in *Endangered Wildlife and Plants of the World* are as follows:

Extinct: A species is extinct when there is no reasonable doubt that the last individual has died.

Extinct in the wild: A species that is known only to survive in captivity, well outside its natural range.

Critically endangered: A species that is facing an extremely high risk of extinction in the wild in the immediate future.

Endangered: A species that is facing a very high risk of extinction in the wild in the near future.

Vulnerable: A species that is facing a high risk of extinction in the wild in the medium-term future.

Lower risk: A species that does not satisfy the criteria for designation as critically endangered, endangered, or vulnerable. Species included in the lower risk category can be separated into three subcategories:

  Conservation dependent: A species that is part of a conservation program. Without the program, the species would qualify for one of the threatened categories within five years.

  Near threatened: A species that does not qualify for conservation dependent, but is close to qualifying as vulnerable.

  Least concern: A species that does not qualify for conservation dependent or near threatened.

Data deficient: A species on which there is inadequate information to make an asssessment of risk of extinction. Because there is a possibility that future research will show that the species is threatened, more information is required.

The categories from the *IUCN Red List of Threatened Plants*, used in *Endangered Wildlife and Plants of the World*, are as follows:

Extinct: A species that has not definitely been located in the wild during the last 50 years.

Endangered: A species whose survival is unlikely if the factors that threaten it continue. Included are species whose numbers have been reduced to a critical level, or whose habitats have been so drastically reduced that they are deemed to be in immediate danger of extinction. Also included in this category are species that may be extinct but have definitely been seen in the wild in the past 50 years.

Vulnerable: A species that is thought likely to move into the endangered category in the near future if the factors that threaten it remain.

Rare: A species with small world populations that are not at present endangered or vulnerable, but are at risk. These species are usually in restricted areas or are thinly spread over a larger range.

Long-wattled Umbrellabird

(Cephalopterus penduliger)

IUCN: Vulnerable

Class: Aves
Order: Passeriformes
Family: Cotingidae
Length: 18¾–20 in. (48–51 cm)
Diet: Fruits, large insects
Habitat: Low montane forests
Range: Colombia from the San Juan River southward through Ecuador

THE LONG-WATTLED umbrellabird has the same jet-black plumage as the American crow (*Corvus brachyrhynchos*), and is as big or even a little bigger. However, unlike the crow, it has a deep blue sheen to its plumage and large white patches under the wing.

The umbrellabird has a wattle, a pendulous organ that hangs from its throat. Also known as a lappet, the wattle may reach almost 12 inches (30 centimeters) long. It is black and fully feathered.

Umbrellabirds derive their peculiar species name from the large mop of hairlike feathers that forms a bowl-shaped crest on the top of their head. This crest hangs down and projects forward to the tip of the beak. In many respects it resembles a small umbrella held close above the bird's head. Females have a more modest crest that does not form the same large mop, and the lappet is much smaller.

Umbrellabirds differ from crows in many other ways, as reflected in their classification. Crows belong to the family Corvidae, with jays, ravens, and magpies. Umbrellabirds are placed in the cotinga family (Cotingidae), which is often combined with the tyrant flycatcher family (Tyrannidae). Cotingas are New World birds.

Only one species, the rose-throated becard (*Pachyrhamphus aglaiae*), ranges into the United States in extreme southern Texas and Arizona. Ornithologists recognize up to 79 species of cotingas, but some place several species in the tyrant flycatcher family. The three umbrellabird species are clearly cotingas.

Distribution

The Amazonian umbrellabird (*Cephalopterus ornatus*) ranges over much of the Amazon Basin, including portions of Bolivia, Peru, Ecuador, Venezuela, Guyana, and western Brazil.

The bare-necked umbrellabird occurs only in Costa Rica and Panama. The long-wattled umbrellabird lives in well-developed forests that cover the lower slopes on the west side of the Andes. It is found as far south as southern Ecuador and as far north as the San Juan River, about halfway between the Panamanian and Ecuadorian borders of Colombia.

This species actually occupies a very narrow belt of habitat that is sandwiched between the Pacific Ocean and the Andes Mountains.

Umbrellabirds have not been studied in great detail, but pieces of information provided by several observers paint a fair picture of these remarkable birds.

Little known

The long-wattled umbrellabird is the least studied of the three species, but it almost certainly follows the general pattern of its relatives.

The male umbrellabird claims a tree during courtship. It sits on just one of two or three select

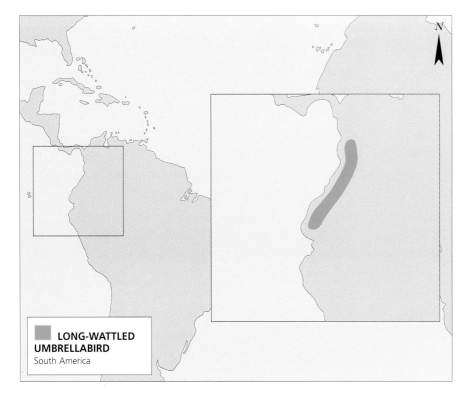

LONG-WATTLED UMBRELLABIRD
South America

branches to perform. Each male is usually within hearing distance of other umbrellabirds. The male leans down and forward so that his lappet dangles. He takes air into his air sacs, then expels it with a quick forward thrust of the head. The resulting call is a deep boom. Females are attracted to the booming, but no one has been able to document whether, after mating, the birds form pairs or the females go off to nest and rear the young on their own.

In the late 1980s and early 1990s there was much publicity about rain forests' vulnerability to commercial exploitation. The long-wattled umbrellabird lives in just such a wet forest. It will be one of the casualties if some of the South American rain forest is not preserved. But habitat loss is only one of the threats that the bird has to face. It is also a prized species for caged bird fanciers, and the local market for the umbrellabird is probably larger and more important than the foreign market.

The future

No specific estimates of the bird's population have been compiled or calculated. The bird still survives in good numbers in some locations and more sparsely in others. The Rio Pitsara in

Not especially beautiful, the long-wattled umbrellabird is valued more for its unusual appearance.

Ecuador was cited as an important population stronghold for the species in the late 1980s.

Unfortunately, no specific preservation or protective work has been initiated for the long-wattled umbrellabird.

If a public education program were implemented with the aim to teach people about the damage caused by caging birds, this could help to prevent the long-term decline of the long-wattled umbrellabird.

Kevin Cook

Unga
(Sarotherodon linnellii)

IUCN: Critically endangered

Class: Actinopterygii
Order: Perciformes
Family: Cichlidae
Length: 6 in. (15 cm)
Habitat: Nearshore and open-water areas
Range: Lake Barombi-Mbo, Cameroon

THE UNGA IS A MEMBER of the family of warm-water fish called Cichlidae, a group that includes about 250 endangered fishes in Africa's Lake Victoria. As with those cichlids of Lake Victoria, the only home for the unga is a single lake, Lake Barombi-Mbo in western Cameroon. The unga is completely dependent upon the continued stability of the lake's ecosystem.

Cichlids scrape algae from underwater surfaces and have pharyngeal teeth in their throat that help break down their food. The unga's gut, which helps digest its food, is very long. It is actually two and a half times the length of the fish. Ungas are not nearly as streamlined as torpedo-like fish. The fairly flat, round appearance of cichlids makes them resemble a plate standing on edge.

The unga and other cichlids have a long, spiny dorsal fin that can extend from the back of their head all the way to the tail. The pectoral fins are long and pointed. This gives cichlids mobility from side to side as they search for food.

The unga is a mouthbrooder. After its eggs are laid and fertilized, one of the parents (depending on the species) will help to pick up the eggs with its mouth and guard them in a chamber in the mouth cavity. The parent incubates the eggs in this manner for one to two weeks. Even after the fish hatch, the free-swimming offspring continue to rely on the parent for protection. If threatened, the offspring will swim back into the parent's mouth.

Appearance

Several physical traits make the unga stand out from many other cichlids. It has large eyes and an unusually large, long head to effectively find and consume food. Adults lack the large spot on the tail end of the dorsal fin called a tilapia mark, but it is present in younger fish. The unga is well armed against predators, with 15 or 16 spines on the dorsal fin to ward off attacks. The overall coloration of this lake dweller is a silvery green; breeding females and young fish are silvery gray. Both sexes may have a dark pigment patch on the throat, but there is individual variability. Likewise, the pelvic fins may be yellow.

Adult ungas, like many cichlids, eat microscopic plant material. Cichlids can extract adequate nourishment from a strictly vegetarian diet, but insects will be consumed when they are available. When young, the unga is omnivorous and will eat whatever is available, if it is a suitable food.

The relatively small range of the unga—one lake—is the main reason why its future is in doubt.

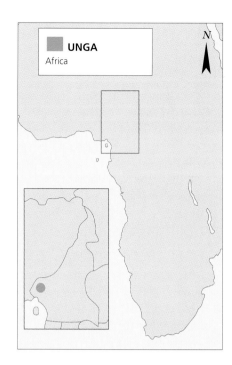

When a species cannot escape adverse conditions, a sudden shift in their environment (such as a change in temperature, salinity, or types of predators) can wipe out the entire population.

Similar species

Because there are species similar to the unga in Lake Barombi-Mbo, interbreeding can also be a problem. One species in particular is the fissi (*Sarotherodon caroli*). This fish is similar to the unga. As a natural means to prevent interbreeding, researchers believe that the breeding cycles of the two species have evolved to occur at different times.

During study expeditions in March and April, mature ungas that had reached breeding condition were captured. The fissi seemed to be ready to breed only after the ungas had passed their breeding peak.

Distinct color patterns that appear only during the breeding season may also be a factor in separating the species.

William E. Manci

Venus' Flytrap

(Dionaea muscipula)

IUCN : Rare

Class: Magnoliopsida
Order: Nepenthales
Family: Droseraceae
Height: Flower stalk to 12 in. (30 cm) tall
Leaves: Spirally arranged in a spreading rosette, up to about 6 in. (15 cm) across and lying fairly close to the ground
Flowers: Late May to early June. White with five spreading petals, each up to 10 mm long, broadest at the tip, which is usually notched
Pollination: By small flying insects. Seeds mature within 6–8 weeks of fertilization
Fruits and seeds: Fruit is a dry capsule, ovoid, up to 4 mm long, irregularly splitting to reveal shiny black pear-shaped seeds. These will germinate immediately on a suitable substrate
Habitat: Sphagnum bogs and damp pineland savanna
Range: Southeastern North Carolina to northeastern South Carolina

THE VENUS' FLYTRAP is a fascinating and unusual plant because it catches insects. This perennial low-growing herbaceous plant is evergreen in sheltered situations. It grows from a slightly bulbous base made up of fleshy scale leaves that can be up to ½ inch (1.5 centimeters) thick. The root system is shallow and diffuse. The leaves of the plant consist of broad flattened stems that may have parallel sides or, more usu-ally, be spatula-shaped. These are abruptly contracted below the leaf blade (trap), which consists of two clamshell-like, rounded to kidney-shaped lobes, which are ¾–1 inch (2–3 centimeters) broad. The midrib acts as a hinge; the edges have stiff, fine teeth (up to 8 millimeters long) that are surrounded at their base by small nectar glands.

The upper (inner) maroon to greenish surface of each lobe is covered by microscopic digestive glands, and in the center of each lobe are three slender trigger hairs arranged in a triangle.

The flowers have spreading petals with five narrow, pointed, green sepals that are of similar length to the petals and alternate with them. The stamens, which usually number around 15, have slender filaments, each 5 to 7 millimeters long, tipped with round, two-chambered anthers. The ovary is superior, with five carpels (female reproductive organs) fused to give one chamber; the style is slender and tufted-branched at its tip. The flowers are borne on the top few inches of a slender stalk up to 12 inches (30 centimeters) tall; the innermost flowers open first, usually in pairs. As the flowers mature, their individual flower stalks elongate to about 2 millimeters.

After several touches, the most remarkable trap in the plant kingdom is triggered in 30 milliseconds, and for the insect caught in the jaws, it is a certain and rather grisly death. The doomed creature's frenzied attempts to escape just alert the plant to the fact that it has succeeded, and the slower second phase of the operation begins.

The outer cells of the leaf enlarge by up to 30 percent, forcing the lobes together, sealing the edges, and crushing the prey. At the same time the digestive glands secrete a mixture of liquids: water, to drown the insect; chitinase to break down its hard outer skeleton; and enzymes to break down its proteins into a soup that the leaf surface can absorb. The relative proportions of this mixture are altered depending on the nature of the prey caught in the trap.

Over the next three to five days the animal is reduced to a dried husk, after which time the trap opens and the remains are left to blow away. Because of the cellular expansion necessary for the closing and opening procedures, it is only possible for each trap to go through this cycle three to four times. To guard against wasteful false alarms, two or more touches on the trigger hairs are needed. Therefore, raindrops or other blown debris do not set off the trap. The varied prey, mainly ants and spiders, are attracted by the trap color and the sugary nectar secreted around its margins. The nectar provides a rich source of the nutrients that are deficient in the acidic soils of the plant's native coastal plain.

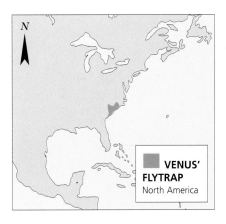

VENUS' FLYTRAP
North America

The species has a rather specialized habitat in this area, most commonly occurring close to the boundaries between long-leaf pine savanna and wet sphagnum bogs, which is ideal rattlesnake and alligator country. Here, in the open, well-lit, damp black peaty sands and pure sphagnum carpets, the species flourishes, but these conditions are dependent on irregular fires to keep down the ranker herbs and woody shrubs.

First mentioned by Arthur Dobbs in 1763, the Governor of North Carolina at the time called it "the great wonder of the vegetable world." Within five years live plants had been introduced to England and led amateur botanist John Ellis to write suggesting the plant's carnivorous nature to the Swedish father of plant nomenclature, Linnaeus. The great American naturalist

The fleshy leaves of the Venus' flytrap are touch-sensitive, triggered to closure by minor irritation.

William Bartram (1739–1823) was clearly convinced of this when he wrote in 1793 of it being "ready on the spring to entrap incautious deluded insects! carnivorous vegetable." Many people doubted its predatory nature, not least because its traps closed so slowly under the cold, dark conditions in which it was often cultivated. It was left up to Charles Darwin to prove its abilities to catch and digest with a series of experiments, on what he justifiably considered to be "one of the most wonderful plants in the world."

So many people have been enthralled by this plant that the demand has all too often been met by the wholesale removal of plants from the wild. Widespread commercial cultivation, the use of micro-propagation techniques, and growing public conservation awareness may have helped lessen the effects of this poaching, but it still poses a threat. Similarly, habitat destruction

through drainage and inappropriate management (for example, the prevention of regular fires) have done much to reduce the plant's already limited range and numbers. Thankfully it is more resilient than many threatened species and can stand a degree of habitat degradation, and it may even exploit some new human-made habitats, such as road banks, but the continued survival of healthy populations of this incredible plant give cause for concern.

The Venus' flytrap is one of the most widely commercially available carnivorous plant species, and no garden center is without it. Unfortunately many of the plants sold do not live for very long, due to a combination of the difficulty in reproducing ideal growth conditions and the small unhealthy plants that are sold. The amount of material available in and still being taken from the wild is unclear.

Fred Rumsey

Large-fruited Sand Verbena

(Abronia macrocarpa)

ESA: Endangered

IUCN: Endangered

Phylum: Anthophyta (flowering plants)
Order: Caryophyllales
Family: Nyctaginaceae
Tribe: Abronieae
Size: To 19 in. (50 cm) tall
Leaves: Gray-green, sticky, hairy leaves with oval, elliptic, or round blades, ¾–2 in. (2–5 cm) long, each borne on a stem ¼–1½ in. (0.5–4 cm) long
Flowers: April. Showy heads of up to 45 fragrant, bright magenta, funnel-shaped flowers, each with a slender tube 18–30 mm long
Fruit: In dense clusters, each papery fruit five-winged and top-shaped, 8–15 mm long and 5–12 mm wide, with tail-like remains of the flower tube attached to the tip
Habitat: Sand dunes and openings in savanna woodlands of post oak
Range: Freestone, Leon, and Robertson Counties in eastern Texas

THE LARGE-FRUITED sand verbena is an erect, spreading perennial that belongs to the same family as the well-known four-o'clock (*Mirabilis jalapa*) and, like this plant, its flowers last for only one day. It is an extremely rare native of a few sandy places in eastern Texas. In fact, it is one of the rarest plants in the United States, known to grow in only three places. It makes a very attractive display in April with its bright magenta flowers, although the grayish foliage may be difficult to see because it is often covered with sand. The fruit of the plant is a small, shiny achene (a dry, single-seeded fruit) enclosed inside a winged, papery structure.

Shortly after the plant has fruited, it lapses into dormancy for the duration of the hot, dry summer, surviving underground as a stout taproot, in which is stored water and nutrients.

Large-fruited sand verbena is well adapted to its special habitat of dry, sandy openings and dunes in savanna woodlands of post oak (*Quercus stellata*).

In such areas the soil is very infertile, largely consisting of sand, and these difficult growing conditions are made worse by low and unreliable rainfall and temperature fluctuations between day and night and between summer and winter.

Large-fruited sand verbena was first discovered in 1968 and described in a scientific journal in 1972. On September 28, 1988, it was listed as endangered by the United States Fish and Wildlife Service. There are only three

Bright magenta flowers decorate the large-fruited sand verbena.

LARGE-FRUITED SAND VERBENA
North America

known populations of the sand verbena, containing about 3,000 plants altogether.

Current threats to the continued existence of large-fruited sand verbena include housing and oil field developments, fire suppression, aggressive competition from non-native plants such as South African lovegrass (*Eragrostis plana*) and weeping lovegrass (*E. curvula*), and the careless use of off-road vehicles. That there are only three known populations makes the plant especially vulnerable to extinction. More research needs to be done to help understand the threats to the large-fruited sand verbena. Conservation could include establishing viable populations in cultivation. Putting seeds into long-term cold storage in a seed bank would provide a backup in case all the growing plants should die out.

Samples of the large-fruited sand verbena are kept at the Mercer Arboretum in Texas as part of the National Collection of Endangered Plants.

Nick Turland

Vicuna

(Vicugna vicugna)

ESA: Endangered

IUCN: Lower risk

Class: Mammalia
Order: Artiodactyla
Family: Camelidae
Weight: 100–120 lb. (45–54 kg)
Shoulder height: 34–38 in. (86–96 cm)
Diet: Grass, herbs
Gestation period: 330–350 days
Longevity: 15–20 years
Habitat: Arid highland grasslands
Range: Argentina, Bolivia, Chile, Ecuador, and Peru

THERE ARE FOUR MEMBERS of the camel family in South America: the llama and the alpaca are domesticated, and the two wild forms are the guanaco and the vicuna.

The vicuna is the smallest member of the camel family. It can be found in small groups of one male and several females. The males are extremely territorial and will battle to the death with any intruder. Female young are tolerated in the family, but males are usually ejected after their first year and often form bachelor herds.

The vicuna is a graceful animal that sports soft camel fur with a touch of russet and light buff underparts. The male develops a long buff apron of fur on its

The vicuna is found only in South America at altitudes from 11,000 to 17,600 feet (3,350 to 5,360 meters). Broad grasslands at these altitudes are called punas.

chest. Its range used to extend across much of the Peruvian highlands, part of Bolivia, part of Chile, and a small part of Argentina.

A long history

The vicuna has been hunted for its fleece since prehistoric times. Prior to 1530, vicuna hair was prized by the Incas. Cloth made from vicuna fleece was reserved for the nobility, and no one was allowed to hunt the vicunas without permission. After the destruction of the Inca empire by the Spanish, this protection disappeared. Vicuna hunting was uncontrolled, and 80,000 animals were slaughtered each year. In 1825, the vicuna was given protection by the revolutionary leader Simon Bolívar. This protection was adopted by most countries, but in name only.

By the 1950s and 1960s, bolts of cloth made from vicuna fleece sold for up to U.S. $2,000, and sources in Peru and Bolivia sold blankets made from the soft neck fleece. The vicuna population dropped so much that by the 1960s, extinction seemed likely. Finally, strong protection measures were instituted in Peru, Chile, and Argentina. Also, the

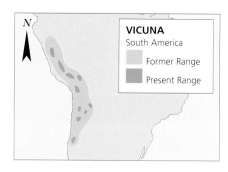

vicuna was listed under Appendix I of CITES.

Population estimates for 1998 to 1999 were 33,000 in Argentina; 45,000 in Bolivia; 20,000 in Chile, and 103,000 in Peru. The vicuna was reintroduced to Ecuador in 1988 and ten years later numbered about 700. With the success in stabilizing the wild population, there is competition for upland grass between the vicuna and domestic alpacas and llamas. The most successful attempt to domesticate the vicuna was near Lake Titicaca during the mid-20th century. Efforts were made to semidomesticate them, with limited success. The second project at Hacienda Cala-cala was to crossbreed the vicuna with the alpaca. The resulting pacovicuna was of some value. There is a small captive population of about 50 vicunas in European zoos.

Warren D. Thomas

VIPERS

Class: Reptilia

Order: Squamata

Family: Viperidae

Vipers are known for their powerful venom, which can often be lethal to human beings. Usually the poison is hemotoxic; that is, it affects blood cells, the lining of blood vessels, and body tissues. Some species also have a neurotoxic venom, which affects the nervous system. Vipers use their tubular fangs to bite, often as a means of killing or subduing prey, but also as a means of venomous defense. They have the unusual ability to tilt their fangs backward against the roof of the mouth when they are not in use. This tilting mechanism is also found in pit vipers, which are not true vipers. They are classified in the family Crotalinae.

Vipers range in size from slender burrowers of scarcely one foot (30 centimeters) in length to those that are nearly six feet (1.8 meters) long. Most are terrestrial, although some live in trees or underground. In general, these snakes feed on smaller mammals—especially rodents.

Vipers are slow and will not chase their prey, but instead wait to strike when victims come within range. After biting its victim, a viper will often release its fangs, allowing the prey to escape. But afterward, it will track down the dead or dying animal and consume it.

Most vipers are oviparous, meaning that they give birth to live young. These offspring are enveloped in a thin membrane from which they immediately free themselves, although the membrane may be ruptured before birth. Only a few vipers lay eggs.

Caucasian Viper

(Vipera kaznakovi)

IUCN: Endangered

Length: Up to 2 ft. (0.6 m)
Reproduction: Oviparous
Diet: Small mammals
Habitat: Wooded slopes and subalpine meadows
Range: The Caucasus range and west Republic of Georgia, south toward Turkey

THE CAUCASIAN VIPER LIVES at elevations up to 6,000 feet (1,820 meters) above sea level. Like all European vipers, it is a member of the genus *Vipera*, to which 15 species belong. The Caucasian viper has a short, broad head that is quite distinct from the neck. Ground color in this species varies from pale yellow to brick red. Along the center of the back is a broad stripe that is black, or brown edged with black. This stripe may occasionally be broken into bars. The top of the head bears dark markings, usually including a V-shaped mark that extends back on either side of the dorsal stripe. A black stripe runs down from the eye to the angle of the mouth and to the side of the neck.

The venom of this viper is more potent than that of many of its close relatives; both humans and cattle are known to have died from the bite of this snake. The main enemy of the Caucasian viper is people. As is the case with many snakes, fear has played a role in the gradual disappearance of this species.

Snakes occupy an important ecological niche wherever they occur. This viper is an important predator of rodents and other pests. Nonetheless, human fear of vipers has helped deplete its numbers, and it has been systematically killed on sight.

All-black vipers are occasionally seen, although they are not as common as the highly patterned forms.

The distinctive markings of the Caucasian viper make it highly recognizable.

While such persecution has influenced the life of this viper for centuries, today new forces are placing pressure on an already weakened population. Habitat destruction from unsound industrial practices, for example, has taken its toll. Georgia has been undergoing enormous political and social change since the breakup of the Soviet Union. It is unlikely that wildlife survival will be a priority there in the coming years.

Elizabeth Sirimarco

CAUCASIAN VIPER
Asia

Cyclades Blunt-nosed Viper

(Macrovipera schweizeri)

IUCN: Critically endangered

Class: Reptilia
Order: Squamata
Suborder: Serpentes (Ophidia)
Family: Viperidae
Subfamily: Viperinae
Length: 26–30 in. (66–76 cm), occasionally longer
Clutch size: 3–8 eggs
Diet: Small birds, small mammals, lizards
Habitat: Rocky hillsides covered with scrub
Range: The island of Milos, and its satellite islands, Kimolos, Polyaigos, and Sifnos, in the Cyclades group, Greece

THE CYCLADES blunt-nosed viper, also known as the Milos viper, is a heavy-bodied snake that can easily go unnoticed on the remote hillsides it inhabits because of its secretive nature and because it rarely comes into contact with humans.

It is active mainly during the twilight hours of the early morning and, especially, in the late evening during the summer. During colder weather, however, it is sometimes abroad during daylight hours, while during the winter it retreats into underground chambers and is rarely seen at all. Its movements are sluggish, although it can strike quickly and accurately, and it rarely moves far except when hunting. Its coloration, of gray with indistinct crossbars, makes it difficult to detect when it is coiled in the dappled shade of small bushes and shrubs that cover its rocky hillside habitat. A small proportion—thought to be about 1 percent—are uniform reddish brown. As its common name suggests, its rounded head has a short, blunt snout. Its eyes are relatively small, with vertical pupils. Each scale on its body has

The gray coloration of the Cyclades blunt-nosed viper makes it difficult to detect in its habitat of bushes and shrubs.

a central ridge, or keel, running along its length, and this gives the viper a roughened appearance, helping it blend into its rocky environment.

Its primary source of food is songbirds, which it catches while they are roosting in shrubs and bushes and into whose nests it climbs. For this reason, its main period of activity is spring, when the birds are nesting. At other times of the year it is less active and feeds only occasionally. It is unusual among the vipers in that it lays eggs—all the other European species give birth to live young—and this may be an adaptation to living in a relatively warm climate. Other than this, very little is known of its breeding habits in the wild.

Threats

Although the viper was heavily persecuted in the past (because it is venomous), the main threat to its continued existence now comes from quarrying. Milos, its main stronghold, is very rich in minerals, especially gypsum, which is used in the manufacture of plaster and plasterboard for the building industry. In order to mine the gypsum, the top layer of limestone must first be removed, along with the plant and animal communities that live there. Mountaintops are sliced off and gently sloping hillsides are sheered into precipices. Roads linking the quarries to a number of small harbors crisscross the island, and trucks carrying the gypsum form an almost continuous stream throughout the working day and into the night. The mining activities not only destroy the viper's habitat, but the heavy traffic crushes large numbers of snakes when they cross roads in the course of their hunting activities. It is difficult to estimate the number killed in this way, but it certainly runs into several hundred, if not thousands, each spring and summer.

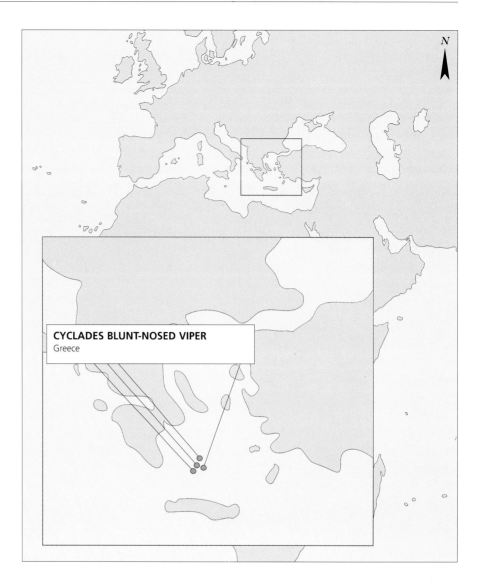

CYCLADES BLUNT-NOSED VIPER
Greece

Conservation

Studies on the movements and habits of the Cyclades blunt-nosed viper have been taking place since 1994, with a view to establishing a program that would help its populations to survive. Basic information is essential; for instance, unless its activity patterns and movements can be established, it will be difficult to know how much land to set aside for its conservation. Radio-tagging projects will hopefully tell scientists more about these factors. So far, most of the mining activities have been concentrated on the eastern part of Milos, and the western end of the island is still relatively untouched. Plans to mine the western half have been put on hold until more is known about the viper's requirements so that areas can be set aside for them. Other recommendations include stopping truck movements to and from the quarries after dusk, when vipers are most likely to come onto the roads and be crushed. Legal protection against collection of the species for private collections has been in place for many years, and visitors to the islands are regularly searched on their departure to ensure this law is enforced.

As a second line of defense, breeding groups of Cyclades blunt-nosed vipers have been set up in a number of zoos, notably the Jersey Wildlife Preservation Trust, Channel Isles, in the hope that young animals can be produced in captivity for possible reintroduction into suitable reserves in the future. Ultimately, though, the fate of the Cyclades blunt-nosed viper is in the hands of the gypsum quarries and the authorities that issue licenses for quarry activities.

Economic considerations

At present, gypsum is the main source of income for the Milos islanders. If an alternative source of income, such as tourism, can be established, the viper's future will be more secure.

Chris Mattison

Danubian Meadow Viper

(Vipera ursinii rakosiensis)

IUCN: Endangered

Length: Up to 21 in. (53 cm)
Reproduction: Oviparous
Diet: Large invertebrates, lizards, and occasionally frogs or rodents
Habitat: Lowland meadows
Range: Danube Valley from eastern Austria through Hungary, southern Romania, and northern Bulgaria

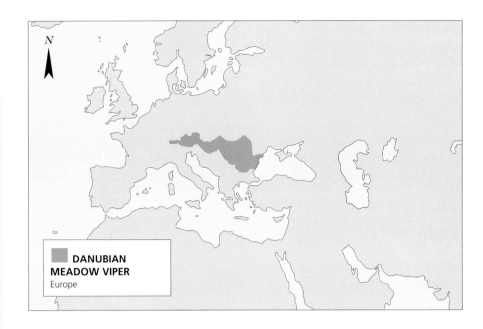

DANUBIAN MEADOW VIPER
Europe

MEADOW VIPERS can be found in various parts of Europe, and the Danubian meadow viper is an especially docile subspecies. It is the smallest of European vipers, rarely reaching more than 19 inches (48 centimeters) in length, and it is the least poisonous. It is, however, one of the most endangered reptiles in Europe.

The color of this meadow viper can be light gray or light brown, darker on the sides than on the top of the body. Males are sometimes golden yellow or greenish gray. The dorsal stripe is always dark edged; undersides are marbled dark gray. The tip of the tail is always dark. The skin has a rough appearance.

This isolated subspecies lives only in lowlands. It prefers sandy habitats of clay, gravel, or similar material. It is found in both dry and moist environments, although damp summer meadows appear to be preferred.

The Danubian meadow viper most often eats large invertebrates such as crickets or grasshoppers, but lizards such as *Lacerta agilis* and occasionally frogs and rodents are also taken. Mating occurs in April, with late summer births; 2 to 20 young may result, depending on the size and age of the female. The species may only breed in alternate years.

Decline

Threats to the Danubian meadow viper are many, but the major reason for its decline is the drainage of land for agricultural use within its range. Modern agriculture has drastically changed the habitat of this viper: once-pristine meadows are now used for vineyards, arable farming, and forestry. Once the viper populations became weakened by this practice, secondary factors began to take their toll.

Agriculture also creates other problems for this subspecies. The use of pesticides and fertilizers has undoubtedly added to the pressure, as has too-frequent mowing, which not only changes the natural constitution of meadows but also kills these snakes directly. Collection of this rare viper for museum or commercial sale is another risk. Humans have also purposely killed this snake, failing to recognize its worth as a predator of insects and rodents. At the beginning of the 20th century, bounties were paid for dead Danubian meadow vipers, even though they were not particularly dangerous. During that time, thousands were killed every year.

A final threat is the introduction of a number of non-native species. Game birds that prey on this small viper are raised in its range, especially in Austria. Elsewhere in the range, livestock—such as pigs and geese—degrades the habitat and directly preys upon the Danubian meadow viper. Other potential predators include the uncommon great bustard (*Otis tarda*) and the introduced pheasant (*Phasianus colchicus*).

No help

People in the viper's range have shown little interest in its decline or in the degradation of its meadow habitat. Reports urging its conservation have been largely ignored, and only small parcels of land have been set aside as nature reserves. Although the snake itself is protected from collection, enforcement of protective legislation is negligible, and the largest known breeding population was decimated in the 1970s by a number of collectors. This highly endangered snake remains virtually unprotected.

Proposals

The most important step in saving the Danubian meadow viper is to set aside more habitat where it would be protected. Pheasants should also be discouraged in areas where the subspecies has been sighted. It has been seen persistently at three sites in Austria; two of these are in Burgenland. The last extensive meadow area in lower Austria should be protected, with implementation of management to conserve and enhance remaining habitats. Surveys to assess the status of this viper are also needed. The Burgenland populations, one of which occurs on private land, should also be protected, with stricter control of collection and of other abusive activities put in place.

All three sites should be designated as reserves to protect these internationally important habitats. Other rare species would also benefit from such protection, including various plants and invertebrates.

The great bustard, the glacial relict lizard (*Vivipara pannonica*), and the southern birch mouse (*Sicista subtilis*) are also known to occur in these areas.

Reintroduction of captive-bred specimens of the Danube meadow viper must also be considered, should the wild populations be too low to allow recovery.

Elizabeth Sirimarco

See also Snakes.

VIREOS

Class: Aves

Order: Passeriformes

Family: Vireonidae

Subfamily: Vireoninae

Vireos are small New World songbirds familiar to most North Americans. The red-eyed vireo (*Vireo olivaceus*) has been described as the most common woodland bird in the eastern United States. All vireos have short beaks with a small hooked tip. Although a few family members have some bright colors, nearly all these birds are drably colored in grays, greens, and dull yellows. Vireos search for their insect prey by hopping from twig to twig and inspecting twig crevices, buds, and leaves. As birds of forests and woods, vireos have declined with habitat loss. Slowly declining populations do not qualify a species as endangered. Two species and one subspecies, however, are seriously threatened with extinction.

Black-capped Vireo

(Vireo atricapillus)

ESA: Endangered

IUCN: Endangered

Length: 4½ in. (11 cm)

Weight: ¼–⅓ oz. (8–9 g)

Clutch size: 3–5 eggs

Incubation: 14–17 days

Diet: Insects

Habitat: Savannas, shrub lands

Range: Summers from southern Kansas through Oklahoma and Texas into Coahuila, Mexico; winters in Mexico from southern Sonora through Sinaloa and Nayarit and on into Oaxaca

THE SHRUBBERY SEEMS alive with a bubbling chatter. A buzzlike trill follows a couple of whistled chirps. The call is busy, quick, and repeated with variations. For all the noise, however, nothing shows itself. No amount of circling or head bobbing and weaving offers even a glimpse of this singing bird. Only after waiting patiently will one see the black-capped vireo.

Smallest of the vireos found in the United States, the black-capped vireo is a busy bird that actively flits about the shrubs in which it lives. Hidden among the shadows of twigs and leaves, the bird sings loudly but can scarcely be seen. Only the quick movement of a shadow within the shrub betrays its location.

The black-capped vireo is one of the so-called spectacled vireos. A thick white ring circles the eye and a white line extends forward through the lore and onto the forehead, resembling a pair of glasses. The bird is unique among American vireos in having a black crown, nape, and cheek, which contrasts sharply with the spectacles. The upperparts are uniformly olive green. The wings and tail are slightly darker, and each wing shows two yellow-green bars. The sides are pale yellow or yellow green. The remaining underparts, from chin to undertail, are clear white. The female has a gray head instead of black. The color of both genders helps to obscure them in the dappled lighting of their shrub land habitat.

Wooded range

Historically, the black-capped vireo inhabited shrubby and partially wooded ravines from southern Kansas southward into Coahuila, Mexico. It slowly disappeared from the northern portions of its range as vital habitat was destroyed. The last black-capped vireos in Kansas were seen in the early 1950s. The extent of its northern range steadily shrank through the 1960s and 1970s until, by the 1980s, it occurred no farther north than central Oklahoma. By 1986, only 51 black-capped vireos could be found in Oklahoma. More than 280 birds were counted in Texas that same year, and another two dozen were found in Mexico. Because it relies exclusively on insects for food, the black-capped vireo vacates its nesting areas every autumn and migrates to the Pacific Coast of Mexico. Habitat loss on the species' wintering grounds may be as critical as habitat loss on its summering grounds.

Landscape

Dry ravines texture the landscape where the black-capped vireo occurs. Woody shrubs grow densely in many of the ravines, and trees often stand in patches. The most important habitat characteristic, however, is a dense

Protecting the black-capped vireo requires preserving both the quantity and quality of its habitat. This may mean restricting cattle grazing and getting rid of cowbirds.

growth of nonwoody, or herbaceous, plants beneath the shrubs and trees. Ornithologists suspect that occasional prairie fires must burn through the shrubby ravines, to stimulate good herbaceous growth and keep the shrubs from becoming too large and dense. Also, light grazing by large animals such as deer (*Odocoileus* sp.) and American bison (*Bison bison*) may have once kept the habitat in good condition for this vireo.

The black-capped vireo may have experienced natural fluctuations in regional populations because of its need for these special habitats. As some ravine habitats matured beyond a certain point, the vireo may have stopped using them until the actions of grazers or fires returned those ravines to more favorable conditions. When people brought livestock to and

planted crops on the Great Plains, vireo habitat rapidly disappeared. Sheep, goats, and especially cattle grazed the land more heavily and in greater numbers for longer periods than did wandering herds of bison or deer. Much of the shrub lands were deliberately destroyed in order to provide more plant life suitable for feeding livestock. Large, con-

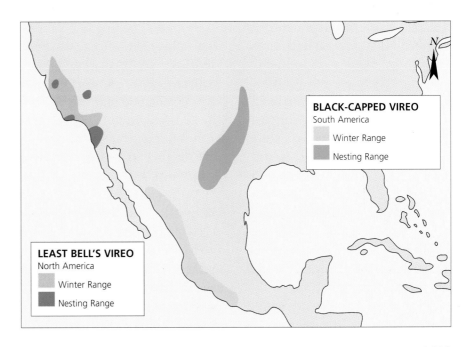

centrated herds of cattle also improved conditions for the brown-headed cowbird (*Molothrus ater*). Cowbirds do not build their own nests but rather lay their eggs in other birds' nests. The host bird then raises the young cowbird. The cowbird egg typically hatches in fewer days than do vireo eggs, so the young cowbird gets a head start on its nest mates. Young vireos rarely survive when cowbirds share their nests.

One of the last large tracts of vireo habitat lies outside Austin, Texas. Urban and suburban expansion threatens to completely engulf this area. If provisions could be made to preserve the vireo's habitat within special greenbelts and open spaces, development would not have such a devastating effect on it. However, many suburbanites prefer lawns and playgrounds over shrub lands where rattlesnakes (*Crotalus* sp.) may live.

Nest disturbance

People further complicate survival for the black-capped vireo. The growing recreation of birding can cause problems. Birders enjoy finding and seeing birds, but they do not necessarily become involved in ornithology—the scientific study of birds. Theirs is a more casual interest. Rare birds are especially exhilarating for birders to find and to watch. The growing number of birders has increased the incidence of nest disturbance. Some vireo nests are visited so frequently by birders thrilled to see an endangered species that the vireo abandons the nest.

Protection of this vireo would demand controlled cattle grazing

and measures to deal with the problem of cowbirds. Restricting cattle grazing has little chance to succeed on private ranches, however, unless some habitat is purchased. Funds for such acquisitions can be especially hard to come by. Therefore, the future for the black-capped vireo appears very uncertain.

Least Bell's Vireo
(Vireo bellii pusillus)

ESA: Endangered

IUCN: Endangered

Length: 4½–4¾ in.
(11–12 cm)
Weight: Probably ¼–⅓ oz.
(8–9 g), based on related subspecies
Clutch size: 3–4 eggs
Incubation: 14 days
Diet: Insects
Habitat: Riparian shrub lands
Range: North-central California to northern Baja, Mexico

THE CASE OF THE least Bell's vireo exhibits many remarkable features. Most important, the vireo's decline demonstrates how the consequences of human activity can make a natural process such as brood parasitism appear evil.

As a full species, the Bell's vireo has a large range. It occurs as far east as Indiana and across the Midwest and Great Plains to eastern Colorado. Small numbers even occupy the Dakotas. It inhabits most of northern Mexico, including nearly all of the

Baja peninsula, and much of the American Southwest. The least Bell's vireo is the subspecies found in California and Baja.

The least Bell's vireo differs from other Bell's subspecies partly through its choice of habitat. This vireo prefers dense willows along streams, especially where good ground cover grows beneath the willows. Before California entered the modern settlement era in the mid-1800s, the least Bell's vireo occurred as far north as Red Bluff in Tehama County, or roughly 120 miles (190 kilometers) north of Sacramento. The vireo occupied nearly all the inland river valley systems southward into Baja. But settlement changed everything.

Intensive farming

People opened the California landscape to agriculture. They brought intensive farming and livestock grazing to the central river valleys where the vireo lived. The brown-headed cowbird (*Molothrus ater*) followed the spread of agriculture around the state. Cowbirds build no nests but lay their eggs in other birds' nests and let the foster parents raise their young. Ornithologists call this behavior brood parasitism. The least Bell's vireo became a regular victim of the cowbird: very few young vireos survive when cowbirds share their nest.

Brood parasitism seems to be a villainous way to survive; but when cowbirds occur in normal numbers in natural habitats, they cannot dominate victims. Only when habitat conditions favor large numbers of cowbirds do nest parasites cause severe problems. Some people look no

People can trap cowbirds forever to help save the least Bell's vireo, but until they address the causes for the cowbird's success, trapping will do little good.

further than the cowbirds to explain the vireo's problems, but behind the cowbirds are the deeds of people.

In Southern California many streams have been dammed, lined with concrete, or drained dry. This causes streamside vegetation to change. Exotic shrubs, particularly tamarisk (*Tamarisk* sp.), have invaded the river valleys and changed the character of the riparian plant communities. When tamarisk moves into a riparian area, it soon takes over and becomes the dominant woody plant. Its presence almost

invariably degrades the habitat needed by the vireo. In altered habitat, the vireo becomes more vulnerable to any disturbance. A host of problems or factors that interfere with the habitat can lead to a decline in population: illegal garbage dumping, oil pipelines, flood control, diverting water for irrigation, expanding suburban and urban communities, herbicide runoff from nearby farms, and more cowbirds.

Conservation history

In 1980 the State of California designated the least Bell's vireo as endangered. Hopes grew that the vireo was benefiting from protective measures, particularly the trapping of cowbirds. Some localized vireo populations showed slight increases in numbers.

The U.S. Fish and Wildlife Service recognized the vireo as endangered in 1986, but just putting a species' name on a list does not save it. The vireo has continued to decline as populations have died out.

By 1992, the least Bell's vireo occupied less than 5 percent of its historic range in California, and only 400 birds were known to survive in the state. The status of the Baja population was not well known.

The vireo population did not drop so remarkably due to brood parasites, but rather because of too many factors changing its habitat at once. The combination of actions and consequences has imperiled the least Bell's vireo, perhaps permanently.

Kevin Cook

San Andrés Vireo

(Vireo caribaeus)

IUCN: Critically endangered

Class: Aves
Order: Passeriformes
Family: Vireonidae
Length: 5 in. (13 cm)
Weight: ½–¾ oz. (16–20 g)
Clutch size: 2
Incubation: 12–14 days
Diet: Insects and fruit
Habitat: Mangroves, bushes, scrubby pasture
Range: San Andrés island, Colombia

FOR MOST COLOMBIANS, the Caribbean island of San Andrés, about 125 miles (200 km) off the east coast of Nicaragua, is best known as a rather exotic holiday destination. It is beautiful, surrounded by warm seas and under blue skies for much of the year. San Andrés also boasts coconut palm plantations, mangrove swamps, overgrown pastures with thickets, and scattered patches of native trees up to 70 feet (20 meters) high. With a prolonged dry season in the first half of the year it is easy to see why the popularity of this small island—of just 17 square miles (44 square kilometers)—has grown so much in the past two decades or so. This development, centered around San Andrés' eponymous capital, has taken over in importance from the traditional economic activities of subsistence farming, coconut plantations, and fishing, and in turn has created problems for the San Andrés vireo, a species of bird found here and nowhere else in the world.

The vireo is not uncommon in those areas of the south of the island that have not been developed. The problem is that these areas are getting smaller. With a quickly growing human population has come the inevitable increase in pressure on land. People want land for the tourist industry; with more people working in this sector of the economy, there is a greater demand for land for housing; and there are more people to be fed, so land improvement for agriculture continues.

Unobtrusive songster

The San Andrés vireo is a small greenish bird that, if not observed closely, would not attract much attention. However, a careful approach in its favored habitat of mangroves and scrubby bushes would reward the observer with views of what is really a very delicately marked species. The olive green of its upperparts is broken by two narrow white wing bars and a pale yellow patch between the eye and

The mangroves and scrubby bushes of the exotic Caribbean island of San Andrés is the perfect location for the San Andrés vireo.

the base of the bill. The underparts are faded yellow, the legs are gray, and its sturdy grayish bill is typical of the vireo family.

However, for the visitor who knows what he or she is listening for, attention is more likely first to be brought to the San Andrés vireo by one of its three songs, a variety of vocalizations that marks it out from other vireo species. The simplest alternative is a single note repeated between 2 and 20 times. Then there is a repeated double note and finally a tri-syllabled call.

Vireos are not the most active of feeders, and they often appear sluggish as they move slowly inside bushes in search of insects. The San Andrés vireo, though, is the most active forager of the Caribbean vireos, probably because it eats a greater proportion of insects to fruit than other members of the genus. It stalks these insects among leaves and branches in trees from ground level to heights of up to 3 feet (10 meters).

Unlike some endangered species, the distribution of the San Andrés vireo is quite well known, as are its habitat preferences, but that does not make it any easier to find a way to ensure the continuity of a viable population, particularly as it is now thought to occupy just 7 square miles (18 square kilometers) in the southern third of the island.

Shared nest duties

Despite its inhabiting only a very small area, one thing working in this species' favor is that its territories are relatively small. The breeding season from May to July is timed to precede the rainy part of the year, which runs from July to December. A nest is constructed in the fork of branches, between 3 and 7 feet (1 and 2 meters) above the ground. It is a deep cup construction, the interior lined with fine grass and the exterior covered with moss and bits of leaves. The female lays two eggs (white with small brown spots), which are incubated by both sexes; both parents also care for the young.

Protection needed

What can be done to preserve the future of this highly localized bird? It is never easy to balance the interests of human development and habitat conservation, especially with a growing human population on a very small island. But some way must be

SAN ANDRÉS VIREO
Colombia

found to give protected area status to the surviving mangrove swamps and areas of scrub, even if it means giving compensation to prospective developers and agriculturalists. Only in this way will it be possible to ensure that the San Andrés vireo continues to sing in the mangroves.

Tim Harris

VOLES

Class: Mammalia

Order: Rodentia

Voles are small mammals that are often mistaken for mice. Like mice, voles are rodents. They can be as large as a small rat—or small enough to climb a rosebush and eat the new leaves. Voles are found in North America from the Central American isthmus to the Arctic tundra. In the Old World, voles are found in Europe from Italy to the Arctic and across Russia to the Siberian plain.

Voles do not hibernate and are active year-round, seeming to prefer nights from sundown to early morning.

Unlike other rodents, voles also breed year-round, and, depending upon the species, may have between four and eight young two to three times a year. Voles live primarily underground and burrow large networks of tunnels, nests, and storage rooms.

Because they live underground, they have evolved to cope with life in a tunnel. Their ears are small and covered with fur, their eyes are small, and their nose is short and blunt. The front claws are lengthened to allow for digging.

Voles are found in just about every possible habitat, from high mountain forests to sea-level salt marshes. Wherever they are found, they construct their homes near grass and running water, burrowing in the region just above the underground water table. Even though they make their home in the ground, they can swim and even dive well. They are strictly vegetarian and often, within a 24-hour period, will eat their weight in grass, twigs, leaves, bulbs, tubers, seeds, nuts, and other plant matter. They store their food to last through the winter.

Voles gather in colonies of 100 to 200 individuals. Populations appear to rise and fall in cycles depending on the season and the amount of food and water available. When populations become high, voles can be pests to humans: they are known to destroy crops, young forest trees, hay, and other cultivated plants such as potatoes and alfalfa.

Voles are slow-moving and easily captured and tamed. They also have more than their share of enemies, including predatory birds, dogs, cats, snakes, and humans. Human expansion into vole habitat may be the main cause of decline in vole populations.

Recently there has been some good news for endangered voles. The Amargosa vole (*Microtus californicus scirpensis*) was discovered in isolated marshes near Death Valley, although it was long believed to be extinct. Two Florida species, the Muskeget Island meadow vole (*M. breweri*) and the Block Island meadow vole (*M. pennsylvanicus provectus*), have both been removed from the endangered species list.

Amargosa Vole

(Microtus californicus scirpensis)

IUCN: Vulnerable

Weight: ½–1½ oz. (15–40 g)
Head-body length: 5½ in.
(14 cm)
Tail length: 1¼ in. (3 cm)
Diet: Various grasses, seeds,
herbs, and other plant material
Habitat: Marshland
Range: Amargosa River, Mojave
Desert

THE POPULATION OF the Amargosa voles has decreased substantially. While its range once covered the area between Shoshone and the upper end of Amargosa Canyon, it is now restricted to the Amargosa River drainage region of the Mojave Desert, California.

A medium-sized rodent, the Amargosa vole resembles a mouse. It is a thickset rodent, covered in a dense layer cinnamon-colored fur. The rest of its features appear to be rather understated: it has small eyes, barely visible ears, a short tail, and short legs ending in delicate pale feet.

A dense layer of cinnamon-colored fur covers the Amargosa vole, which is a medium-sized rodent.

The Amargosa vole is found in habitats that are close to, or bordered by, a permanent water source such as a spring or a river, so it is frequently found in marshland dominated with bulrush plants.

Recent research has shown that it is able to utilize three different elevations of the marshland it inhabits. While the lowest elevation is able to provide optimal conditions for the animal in terms of substrate, food, and so on, it has the disadvantage of being susceptible to annual flooding. Because of this, where the river swells above the height of the first elevation, the Amargosa vole switches location to the second level. The highest elevation is used only during particularly extended periods of rainfall.

Little is known about the feeding habits of the Amargosa vole. However, it is thought that its diet consists of a variety of grasses, seeds, herbs, and other such plant material.

The Amargosa vole breeds throughout the year. It has a relatively short reproductive cycle and life span, and the young reach sexual maturity at an early age. As a consequence of this fast population turnover, and as is characteristic of the Microtinae subfamily, populations of the Amargosa vole can expand and contract extremely quickly. So rather large population increases tend to occur over a two- to four-year cycle.

Like so many other rodent species, the Amargosa vole is highly adapted to a specific narrowly defined habitat, but much of its habitat has suffered extensive destruction. The vole's

AMARGOSA VOLE
North America

range is further restricted by its need for permanent water sources. As many stretches of the Amargosa River are subject to seasonal dehydration, the vole is often left to survive in the small pockets of remaining habitat.

Added to this desperate situation are the continual threats of overgrazing, diversion of water sources, marsh drainage, and vegetation burning that tend to accompany the sprawl of agricultural and urban development.

The Amargosa vole is also faced with considerable competition from exotic species such as the house mouse. The vole's habitat is at risk as plant species such as tamarisk and salt cedar, which are tolerant of different environmental conditions, can hinder the growth of more specialized marshland plant species.

A recovery plan for the species has been established, and the springs and marshes near Tecopa, California, on land owned by the U.S. Department of the Interior's Bureau of Land Management have been designated an Area of Critical Concern. In addition, the agency plans to negotiate with private landowners in order to acquire more of the marshland that lacks government protection.

Adrian Seymour

Hualapai Mexican Vole

(Microtus mexicanus hualpaiensis)

ESA: Endangered

IUCN: Vulnerable

Weight: ½–1½ oz. (15–40 g)
Head-body length: 5½ in. (14 cm)
Tail length: 1¼ in. (3 cm)
Diet: Various forest grasses
Habitat: Mountain forests
Range: Hualapai Mountains, Arizona

The Hualapai Mexican vole is a small, thickset animal with a bluntly rounded muzzle, and a tail that is less than half the length of its body.

THE HUALAPAI VOLE is thickset, blunt-nosed, and short-legged. It has tiny ears almost completely hidden by coarse, dark, cinnamon brown fur and lives high in the forests of the Hualapai Mountains in Mohave County, Arizona.

This vole builds its burrow near grass-lined streams to be near the water and food it needs in order to survive. It lives on a diet of lush grasses found near these high mountain streams.

The Hualapai vole has a very limited range. Only four locations are home to this small rodent.

Little is known about this vole. It is one of 12 subspecies of the Mexican vole (*Microtus mexicanus*), which has a much larger range from the state of Oaxaca in Mexico to the American states of Arizona, Colorado, New Mexico, Texas, and Utah.

Little information

What is known of the Hualapai vole are just guesses or assumptions based upon what researchers have found out about the other Mexican vole subspecies. It probably has small litters, based on the fact that females have only two pairs of mammary glands, limiting the number of young to four. Observations have shown that between two and three young are born each season.

Aggression

Voles in general have a tendency to live in large colonies, sometimes numbering in the hundreds, yet they appear to be very aggressive with each other. Furthermore, the larger the colony, the more aggressive they become. Why they should become more violent and still group in large numbers is not well understood, but it may spur population segments to seek other nesting sites.

The life span of this vole and the number of voles alive today is unknown. There are many predators that feed on this small rodent, including owls, hawks, foxes, dogs, coyotes, and snakes. But the principal reason that the population continues to decline is the encroachment of humans. Grazing cattle consume grass and drink water that is already in short supply during periods of little rain. Mining operations and roads constructed to support them have also destroyed habitat. Finally, people's recreational activities, such as camping and using off-road vehicles, and development to support these activities have destroyed much of the habitat that is needed by these animals to survive.

Government protection

The Hualapai vole is protected by the governments of both Arizona and the United States. Current plans are in effect by the Bureau of Land Management to restore and protect its habitat.

In addition, both state and federal authorities are negotiating to buy (or exchange for federal property) privately owned land to increase the size of protected vole habitat.

Salt Marsh Meadow Vole

(Microtus pennsylvanicus dukecampbelli)

ESA: Endangered
IUCN: Vulnerable

Weight: 1–2½ oz. (28–70 g)
Head-body length: 3½–5¼ in. (9–13 cm)
Tail length: 1½–2½ in. (3.5–6.5 cm)
Diet: Grasses, bark
Habitat: Salt marshes
Range: Waccasassa Bay, Florida

VERY LITTLE IS KNOWN about the salt marsh meadow vole. Its habitat is restricted to a single salt marsh on Waccasassa Bay in Florida. There is no population information available.

Researchers believe that this vole is much like most other subspecies of *Microtus*: it has dark fur, a limited litter size, and most likely is very aggressive—even to its own kind.

Scientists view the social life of voles as an oddity. These animals are very aggressive, both against predators and each other. The males fight viciously and, in some species, are often dominated by females. One study revealed that a little less than half the voles sampled from one colony showed wounds and scars from earlier battles.

Voles are thought to be particularly aggressive toward each other as a way to force expansion of their overall territory. Despite normal adult animals caring for

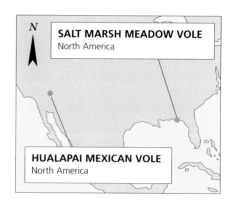

the young and the intricate networking of tunnels and burrows, there is no evidence of lasting pairs or social structure among the voles.

Observers are still anxious over the fate of this tiny vole, as it is believed that a single Gulf hurricane or other catastrophe could destroy the remaining habitat and, in turn, the entire population, making the species extinct.

George H. Jenkins

Cinereous Vulture

(Aegypius monachus)

IUCN: Lower risk

Class: Aves
Order: Falconiformes
Family: Accipitridae
Length: 39–43 in. (100–110 cm)
Weight: Male, 15½–25½ lb. (7–11.5 kg); female, 16½–27½ lb. (7.5–12.5 kg)
Diet: Carrion
Habitat: Diverse
Range: Parts of Europe, North Africa, and Asia

A DEAD HORSE CAN BE a heartbreak, nuisance, or a delight. For people, a horse carcass can be a health hazard. For a cinereous vulture, it is food for a week or longer.

The cinereous vulture is an immense bird, the size of a California condor (*Gymnogyps californianus*). It has a large beak, short neck, long and broad wings that span more than 9 feet (2.7 meters) in some females, and a short and broad tail. The entire body plumage is a brownish or sooty black. The flight feathers are a little grayer. A collar of long, shaggy feathers (called a ruff) shows more brown; and the light, sparse, downlike feathers of the upper nape and hindcrown are gray. This vulture takes its name from its head color, because *cinereous* means "ashy gray." The bare skin about the face, chin, and throat is darker gray, sometimes washed over with a little pink. The pale base of the beak contrasts sharply with the dark tip. Some observers have written that the cinereous vulture looks somber or even morose.

This species is not gregarious or flocking, like some vultures. When it arrives at a carcass, it quickly chases away other scavenging birds. Its aggressive behavior and great size make it intimidating. Written accounts of the vulture's seasonal movements indicate that European populations behave differently than some Asian populations. European vultures apparently remain in their territories all year round. Only the immature birds roam, and their dispersal is not regarded as a true migration. Most Asian vultures also remain attached to territories yearround. However, those individuals in the northern extreme of the species' range do flock to central India and southern China in the winter months. The presence of adults among these wintering birds indicates migratory behavior.

Tree life

The cinereous vulture prefers nesting in trees, particularly those on steep slopes. It does not seem bound to forests or woodlands, however. When hunting, it patrols woodlands that are often inaccurately described as forests. If the vulture hunted over true forest, it would not be able to see through the canopy to spot carcasses on the ground. Nor would it be able, with its huge wings, to maneuver through the canopy to get to the ground. It also hunts over shrub lands and agricultural fields. The cinereous vulture does not prosper around people.

Where does it breed?

Many former breeding areas of the cinereous vulture have been vacant for decades. Areas where it used to soar above the land have not been visited by a vulture in many years.

Several factors may explain this decline. First, people have directly persecuted the cinereous vulture. In some areas, the bird reportedly has taken the lambs of domestic sheep. Second, dwindling herds of large wild animals yield fewer carcasses for the vulture. Third, careful animal husbandry results in fewer available livestock carcasses than in past centuries. Fourth, the spread of croplands, urbanization, and other land uses that do not favor wildlife or the occurrence of and

access to carcasses has probably had very serious effects. Inadequate food supplies initially cause breeding failure, which eventually leads to localized populations dying out altogether.

A shrinking range

The cinereous vulture once ranged over all of southern Europe, and occasional birds wandered into northern parts of the continent.

The species has entirely disappeared from many countries: France, Austria, Germany, Poland, Czechoslovakia, Hun-

The cinereous vulture has a powerful beak for tearing flesh. The cere (base of the beak) is mauve, becoming darker at the tip.

gary, Romania, and Albania. In the mid-1970s, ornithologists estimated that about 600 birds survived in Spain, with that figure representing 250 nesting pairs. By the late 1980s, that figure had been revised to about 365 pairs and maybe 1,000 birds.

Cinereous vultures require five to six years to reach breeding age, so the total population should greatly exceed the number counted in breeding pairs.

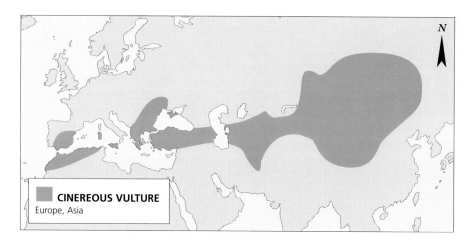

CINEREOUS VULTURE
Europe, Asia

Some nesting still occurs in Greece and Turkey. The vulture does inhabit portions of North Africa—notably Morocco and Algeria—but it has never been proved to nest there.

Cinereous vultures in Asia have fared little better than those in Europe. The larger size of most Asian countries masks the severity of the problem there. Whereas entire European countries have lost these vultures altogether, in Asia the larger countries have merely experienced a sharp decline in vulture populations.

However, populations still occur in all Asian countries within their historical distribution. Long wars in eastern Europe and portions of Asia certainly must have taken a toll on the vultures. War disrupts nesting cycles, and birds are sometimes shot.

Help strategies

Cinereous vultures naturally occur in low densities. They generally do not flock, nest in colonies, or form large social groups. Because of their size and habits, they tend to spread out. Developing practical strategies to help this species is not easy. Several environmental groups are studying the current status and plight of the cinereous vulture, and in 1988, the Spanish government designated a 66,825-acre (27,043-hectare) nature park in Cabaneros that should help the bird. Internationally, no specific actions have been taken on a broad scale to help the bird.

Kevin Cook

Bridled Nailtail Wallaby
(Onychogalea fraenata)

ESA: Endangered

IUCN: Endangered

Class: Mammalia
Order: Marsupialia
Family: Macropodidae
Weight: 3½ lb. (1.5 kg)
Tail length: 20½ in. (52.5 cm)
Diet: Roots, bark, grasses, fruit
Habitat: Woodland and grassland
Range: Queensland and New South Wales, Australia

NAILTAIL WALLABIES are shy and solitary marsupials often mistaken for tiny kangaroos. About the size of a small rabbit, they are banded by white shoulder stripes against dark fur that form a crescent around the back of each shoulder. The bands do not extend to the neck, which is covered only with the same dark fur.

The hips are also banded with white stripes, but are often so faint as to be almost indistinguishable. The underbelly is covered in white or cream fur.

Marsupials include kangaroos, opossums, koalas, and

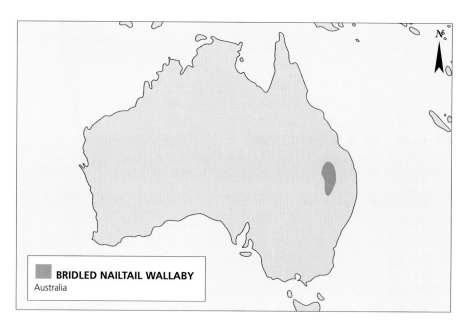

BRIDLED NAILTAIL WALLABY
Australia

cuscuses. They are usually found in the Southern Hemisphere, mainly in Oceania (Australia, New Zealand, and New Guinea) and South America.

Creatures of the night
Nailtail wallabies are mostly nocturnal. They will move about during the day but spend most of their time in shallow trenches scratched into the ground under brush or a thicket of tall grass, depending upon vegetation for cover.

Nailtail wallabies pump their arms while hopping, a trait that encouraged early settlers to call them organ grinders.

Very little is known about the reproductive habits of this animal. Females are believed to give birth to a single young each spring, probably in May.

Nailtail wallabies have a spur or nail at the tip of their tail. It is not known why or how this spur is used, but presumably it is either a remnant from some ancient evolutionary need or it is used for fighting.

Potential for recovery
The population of this animal was quite extensive in the early 18th century. However, the introduction of non-native species contributed greatly to its initial decline. Dogs and foxes preyed on them, and cattle and sheep destroyed much of the grassland so critical to the survival of this species.

Grazing livestock eat so much of Australia's grassland that the grass cannot grow back fast enough—if it grows back at all—for other animals to use as a food source. This is one of the many things that has reduced populations of nailtail wallaby.

Wallabies were hunted for food by the aborigines of Australia, who passed on their practice of consuming this native delicacy to the new settlers.

Species' territories
There are three species of nailtail wallabies: *Onychogalea unguifera*, ranging from northern Western Australia to northeastern Queensland, and still common but losing ground; the very rare *O. lunata*, ranging from southern Western Australia, southwestern Northern Territory, South Australia, and probably southwestern New South Wales; and, finally, the bridled nailtail wallaby, at one time believed to be extinct and formerly inhabiting the inland parts of southern Queensland, New South Wales, and Victoria.

Protected reservation
In 1974, a small population of the bridled nailtail wallaby was found in central Queensland in an area of about 65 square miles (168 square kilometers). Since then, the Australian government has purchased roughly half of the bridled nailtai wallaby's current territory to form a permanent reservation.

If this protected area can remain undisturbed and free from exotic predators and overgrazing livestock, this wallaby will possibly recover.

George Jenkins

WARBLERS

Class: Aves

Order: Passeriformes

Warblers are delightful and fascinating birds. They sing jubilant songs, and bright colors and brilliant patterns liven up their appearance.

Most warblers eat insects as their main food. They catch them by picking, gleaning, and chasing them through the air. Some warblers eat small fruit, such as berries, during the winter months. As a general group, warblers occupy a broad diversity of habitat, from forests and woodlands to shrub lands, swamps, and other wetlands. Some are terrestrial while others are strictly arboreal. The more abundant warblers usually have the most generalized habitat requirements.

The warblers represent two very different families of songbirds. The Old World warblers are Sylviinae, a subfamily of the Old World flycatcher family (Muscicapidae). The New World warblers are usually called wood warblers by ornithologists, and they belong to the family Parulidae. A few Old World warblers also occur naturally in North America. They include the familiar ruby-crowned kinglet (*Regulus calendula*).

Wood warblers have occasionally strayed into Europe, but none live there. Most wood warblers in the United States are migratory. Some move to southern states only for the winter, but many move to Central America, the West Indies, or northern South America.

Several warbler species in both groups now require protection from deteriorating habitat. However, preserving rare or endangered wood warblers must also take into consideration the migratory habits of the birds.

Bachman's Warbler

(Vermivora bachmanii)

ESA: Endangered

IUCN: Critically endangered

Length: 4¾ in. (12 cm)
Weight: Probably ¼–½ oz. (7.5–14 g)
Clutch size: 3–5 eggs, usually 4
Diet: Insects
Habitat: Swamps
Range: Southeastern United States, Cuba, Isle of Pines

IN 1832, A MINISTER named John Bachman who lived in Charleston, South Carolina, collected a female specimen of a warbler he had never seen before. It had a yellow forehead that continued over the eye as a short eyeline. The crown and nape were pale gray. A bit of yellow-gray smudged the cheek on an otherwise yellowish face. The chin and throat were yellow, as were the sides and belly, but a black patch crossed the breast like a bib. Her back, unmarked wing, and tail were an olive color.

Eight months later, in March 1833, Bachman collected a second bird similar to the first, but this time it was a male. It differed from the female in having a greener cheek and lore and a black forecrown. Both specimens had dark beaks and pinkish feet and toes. Bachman gave the birds to his friend John James Audubon, who named the bird Bachman's swamp warbler. It was 50 years before anyone reported seeing the Bachman's warbler again, and 65 years after the species was discovered and named that a nest was finally found.

Through the closing decades of the 1800s and the early decades of the 1900s, all the wrong people found the Bachman's warbler. One plume collector in Louisiana killed 38 of these small birds in five years. Then an egg collector in South Carolina raided 32 nests in three states between 1906 and 1918, collecting 58 specimens. Such people seldom take an interest in documenting details of behavior or natural history. Their enthusiasm is not for birds, but rather for the profit to be made. These collectors caused opportunities for greater knowledge to be lost.

An unlucky species

Ornithologists generally concede that the Bachman's warbler has always been somewhat rare, but the term *rare* is relative. Some ornithologists point to the 38 birds taken in Louisiana and to another 21 that were killed in March 1889 when they flew into a Florida lighthouse. These numbers suggest that the warbler was historically more abundant than commonly believed. Compared to other warblers, however, the Bachman's warbler was indeed rare. If any other warbler species flew into a lighthouse, hundreds or thousands of birds would be killed. Some flocks of warbler species number 10 times more than the 38 Bachman's warblers killed over five years. What the lighthouse event tells us is that the Bachman's warblers were migrating together.

The Bachman's warbler once ranged as far west as eastern Arkansas and southeastern Missouri. It nested as far north as Kentucky, and at least once wandered to the Washington, D.C., area. The species' primary range swept through the southern states from South Carolina to Louisiana. Nests have been found in widely separated localities of Arkansas, Missouri, Kentucky, and Alabama. Presumably much suitable habitat existed in between, but nests were not found. And it is no wonder—the hot, humid habitat typically harbors mosquitoes carrying malaria, yellow fever, and encephalitis, as well as poisonous snakes, alligators, ticks, fleas, chiggers, and biting flies. Searching for birds in this environment is extremely uncomfortable and possibly hazardous.

A bird of the swamps, the Bachman's warbler succumbed to people's disregard for its habitat. It nested in low vegetation, often over water, but searched for its insect prey up in the trees. As people drained the swamps and cut trees, the warbler's habitat disappeared. But this explanation is general and speculative. Too little of the bird's natural history is known for experts to be certain that this is the main reason for its decline. Certainly, some swamplands remain in the southern United States, and the Bachman's warbler could presumably have survived. Some essential detail of habitat was probably lost before anyone knew what it was.

In the case of the Bachman's warbler, virtually 100 percent of the species' population wintered on Cuba and the Isle of Pines. The landscape on the Isle of Pines has been almost completely altered by humans.

Nearly all the swamps of Cuba have been lost to cutting and agricultural development. Without wintering habitat, then faced with dwindling summer habitat, a rare bird can quickly become rarer. Egg and specimen collecting may have contributed a secondary pressure that the bird could not withstand.

Sightings

Years went by with no reports of the Bachman's warbler. Sightings did increase in the 1930s, 1940s, and 1950s, but began declining again in the 1960s. The increased

The Bachman's warbler has been so rare for so long that no one has been able to study it in any useful detail.

sightings are almost undoubtedly due to a growing army of recreational birders who have added the Bachman's warbler to their sighting lists. A sighting in Florida in 1977 is accepted by most ornithologists as the last reliable report of the species. More recent sightings in Cuba are unconfirmed. This bird quietly avoided bird enthusiasts for 50 years after it was discovered.

The question now is if it can avoid far greater numbers of people deliberately looking for it. Until more is known it will be listed as critically endangered by the IUCN.

Golden-cheeked Warbler

(Dendroica chrysoparia)

ESA: Endangered

IUCN: Endangered

Length: 5½ in. (14 cm)
Weight: 8.7–12 g
Clutch size: 3–4 eggs
Incubation: 11–12 days
Diet: Insects
Habitat: Mature juniper woodlands
Range: Summers in Texas; winters in Guatemala, Honduras, and Nicaragua

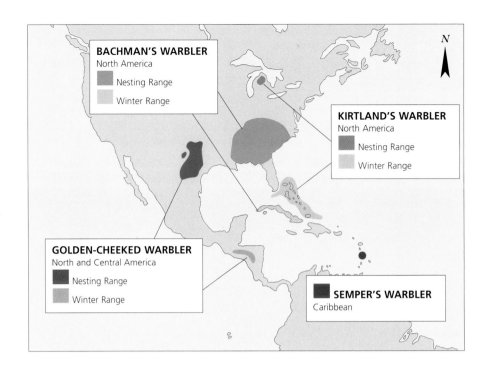

THREE DIFFERENT TREES in the family Cupressaceae cover the hilly landscape of Edwards Plateau in Texas. Botanically, they are junipers, but most people know them as cedars. The eastern red cedar (*Juniperus virginiana*) and white cedar (*Juniperus pinchotii*) contribute to the overall wooded character of the land, but the Ashe juniper (*Juniperus ashei*) dominates the woodland. It also provides the key element in the natural history of the golden-cheeked warbler. As the Ashe juniper matures, its outer bark naturally shreds into long strips. The female golden-cheeked warbler collects strands of these bark strips and uses them to fashion her nest.

Appearance

The female golden-cheeked warbler is dull green from the forehead, over the crown, down the nape, and onto the back. Fine blackish green streaks darken the dull green. Each dark wing shows two white bars, and the dark tail shows white underneath. The breast and belly are clean white. Short stripes pattern the sides. The black feathers of the chin and throat have white edges and tips, making them look scalloped. The entire face, including the lore, the stripe over the eye, and the cheek, is bright yellow, and there is a dark green line through the eye. The male shows the same pattern as the female, but his upperparts, chin, throat, and upper breast are not streaked.

The male's brighter colors attract attention to him and away from the female and her nest. The male assumes responsibility for defending his territory against others of his kind. This probably protects the food supply essential for feeding the young.

The female incubates the eggs in a nest she built by herself. She may use hair, fine grasses, rootlets, and feathers to line her nest; but she always uses strips of bark from the Ashe juniper to build the base structure. The bark strips are carefully secured with spider webs, which she also gathers from the junipers.

The female golden-cheeked warbler usually builds her nest in an Ashe juniper, but not always. Occasionally she will locate her nest in one of the other juniper species or even in an oak, elm, or hackberry tree.

Tree homes

The juniper woodlands of Edwards Plateau are frequently called cedar brakes. The term *brake* means an area densely grown with woody, shrubby vegetation. It is a colloquial, rather than a botanical, term, and people in different parts of the country apply it to different portions of the American landscape.

Since the early settlement days in Texas, people have looked upon the cedar brakes as a mixture of a valuable resource and a cursed wasteland. The junipers or cedars can be cut for fence posts and rails that will withstand the ravages of weather for a long time. Cedar stumps can also be rendered for commercially valuable cedar oil. Small prairie expanses interrupt the brakes, and livestock often graze there. Small fires or a couple of bulldozers with a stout chain slung between them are used to fell the problem trees and open the land for growing grass and grazing cattle.

Woodlands disappear

While deliberate assaults have reduced the total area of juniper woodlands, indirect loss has also taken its toll. Expanding urban and suburban areas, golf courses, campgrounds, and road improvements have all destroyed portions of woodland vital to the golden-cheeked warbler.

Some effort has been made to calculate the past extent of the

The golden-cheeked warbler has a dark eye line, and no clear ear patch. Its is black above, with a black crown and bib and black-streaked sides.

woodlands and compare historical size with present size, but these estimates are extremely difficult to calculate and their value is suspect.

Moreover, natural history research on the warbler indicates that the amount of total habitat is probably less critical than its quality. Golden-cheeked warblers do not need numerous junipers as much as they need mature Ashe junipers.

Even if the juniper woodland has spread on Edwards Plateau in the last century, many of the newer areas have trees that are too young to contribute the bark strips that the warbler needs for its nest. Further habitat problems may be affecting the golden-cheeked warbler.

Its primary wintering grounds in Central America are still poorly known, although the general area was identified many years ago.

Heavy forest cutting and other habitat changes could be reduc-

ing the amount of wintering habitat that is available to the golden-cheeked warbler.

Continuing decline

Despite the general awareness of the warbler's survival problems, and despite its legal listing as an endangered species, the golden-cheeked warbler continues to decline. Ornithologists are not sure why, although habitat quality seems to be a likely factor.

A common attitude that people and communities adopt is that their own activities cannot be harmful to the warbler, because they truly believe that the warbler can go somewhere else. The total habitat loss accumulated through hundreds of small, unconnected activities continues almost without a break. The golden-cheeked warbler will eventually run out of suitable space. The only future for the species lies in preserving large tracts of mature woodland grown with Ashe juniper.

Kirtland's Warbler

(Dendroica kirtlandii)

ESA: Endangered

IUCN: Vulnerable

Length: 5¾ in. (14.5 cm)
Weight: (2–16 g)
Clutch size: 3–6 eggs, usually 4–5
Incubation: 13–16 days
Diet: Primarily insects but occasionally small fruits
Habitat: Nests in pine woodlands
Range: Summers in lower peninsula of Michigan; winters in the Bahamas

The unusual nesting habits of the Kirtland's warbler have played a role in its decline. It builds its nests only under jack pines and as those disappear, so too does the warbler.

THE KIRTLAND'S WARBLER has earned more fame than any other songbird in North America. People may more quickly recognize the red-winged blackbird (*Agelaius phoeniceus*) and the American robin (*Turdus migratorius*), but romance surrounds the warbler.

In May 1851, Charles Pease collected an unfamiliar wood warbler near Cleveland, Ohio. The head, upperparts, wings, and tail were bluish gray. Black stripes patterned the back, and two faint bars decorated each wing. White eyelids formed an incomplete ring around the eye. Brilliant yellow covered the specimen from chin to lower belly, but the undertail was white. Black spots and stripes marked the sides. Pease gave the specimen to his father-in-law, Jared Potter Kirtland. A well-known physician and naturalist, Kirtland sent the bird to a renowned ornithologist, Spencer Fullerton Baird, who named the species in honor of Kirtland.

The bird remained a mystery for a century after its initial discovery. The first nest was not found until 1903, about 50 years after the first specimen was found. As decades passed, the Kirtland's warbler story gradually unfolded. Portions of its life story are still not understood.

Kirtland's warbler migrates between the Great Lakes area in Michigan and the Bahama Islands off the Atlantic Coast of Florida. It is seldom seen in migration and is difficult to find in the Bahamas. During summer, the Kirtland's warbler congregates in an area of 4,800 square miles (12,430 square kilometers). Its nesting grounds lie between Saginaw Bay of Lake Huron on the east and Lake Michigan on the west.

Individual males have been found in Michigan's upper peninsula, Wisconsin, and Ontario, but no nesting sites have been found outside Michigan.

Within its limited nesting range, this warbler nests only in jack pine (*Pinus banksiana*) woodlands. Specifically, it nests beneath young jack pines variously reported as 3 to 16 feet (0.9 to 4.9 meters) and 6 to 20 feet (1.8 to 6 meters) tall. The warbler builds its nest directly on the ground among grasses or other non-woody vegetation growing immediately under the jack pines. Once the jack pines grow too large, the ground cover beneath them changes and the Kirtland's warbler stops nesting there. Occasional fires set up conditions for jack pines to grow back in patches. As one patch matures beyond the warbler's use, others emerge as suitable nesting sites. However, the actions of humans have disrupted this cycle.

Fire benefits

When professional forestry first began developing in the United States, fire was regarded as a great evil to be prevented and avoided. All fires were extinguished without thought to their part in a natural process. The jack pine is one species that actually benefits from light fires. Heat scorches the cones and improves germination of the seeds. In Michigan, one result of fire fighting was a gradual decline in suitable jack pine habitat vital to the Kirtland's warbler. By the time ornithologists and foresters combined their views and developed a fire plan to help the warbler, another problem had developed.

Human intervention

The expansion of human populations throughout the Midwest brought more changes to the landscape. Forests and woodlands were opened up for farming and livestock grazing. The brown-headed cowbird (*Molothrus ater*) found its way into this new habitat.

Cowbirds lay their eggs in other birds' nests, then abandon them to the host birds for parenting. This behavior is called brood parasitism. Usually cowbird eggs hatch before the host birds' eggs. This early hatching gives young cowbirds a competitive advantage over the hosts' true offspring. Once brown-headed cowbirds moved into the warbler's habitat, they steadily victimized the warblers and hastened their decline. For some

unknown reason, the Kirtland's warbler suffers an unusually high loss of young birds between the time that they first leave the nest and the end of their first year. The naturally high mortality of young birds makes cowbird parasitism a far more serious issue.

If the warbler population drops too low, heavy parasitism could severely threaten the population. Since the 1970s, people have erected traps to catch brown-headed cowbirds, but turning them loose somewhere else only compounds the parasitism problem for other birds. Cowbird trapping has increased over the years, but the Kirtland's warbler has not responded with a dramatic increase in population.

Other protective actions on behalf of the Kirtland's warbler include public education and controlled burning. The warbler has become a local celebrity, and residents welcome visiting birders who come to Michigan for a chance to see the famous bird.

To make sure that Kirtland's warblers remain in the area, forestry officials now intentionally burn some selected areas to encourage the proper growth of jack pines for the warbler.

The U.S. Fish and Wildlife Service has set a goal of 1,000 nesting pairs of Kirtland's warblers. Something about the bird's natural history apparently interferes with achieving this particular goal, however, as the population has stabilized at around 500 birds for many years, with year-to-year gains and offsetting losses.

The annual effort to monitor, count, and protect the Kirtland's warbler has developed into an American pastime.

Nauru Reed Warbler

(Acrocephalus rehsei)

| IUCN: Vulnerable |

Length: 5½–6 in. (14–15 cm)
Diet: Insects
Habitat: Shrub lands
Range: Nauru Island in the western Pacific Ocean

THE NAURU REED WARBLER is imperiled by an unusual set of circumstances caused by the fertilizer industry on its island home. The guano industry, which produces a fertilizer mainly from seafowl excrement, is the only significant industry on the island and is the major source of revenue for the people who have settled there.

Little more than a low plateau that rises from the sea, Nauru provides ideal nesting conditions for many seabirds.

The diets of these birds include mostly crustaceans, squid, and fish. Their body wastes are consequently rich in minerals and compounds that can be processed into high-quality plant fertilizers. The phosphates in their droppings are particularly valuable to plants. During centuries of nesting on the island, seabirds have left a thick layer of droppings, ready for mining. The industry may not last much longer, however, because the guano mining progresses faster than the birds can replenish the supply. The mining also destroys the habitat that the birds need for nesting. The Nauru reed warbler does not contribute appreciably to the guano supply, but it does suffer from the loss of habitat.

Nauru lies just one degree south of the equator. It is an island with a checkered political history. It was discovered by British sailors in 1798, but Germany controlled it from 1888 through World War I. The League of Nations then assigned the island to Australia, but Japan seized it during World War II. After the war, Australia resumed control of Nauru.

This dot in the Pacific finally became a nation in 1968. About 9,000 people now live on Nauru's 8 square miles (21 square kilometers).

For many years they enjoyed one of the highest incomes per person of any nation in the world. Their wealth was not based on oil or gold but on the phosphate content of bird droppings, or guano.

Species or subspecies

The Nauru reed warbler is considered by some ornithologists to be a subspecies of the nightingale reed warbler (*Acrocephalus luscinia*). Both birds belong to the subfamily of Old World warblers (Sylviinae). The nightingale reed warbler occurs on several of the Mariana Islands northwest of Nauru. The Nauru reed warbler lives nowhere else but on Nauru. The Nauru reed warbler is smaller than its cousin and is a dull gray to brownish gray overall. It has a thin, straight beak that it uses for catching insects.

There is very little information about this warbler except that its habitat is being eroded by mining activities.

A shy bird of shrub lands and shrubby forest undergrowth, the Nauru reed warbler needs the plant communities that are constantly being removed in the process of mining guano. Ironically, as the mining continues, more shrubbery is destroyed and more guano is removed. Eventually the Nauru people will have no minable quantities of guano and no shrub lands left. Without the shrub lands they will have no place for either the seabirds or the Nauru reed warbler. Unless specific protective measures are taken, Nauru will have no industry, no seabirds, and no reed warblers.

Some estimates in the early 1980s predicted that Nauru would deplete its guano supplies by the early 1990s. As of 1983, the reed warbler still inhabited the remaining fragments of shrub land on Nauru. No recent investigations or surveys have been conducted on the island, so the status of the Nauru reed warbler remains a mystery.

Before recommendations can be made, studies are needed to determine the current status of the bird, and mining must be controlled to reduce further habitat loss.

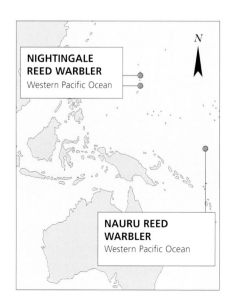

Nightingale Reed Warbler
(Acrocephalus luscinia)

ESA: Endangered

IUCN: Vulnerable

Length: 7 in. (18 cm)
Diet: Insects
Habitat: Wetland thickets, forest undergrowth
Range: Mariana Islands in the western Pacific Ocean

THE NIGHTINGALE reed warbler is slowly disappearing due to predation and the loss of its wetland habitat, and it can now only be found only on the islands of Saipan and Alamagan located in the Mariana group.

This reed warbler appears to be a long, slender bird. Its length is exaggerated by its beak, which is especially long and slim for a warbler. A plainly colored bird, it is a dull, golden yellow below and a golden brown above. A pale line runs over the eye. The unmarked wings and tail are the same golden brown as the upperparts. The outer tail feathers are shortest, and the feathers get a little longer with each pair toward the center, giving the tail the appearance of being graduated when folded and rounded when spread out.

The nightingale reed warbler has a distinctive and complex song that sounds similar to songs of many familiar birds, yet it has a definite quality of its own. When nothing seems at home in the marsh, the song of the reed warbler says otherwise. Once common on Guam and several of the Mariana Islands, the nightingale reed warbler has disappeared entirely from Guam and probably from the islands of Aguigan and Pagan as well. It seems to be surviving on Saipan and Alamagan. Many birds unique to Guam have disappeared from that island. Much of the blame has been leveled against the brown tree snake (*Boiga irregularis*). An exotic species to Guam, the snake is native to Southeast Asia. It probably came to the island as an uninvited hitchhiker in ships' cargo; it first appeared on Guam at the end of World War II. At first, people tolerated—even welcomed—the snake as a way to control rats on the island. But the brown tree snake favors bird eggs and nestlings. It can climb trees well and explore small crevices that larger predators could never reach. A mild venom improves the snake's predatory abilities.

The decline of many birds unique to Guam corresponds closely with the arrival and proliferation of the brown tree snake. The snake, however, was only one element in a whole series of problems.

Other exotic species that could work against the nightingale reed warbler include rats, monitor lizards, pigs, house cats, and dogs. All of them have the ability to find nests and take eggs and nestlings. Some of them can even catch adult reed warblers. Most of these exotic animals were already on Guam by the late 1800s. They had been working on Guam's native birds for several decades before the brown

tree snake arrived. The snake inherited a damaged island; and not all the changes were caused by exotic species.

Other threats

The chemical DDT came into popular use as a compound for killing lice during World War II. Its insecticidal properties became well known. After World War II, the chemical was sprayed heavily on Guam for years. The spraying was mainly intended to eradicate mosquitoes and secondarily to control insects that damaged crops, but ornithologists suspect that DDT killed more than just insects. The chemical interferes with calcium use in birds. Females exposed to DDT lay eggs with very thin shells. Exotic predators and devastating chemicals together could have exterminated these birds, but yet another factor enters the tale of the nightingale reed warbler.

Most of Guam's naturally occurring freshwater wetlands were drained and filled in the 1960s and 1970s. The warbler disappeared quickly during this period. People on Guam needed space for living and growing food

crops. The demand for space claimed wetlands. When they were destroyed, the birds that depended upon them also disappeared. Apparently no one thought to preserve part of the island's natural wetlands, so all the wetlands were lost, either by thoughtless planning or by random consequence.

The combination of events on Guam is as severe as those on any of the Mariana Islands. Some islands had no reed warblers because they had no natural wetlands to support them. Not all the islands have brown tree snakes. One of the islands where the nightingale reed warbler still thrives, Saipan, has both natural wetlands remaining and no snakes. Recovering the reed warbler on other islands will require restoration of the wetlands and aggressive control of exotic predators.

Maintaining trees

Other measures could include the maintenance of trees that this warbler is known to nest or forage in, such as the Madras thorn (*Pithecellobium dulce*) or sea hibiscus (*Hibiscus tiliaceus*).

Warblers occupy a variety of habitats all around the world.

Semper's Warbler

(Leucopeza semperi)

ESA: Endangered

IUCN: Critically endangered

Length: 5¾ in. (14.5 cm)
Diet: Insects
Habitat: Montane forests
Range: Saint Lucia in the Lesser Antilles of the West Indies

TIME MAY HAVE RUN out for one of Saint Lucia's most distinguished inhabitants, the Semper's warbler. In decline for many years, the bird has not been observed since 1972.

The Semper's warbler is not distinguished by its impressive size or dazzling color: it is a small bird with dark gray upperparts that blend softly into a dull white. The bird is unique for living only in the montane forests of Saint Lucia. It has no near relatives among all the many wood warblers. Ornithologists classify it in a genus by itself.

The island of Saint Lucia is a a 238-square-mile (595-square-kilometer) volcano top that protrudes above the water. To the east of the island sprawls the Atlantic Ocean; to the west lies the Caribbean Sea.

Saint Lucia, the second largest of the Windward Islands in the Lesser Antilles, is situated near Martinique to the north, Saint Vincent to the southwest, and Barbados to the southeast. Mount Gimie at the island's southern end towers 3,145 feet (959 meters) above the sea. Its flanks were once well covered by forest. Dry forests, woodlands, and shrub lands occurred at lower elevations. Wet forests covered the higher slopes.

Most of Saint Lucia's native plant communities have been damaged or destroyed. The island was discovered during the colonial years of the European nations, coming under British rule in 1814. By then the pattern of clearing the land to grow exportable crops was well established. Saint Lucia became an independent nation in 1979. The government looked for ways to improve the island's primarily agricultural economy, which was based on bananas, coconuts, and cocoa, so tourism and light manufacturing became important. In the 1980s, plans were drafted for making Saint Lucia a port for oil tankers.

During the last two centuries, Saint Lucia has changed. Many of its woodlands and forests have been cut for local building materials, exporting lumber, and firewood to make charcoal. Other tracts have been cleared to make room for plantations, and still others have been replaced by resorts and related tourist facilities. Nearly all the lower-elevation forests and woodlands have been destroyed or severely modified.

Very little is known about the natural history of the Semper's warbler. Ornithologists do know that it spends considerable periods of time on the ground amid low plant life beneath the forest canopy. Such a lifestyle made the warbler extremely vulnerable to black rats, which are known to take eggs and nestlings. Black rats came to Saint Lucia as stowaways in ship cargo. As an exotic species, they have caused enormous problems for island wildlife all around the world. In the 1870s, Indian mongooses (*Herpestes auropunctatus*) were deliberately released on many islands where rats had become established. The good intention was that the mongooses would eat the rats and perhaps eliminate them. But instead of stocking a few islands with mongooses and monitoring the results, mongooses were introduced to many places around the world, including Saint Lucia. The mongooses did little to control rat problems, and quickly added to the problems of exotic species on many islands.

Exotic endangerment

The Semper's warbler encountered steady habitat loss when people converted its island home to plantations and resorts. Any portions of habitat that remained were first degraded by exotic rats that stole eggs and nestlings by night, then by exotic mongooses that preyed on eggs, nestlings, and adults by day.

Other factors may have contributed to the decline of the Semper's warbler, but the exotic species and habitat loss together were probably sufficient to endanger this unique bird.

The last report of a live Semper's warbler was in 1972. About 15 years later, some field ornithologists spent 10 days searching the island for the bird. They set up nets and used other techniques to detect this warbler, but they did not find one specimen. No extensive searches have been made since 1987. Other birds have disappeared for longer periods and reappeared, but when an island bird goes unseen for over two decades, the hope that it survives soon outweighs the probability that it does not.

Rodrigues Brush Warbler

(Bebrornis rodericanus)

ESA: Endangered

IUCN Critically endangered

Weight: 11–12 g
Clutch size: 3 eggs in recent nests; 4–5 reported in 1875
Diet: Small insects
Habitat: Forest undergrowth and forest edges
Range: Rodrigues Island in the Indian Ocean, east of Madagascar

CONSUMING INSECTS can be noisy work: it is easy for a listener to hear the Rodrigues brush warbler snapping its beak as it eats small insects. The difficulty is actually finding the warbler.

Rodrigues is one of three islands in the group known as the Mascarene Islands. Covering only 43 square miles (112 square kilometers), it lies 500 miles (800 kilometers) east of Madagascar. The other two Mascarene Islands, Mauritius and Réunion, are farther west, closer to Madagascar. Rodrigues sits inside the Tropic of Capricorn at about the same latitude south of the equator as Puerto Rico is north of the equator. Its climate is tropical and strongly influenced by the

Indian Ocean. Before people discovered Rodrigues, forests grew over most of the island. Human settlement in the 1600s brought many different changes to the terrain.

Habitat disruption

People cut down the forests for several reasons. At first they simply needed firewood, then they needed building materials, and finally they required space. Forest grazing offers less total food to animals than prairie land, so the forests were cleared to open the land for grass production. Cattle, goats, and pigs were all brought to Rodrigues by humans. The island had never supported large grazing animals before. Their eating habits changed the character of the island's plant communities. They ate seeds, seedlings, and saplings of shrubs and trees so that woody plants could not easily replace themselves. As old trees and shrubs died, no young plants matured in their place. Being a small and remote island, Rodrigues has never attracted the same attention as its sister islands. The island's human population grew for some time, then steadily declined. Many livestock

animals were abandoned or allowed to escape, and they continued to damage the island after the people had left. The changes on Rodrigues made it very difficult for some birds that are unique to the island to survive, including the Rodrigues brush warbler.

A drab little bird, the brush warbler has uniformly olive-green upperparts and paler, more yellow underparts. The long, thin beak is gray, as are its feet and toes. When excited or agitated, it often holds its short crown feathers erect so that its head has a shaggy look. It also cocks its long tail upward.

Today, the brush warbler inhabits thickets and forest undergrowth, particularly along forest margins. Observers have also reported seeing it in mahogany plantations. Such observations do little to clarify the species' habitat preferences. The plant communities of Rodrigues have been so thoroughly altered and the native forest growth survives in such small, isolated patches that no one can be certain what the brush warbler needs or favors as habitat. Its regular occurrence at forest margins would suggest that

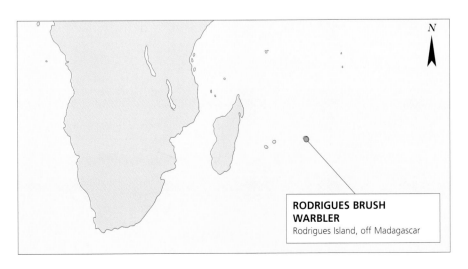

N

RODRIGUES BRUSH WARBLER
Rodrigues Island, off Madagascar

opening the forest on Rodrigues and creating clearings and edges should have benefited the bird. Apparently, this was not the case. Estimates in the early 1970s figured the population at close to 60, but by the late 1970s the Rodrigues brush warbler had declined to just 30 birds. If forest clearings and edges were important to it, its population should have increased over the decades.

Cyclone damage

Some people have blamed cyclones for the species' troubles, but this ignores the thousands of years that brush warblers survived cyclones on Rodrigues before people arrived. However, as people cleared the forests from Rodrigues, the small remaining patches of trees could not provide the same protection from cyclones as a more expansive forest cover. The effects of cyclones on Rodrigues are probably more severe since the native plant communities were removed.

People cannot change the course of cyclones or prevent them from happening. They can, however, reduce the devastation of cyclones by restoring forest communities. Some minor steps have been taken on Rodrigues. The island is under the dominion of Mauritius, which is an independent and sovereign nation.

Protection

Revised wildlife laws have improved legal protection for the islands' birds, but they do not help the bird to feed or nest. The Mauritius government has supervised the removal of feral livestock from Rodrigues, which is a vital step, but too many domestic animals remain.

The forests on Rodrigues are administered under forestry laws that view trees as commercial products rather than as habitat for birds.

Black rats (*Rattus rattus*) are suspected to have invaded Rodrigues. Known for killing birds and taking eggs, they could be the final blow to the imperiled brush warbler.

By 1990 the Rodrigues brush warbler had declined to only two dozen birds. Despite its critically low numbers, this small bird has not been targeted for recovery work. If the trend established in the last few decades continues through the 2000s, the Rodrigues brush warbler will become extinct in the 21st century.

Kevin Cook

Banded Wattle-eye

(Platysteira laticincta)

ESA: Endangered

IUCN Vulnerable

Class: Aves
Order: Passeriformes
Family: Muscicapidae
Subfamily: Platysteirinae
Length: 7½–8 in. (19–20 cm)
Clutch size: Possibly 3 eggs (known from 1 nest)
Diet: Insects
Habitat: Montane forest
Range: Bamenda Highlands in Cameroon, Africa

ORDINARILY, a goat would seem to pose no threat to a bird. In a narrow human view of animal relationships, goats eat plants and therefore are herbivores, not carnivores. The banded wattle-eye should have nothing to fear from domestic goats (*Capra hircus*). A wider view of natural history, obtained through the science of ecology, reveals links between animals that are not so obvious. In fact, the banded wattle-eye has suffered decline from the habitat loss caused by the grazing habits of goats.

African species

A quiet, even shy, little bird, the banded wattle-eye deserves its name. The male is white from chin to undertail except for a shiny blue-black band that crosses the lower breast and belly like the cummerbund on a tuxedo. His entire upperparts, including forehead and face, wings and tail, are deep black with a blue sheen. As the bird moves about, a green glint shines off the dark feathers. A bare patch of ruffled pink skin circles the eye like a flower. The bare skin is called a wattle, which becomes enlarged with blood when the bird becomes excited. Another trait is not reflected in the bird's name. The inner flight feathers of each wing have fringed edges. When the bird folds its wings, the fringes puff out like a tuft of fine hair.

The banded wattle-eye is just one of eight wattle-eye species. All eight occur in Africa, where the banded wattle-eye may have the smallest range of them all. It inhabits only the montane forest of the Bamenda Highlands in western Cameroon. As small as its range naturally is, it has

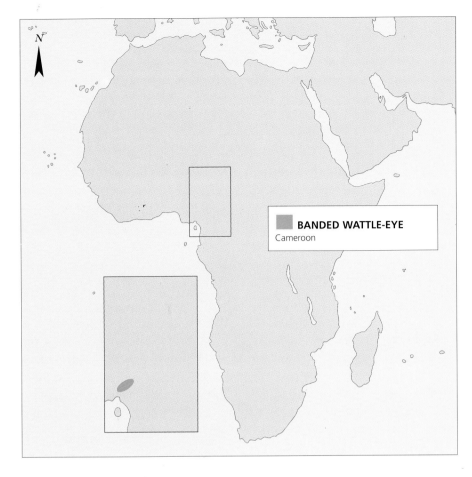

BANDED WATTLE-EYE
Cameroon

A somewhat arboreal species, the banded wattle-eye is dependent on the trees and forest. It continually searches from the ground through the understory and into the canopy for insects. The goat only symbolizes the travesty that has befallen the great forest that once completely covered the Bamenda Highlands of Cameroon.

Praise

The Cameroon government has received high praise from the International Council for Bird Preservation (ICBP) regarding habitat preservation. The people of Cameroon have protected 7,700 square miles (20,000 square kilometers) of savanna and other lowland habitat in nine national parks. Forest fragments of the Bamenda Highlands are protected by forest preserve status, but preserves, unlike national parks, do not receive enforcement protection.

Human threat

Despite their status as forest preserves, people still cut, burn, till, and graze the remnants of highland forest. Recommendations have been made to the Cameroon government regarding protection of the remaining large tract of highland forest found on Mount Oku. It is the last significant tract of primary forest and still supports fair numbers of banded wattle-eyes. The ICBP has coordinated field studies of the Bamenda Highlands forest and its bird life. The ornithologists of that organization believe that if the Mount Oku forest is not preserved, the banded wattle-eye will become extinct.

Kevin Cook

steadily dwindled. Only isolated fragments of a once extensive forest system now survive in the highlands. Some fragments still support the banded wattle-eye, but even these fragments have been altered. The loss of forest has been caused by a combination of factors.

Consumption

Many villagers in Cameroon depend on firewood for their basic cooking needs. They walk many miles to cut bundles of wood. Each time they cut, a little more forest disappears. Week by week, month by month, they must walk farther and farther to obtain the wood they need. People also need space to grow crops, both for commerce and for eating. Much of the forest has been cleared to develop plantations of palms for producing palm oil. These plantations now creep right into the foothills of the highlands. To increase plantations further, people burn the land to kill small trees and shrubs that make farming difficult. The fires can burn out of control, however, and destroy more forest than people need. Farmers even clear undergrowth and ground cover to plant beneath the trees.

Livestock also graze in the forest. Goats, sheep, cattle, pigs, and horses all eat the native vegetation. They consume everything, including leaves, twigs, fruits, seeds, seedlings, and saplings. So many domestic and feral livestock feed in the area that the plants, particularly the trees, cannot grow fast enough to survive. The forest has, in part, disappeared because no young trees are growing to replace old trees that die or are cut down.

WEAVERS

Class: Aves

Order: Passeriformes

Family: Ploceidae

Subfamily: Ploceinae

Weavers select fine grasses and hair to make their nests. They carefully weave their building materials either in solitary nests or in large communal nests that may fill an entire tree. All the nest structures are domed in some way, and birds enter from the side or the bottom.

A fascinating family of approximately 143 species, the weavers naturally occur only in the Old World. Different species range through Europe, Asia, and the East Indies, but the greatest diversity occurs in Africa. Many of the weavers have brilliant hues of red or yellow, although some are plain black, while others are different shades of gray or brown.

The weaver most familiar to Americans is the house sparrow (*Passer domesticus*). This bird, also called the English sparrow, is native to northern Africa, southern Europe, and the Middle East. People intentionally brought it to North America, where it has proved extremely adaptable to urban living.

The birds known as queleas (*Quelea* sp.) congregate in groups of thousands, and flocks in the hundreds of thousands are regularly reported. There have even been groups of one million. Such large groups present enormous problems to grain farmers. In just minutes, a giant flock of queleas can demolish an entire millet field. However, not all weavers thrive in such great numbers.

Many weaver species inhabit only small areas. As human populations have grown and exerted more influence on the character of the land, some weavers have declined. At least three species of weavers need special consideration by conservationists if they are to avoid extinction.

Bannerman's Weaver

(Ploceus bannermani)

IUCN Vulnerable

Length: 5¼–5½ in. (13.5–14 cm)

Clutch size: 2 eggs (2 nests)

Incubation: Probably 12–14 days

Diet: Probably seeds and insects

Habitat: Forest edges

Range: Eastern Nigeria, western Cameroon

THE AFRICAN LANDSCAPE is changing so rapidly that many of the creatures that live there are fading into history. Most of them could be saved if more were known about their natural histories. But for all the time the humans have lived among these creatures, the basic details of their lives have remained unrecorded—if they were ever known at all. The Bannerman's weaver is just such a species.

Ornithologists know what kind of bird it is and generally where to find it. They know little else, however, except that it is one of the many species that is slowly disappearing.

Golden bird

The Bannerman's weaver is golden overall. The upperparts, including the crown and the nape, are greenish gold; the underparts from lower throat to undertail, are brighter yellow. The wings and the tail are darker and browner than the back. The black eyes are surrounded by a black mask that includes the lore, cheek, chin, and throat. A golden yellow border separates the mask from the greenish gold of the crown and neck.

Neither a forest nor a prairie species, the Bannerman's weaver inhabits forest edges and the dense shrubbery that grows in the woodlands surrounding the forests and in strips through ravines and along streams. Since its discovery in 1925, the Bannerman's weaver has never been abundant. Even early references to it mention that it is rare. As the forest cover of its range disappears, the weaver has been disappearing with it.

The native forests have been cut and replanted with eucalyptus trees (*Eucalyptus* sp.) as a lumber crop. They have also been cleared for livestock grazing and food crops. Local people tend to use fire to clear away young trees and woody shrubs. The fires often burn out of control and consume far more forest than necessary to meet the people's needs. Although this weaver inhabits forest edges, it does not seem to benefit from these burnings, even though they reduce the forest and create openings or patches. Any increase in habitat at the forest edges should promote population growth.

One theory to explain why this weaver has not prospered is that because so much forest has been lost, the amount of forest-edge habitat has not in fact increased at all. Where it still occurs, the Bannerman's weaver is regarded as common. But it does not occur in many places today. No estimates of population size have been calculated, and no specific measures to protect this bird have yet been implemented.

However, Cameroon has preserved 7,770 square miles (20,000 square kilometers) of savanna and other lowland habitat in nine national parks.

Proposals have been made to preserve the last natural forest tracts in western Cameroon. If accepted, a national park to protect montane forests would extend some protection to the Bannerman's weaver.

Clarke's Weaver

(Ploceus golandi)

ESA: Endangered

IUCN Vulnerable

Length: 5–5½ in. (12.7–14 cm)
Habitat: Forests, woodlands
Range: Sokoke Forest in Kenya

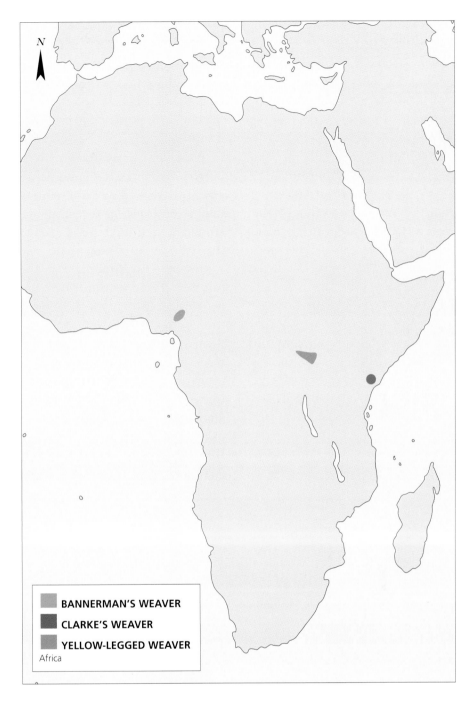

BANNERMAN'S WEAVER
CLARKE'S WEAVER
YELLOW-LEGGED WEAVER
Africa

WHEN TIMBER cutting outstrips the rate at which new trees can grow, it ceases to be a profitable activity. Logging has a profound effect on the wildlife that depends on those trees and the plant community that forms around them. Their habitat is lost and, as a consequence, they will simply decline.

Clarke's weaver is one such species to suffer due to this habitat loss. The bird was first collected and described in 1913, but 42 years passed before another specimen was collected. Many ornithologists discounted Clarke's weaver as a legitimate species. They reasoned that if it were a separate species, it would be observed and collected more often. Because the bird was not seen or collected, it was believed to be another form of masked weaver (*Ploceus intermedius*).

Today, ornithologists acknowledge the Clarke's weaver as a full species and believe the bird is actually more closely related to the Weyns' weaver (*Ploceus weynsi*) of central Africa.

Clarke's weaver is a yellow-and-black bird with a black hood that covers the entire head, neck, chin, and throat. The black extends down onto the breast and the back. The wings, rump, and tail are dark green. The underparts fade from bright yellow on the lower breast to yellowish white on the undertail. The beak is dark gray.

The Clarke's weaver typically gathers in flocks of up to 30 birds, but occasionally groups as large as 100 congregate. While flocking, the Clarke's weaver is conspicuous enough to be noticed. During the breeding season, it seems to disappear. If the bird migrates to other areas to breed and nest, it must spread out so much that it becomes nearly invisible. The location of Clarke's weaver's nests needs more investigation.

The Clarke's weaver occurs only in a wooded tract along the coast of Kenya. Known as the Sokoke Forest, the area hosts several unique species of plants and animals besides the weaver. The Sokoke Forest is actually a mosaic of four major plant communities.

Woodlands, not forest, make up the largest part of the area's 160 square miles (400 square kilometers). This forest-woodland complex stretches between the villages of Sokoke on the southwest and Arabuko on the northeast. People in the local villages turn to the Sokoke Forest to graze their livestock, grow their food, and cut their firewood to cook the food; they earn their wages by cutting down trees. The lumber industry situated around the Sokoke Forest once maintained three sawmills. But all three were forced to shut down when they ran out of trees and could no longer operate profitably. People still cut down trees in the Sokoke Forest, even though the mills are gone and the area is protected as a forest reserve.

Clearance

Portions of the reserve have been cleared to make way for plantations of exotic trees that are being grown for their lumber value. Whether by cutting, grazing, farming, or burning, the Sokoke Forest has been dramatically altered over the past several decades. Even the nature reserve that covers about 16½ square miles (43 square kilometers) within the Sokoke Forest Reserve offers only modified habitat. Much of the nature reserve still offers good habitat

Weavers occur naturally only in the Old World. Different species range throughout Europe, Asia, and the East Indies, but the greatest diversity of weavers occurs in Africa.

for the Clarke's weaver, but no estimates of this bird's population have yet been made. However, a small population spreading out in the nature reserve to nest could be so dispersed that it would be very difficult to find.

More land recommended

The International Council for Bird Preservation (ICBP) recommended to the Kenyan government that the size of the nature reserve should be substantially increas-ed. The ICBP proposal was developed in the early 1980s, but by the early 1990s no action had been taken. Meanwhile, fire-wood cutting, livestock grazing, and some timber cutting all continue both within the Sokoke Forest Reserve and inside the nature reserve.

Yellow-legged Weaver

(Ploceus flavipes)

IUCN Vulnerable

Length: Probably 5–5½ in. (12.7–14 cm), as in related species
Diet: Unknown, but probably insects
Habitat: Lowland forest
Range: Eastern Democratic Republic of the Congo

WHEN THE YELLOW-LEGGED weaver was discovered in 1913, its only known homeland was the Ituri Forest in the Belgian Congo. The land, forest, and bird have lasted since that discovery, but interests have changed. The country is now called the Democratic Republic of the Congo, and both bird and forest are harmed by the ways people use land.

Appearance

The yellow-legged weaver is an unspectacular bird. Overall black plumage makes its yellow feet and toes stand out. Immature birds show some dark greenish cast to their plumage, but otherwise the species has no distinguishing traits. It lives in the upper canopy of wet lowland forests. Dark birds in such places can be very difficult to detect, as the example of the yellow-legged weaver proves.

The first specimen of the species was collected in 1910, but it was misidentified as a golden-naped weaver (*Ploceus aureonucha*). After the species was formally described in 1913, additional specimens were collected in 1921, 1950, 1952, and 1953. The total was only seven birds. The yellow-legged weaver was not seen again for 30 years. During that time, some ornithologists feared that the bird had become extinct before anything could be learned about it. Many observers reported seeing the yellow-legged weaver through the 1980s; however, ornithologists still know almost nothing about the bird.

Insect diet

The stomach contents of one yellow-legged weaver held parts of some caterpillars, which indicates a possible diet of insects. Because the yellow-legged weaver lives in the treetops, an insect diet would be expected.

A very localized species, the yellow-legged weaver is undoubtedly at risk from habitat destruction. The same problems that threaten the bird also threaten local people and their culture. These problems are meshed in the country's history.

The Democratic Republic of the Congo has an area of 905,063 square miles (2,344,113 square kilometers), and more than 33 million people live there.

Political conflict

The Belgian Congo became an independent nation in 1960 and was renamed the Republic of Zaire in 1971. It became known as the Democratic Republic of the Congo in May 1997. Intense conflict among the country's more than 200 distinct tribes caused much bloodshed during the 1960s and 1970s. The violence prevented scientists from studying the nation's land and wildlife. Species such as the yellow-legged weaver remained mostly obscure and their status uncertain. As the country has worked to modernize, the consequences to wildlife have been predictable.

Forest threat

The Ituri Forest in the republic suffers all the same threats as other tropical forests. People are cutting it down for lumber products and firewood and to open up the land for agricultural use.

Some organizations have recommended the development of stronger protection for the forest. Virunga National Park lies east of the Ituri Forest. If it were expanded, Virunga could incorporate specially protected habitat for the yellow-legged weaver within its borders.

Kevin Cook

GIANT WETAS

Class: Insecta

Order: Orthoptera

Wetas are cricketlike insects that live on the islands of New Zealand. Isolated in the southern Pacific for nearly 100 million years, New Zealand harbors some of the most primitive creatures known in the world, of which giant wetas are a very good example. The giant wetas of the genus *Deinacrida* are among the world's largest insects, weighing as much as 2½ ounces (70 grams), which is nearly three times as much as the average house mouse. They typically measure 4 inches (10 centimeters) or more in length.

Giant wetas rank among the most endangered insect species in the world.

In the absence of land mammals, snakes, crocodiles, and other predators, many of New Zealand's birds became flightless and many insects grew to huge proportions. The flightless kiwi, for example, is New Zealand's national emblem.

Giant wetas are not only large, but they are also flightless. These insects even lack wings.

Prior to human settlement in New Zealand, the herbivorous wetas filled the ecological niche or function of rodents in New Zealand; indeed, they are often called invertebrate mice. About 1,000 years ago, humans arrived from Polynesia, bringing carnivorous *kiore* rats with them. European settlers colonized New Zealand in the 1880s, bringing several mammalian predators—notably more rats—that have resulted in the decline of the flightless wetas throughout much of their historical geographical ranges.

Predation by introduced rodents and cats has been especially devastating to weta populations.

Because of the introduction of numerous non-native predators and pests, New Zealand now harbors about 10 percent of the endangered plant and animals species that are recognized in the world today.

Description

Wetas are primitive members of the insect order *Orthoptera*, which includes grasshoppers and crickets. Like all insects, wetas have three main body regions: a head, a thorax, and an abdomen. A typical adult weta resembles a giant cricket: its body is squat and amber, but it lacks wings. The hind legs are armed with long spines, which are used to fend off predators.

Wetas have very large mandibles, or jaws, for chewing on plants. They feed at night on the leaves of trees, shrubs, grasses, and forbs (an herb other than grass).

Giant wetas are believed to live as long as two or three years. They usually live alone except during the spring or summer mating season, depending on the species. Eggs are laid in moist soil, either singly or in small groups. A single female may lay as many as 600 eggs during her life span, but 200 to 300 are more typical.

The vigorous movement of weta legs creates a loud rasping sound from filelike ridges on its body. When a weta is threatened, this noise is used to startle its potential predator.

Types of wetas

Some of the giant wetas, such as the wetapunga (*Deinacrida heteracantha*) and the poor knights weta (*Deinacrida fallai*), are tree-dwelling species; while others, such as the Stephens Island weta (*Deinacrida rugosa*) and Herekopare Island weta (*Deinacrida carinata*), are ground dwellers, hiding under rocks and logs during the day.

Endangered species

After the introduction of rats on New Zealand, the giant wetas nearly disappeared. By the 1970s, they survived on only three rat-free islands in the Cook Strait region, and only one of the islands—Mana—supported a large population. Because Mana lies close to the mainland, conservation-oriented entomologists knew that the island would probably not remain completely rat-free forever.

Thus, in 1977, the entomologists captured individuals of all the giant weta species, studied them in captivity to learn more about their biology and diet, then moved some of them to rat-free Maud Island.

Annual census counts have revealed that weta population numbers are gradually increasing on Maud Island.

Ideally, the introduced rats can be eliminated or controlled so that similarly successful translocation efforts can be attempted in other parts of the giant wetas' historical range.

Richard A. Arnold

WHALES

Class: Mammalia

Order: Cetacea

Whales are some of the largest animals in the world. In fact, the largest animal to have ever lived on Earth was not a dinosaur, but a whale. Whales can be found throughout the saltwater oceans and seas from the Antarctic to the Arctic. Baleen whales tend to feed on some of the smallest animals alive: tiny marine animals known as plankton. But some whales, such as the killer whale, feed on large animals. They prey on seals and dolphins and even on baleen whales.

Because whales are mammals, they share many physical characteristics of land-dwelling mammals. They breathe air and therefore must surface regularly to breathe. However, as an adaptation to their aquatic lifestyle, their nostrils are on top of their head, allowing them to breathe quickly without expending much energy to lift themselves above the water.

Toothed whales have a single nostril, or blowhole, while baleen whales have two.

Although whales appear smooth-skinned, all whales have at least a few hairs on their body during some stage of their life, and many have a few hairs even as adults. Whales have a pair of pectoral or side fins (flippers) that are primarily used for steering and stabilization. The large, horizontal tail fins or flukes are their primary source of propulsion.

Whales are similar in another way to land-dwelling mammals. Females feed their young on milk, and for some species the amount of milk produced is large, befitting an animal that may reach more than 65 feet (20 meters) long. Whales' forelimbs have evolved into the shape of fins, giving them a superficial resemblance to fish. But whales have tail flukes that are horizontal, unlike a fish's tail, which is vertical.

Many whale species have been ruthlessly killed by commercial hunters during the last several hundred years for their oil, meat, and other body parts. Other species have been hunted extensively only since the advent of steam power and exploding harpoons.

Hunting has led to drastic reductions in populations of most large whales throughout the world, and even to extinction (the gray whale of the Atlantic is the first whale species to become extinct). Only since the 1960s has there been any real attempt to regulate or halt whale hunting.

Although the taking of whales for commercial purposes in now banned temporarily, it is not yet clear whether this action was taken in time. For some of these widely dispersed, slow-breeding giants, it will be many years before their survival is assured, if this can ever be achieved.

As most species of whales are migratory, special efforts must be made to ensure that productive polar waters are not damaged or destroyed by excessive fishing or pollution, and that breeding areas remain free of human disturbance so that depressed populations of these ocean giants can return to anywhere near their former numbers.

Nearly all whale population estimates, particularly for the balaenopterid and sperm whale species, are questionable. They are not guaranteed to be accurate because they are what is known as soft—that is, they may be incorrect.

Surveying endangered species such as the whales, in something as vast as the world's oceans, is quite a difficult task.

Blue Whale

(Balaenoptera musculus)

ESA: Endangered

IUCN: Endangered

Weight: Up to 200 tons (182 metric tons)
Length: 72–109 ft. (22–33 m)
Diet: Krill
Gestation period: 300–330 days
Longevity: Possibly up to 90 years
Habitat: Open oceans
Range: Northern and Southern Hemispheres

IT MAKES SENSE that the largest animal to have ever lived would be aquatic. Being large means that the structures an organism uses for support (such as limbs or bones) must be huge, and on land the effects of gravity can place an enormous strain on them. However, water can act to support an organism, removing the necessity of having huge internal structures to carry and support a large and heavy body.

It is no surprise that the largest animal to have ever lived is the blue whale, resident of open oceans throughout the world. While the largest dinosaur is estimated to have been around the same length of 100 feet (30 meters) long, much of that length was a thin neck and tail. A blue whale can grow to be much more massive, reaching up to 200 tons (182 metric tons).

Eating machine

Although the blue whale is huge, it's long, slender build gives it a sleek, hydrodynamic look. This

Unfortunately, despite its awe-inspiring size and the huge expanse of ocean wilderness that is home to this giant, the blue whale is threatened with the same fate as that of the largest dinosaur.

shape, combined with large tail flukes driven by powerful muscles, enables the blue whale to reach swimming speeds of up to 30 miles (48 kilometers) an hour. Despite its torpedo-like shape, the blue whale can expand its mouth and throat to an enormous size during feeding. This is possible because of a series of skin grooves, or pleats, that run under its jaw. These pleats can be spread apart, greatly widening the mouth and throat area.

Although the blue whale can open its mouth to such an extent, the foods it prefers to eat are actually tiny. Even more amazing, the blue whale has no teeth. Instead, it has long, brushlike plates of baleen suspended from the roof of its mouth. These baleen plates act as strainers. When feeding, the blue whale moves through the water, mouth and throat open. It then turns on its back or side and uses gravity to force the water out of its

mouth through the baleen plates. The plates capture the food while allowing the water to pass out of the mouth. Although it is completely toothless, the blue whale fetus contains tooth buds. This is true of all baleen whales in the family Balaenopteridae, suggesting that the baleen whales must have once had teeth like their relatives the odontocetes, or toothed whales.

Despite its gargantuan size, the blue whale feeds almost entirely on small planktonic animals. It is highly selective in its eating habits, preferring to feed on shrimplike crustaceans called krill. These are found in the colder waters of temperate and polar regions, where upwelling currents from the depths cause nutrient circulation. These nutrient-rich waters contain millions upon millions of plankton, krill, and other small animals. Many larger animals, including fish and seals, wander these waters to feed on the abundant food source. A single adult blue whale may end up eating 40 million krill every day in these northern waters.

The blue whale, like many other species, migrates to warm

tropical waters to breed. During this period it feeds little, if at all, relying instead upon its fat reserves. It is thought that a female blue whale gives birth to a single calf every two to three years. As might be expected for such a large animal, a baby blue whale is still comparatively huge, and it grows at a phenomenal rate. Toward the end of gestation, while still a fetus, a blue whale calf gains 75 pounds (34 kilograms) a day; and after birth, the 4,400-pound (2,000-kilogram) calf gains about 200 pounds (90 kilograms) every day.

When a whale slips beneath the waters for a lengthy dive, the process is called sounding. Different species have varying methods of this. For example, the blue whale raises its flukes above the surface slightly, then spouts one to four times a minute, followed by 12 to 15 brief dives in a row, gradually deepening the dives and staying under from 10 to 30 minutes.

Reduced numbers

Although the blue whale has been found in all ocean waters from the Arctic to the Antarctic, in historic times the largest population of this whale was found in the Southern Hemisphere. Because of the blue whale's large size and deep-water habits, early whalers rarely took this species. However, when modern methods such as the harpoon gun and the whale factory ship revolutionized the whaling industry, the blue whale came under increasing persecution, first in the Northern Hemisphere, then in the Southern. From an estimated population of more than 200,000, today the numbers have been estimated at less than a few thousand.

Since it seems as if the southern and northern populations never actually meet and interbreed, the small number of blue whales that remain becomes an even more disturbing statistic. While the northern population probably never numbered more than 12,000, today there may be as few as 3,000 to 4,000 blue whales in the north.

While there were once as many as 200,000 blue whales in the Southern Hemisphere, perhaps as few as 500 remain in southern waters. There may also be a few thousand pygmy blue whales left.

It is not at all clear whether these numbers are enough to support the two distinct populations of this whale and allow the species to increase in numbers.

Just finding a mate, even for an animal as large as a blue whale, in the immense area of the oceans of the Southern Hemisphere is a difficult task.

And when there are so few blue whales remaining, this activity becomes an even greater challenge.

Northern Bottlenose Whale

(Hyperoodon ampullatus)

IUCN: Lower risk

Weight: 3–4 tons (2.7–3.6 metric tons)
Length: 23–32 ft. (7–9.8 m)
Diet: Primarily squid, some fish
Gestation: 365 days
Longevity: Up to 37 years
Habitat: Open oceans
Range: North Atlantic Ocean

THE NORTHERN bottlenose whale belongs to a group of little-known, medium-sized cetaceans called beaked whales that are in the family Ziphiidae. These appear to be much more similar to dolphins than to whales in their basic body structure. Beaked whales are much smaller than most baleen whales, with some species being only about as big as a large dolphin. Many of the beaked whales also have a bulging forehead and a long beak similar to those of a dolphin.

There are some fairly obvious differences, however, between dolphins and beaked whales. For example, while the size ranges of the two groups of cetaceans do overlap, most beaked whales tend to be larger than dolphins. Dolphins range from about 5 to 13 feet (1.5 to 4 meters) in length; beaked whales vary from 13 to 43 feet (4 to 13 meters) in length.

Members of the beaked whales also have a pair of grooves that form a V shape in the skin of the throat. Most beaked whales have only one or two pairs of

functional teeth (with the exception of the shepherd's beaked whale, which has more than 50 teeth). The teeth are found in the lower jaw and are frequently so deep within the gums that they cannot be seen. Other vestigial teeth are found below the gum line in both the upper and lower jaws. In females of many species, including the northern bottlenose whale, the teeth sometimes do not erupt. As beaked whales tend to have many scrapes and scars on their bodies, it has been hypothesized that perhaps these odd teeth are used as weapons in fights among males to determine dominance, but this has yet to be proven.

The northern bottlenose whale tends to vary in coloration. Younger animals are usually a dull brown or yellow, but as they age this lightens to almost white. Males are usually much larger than females. The northern bottlenose whale has a large, prominent bulge on its forehead, which is more obvious in mature males. This bulge contains a structure called a melon. Some scientists think that this area of the head is used to regulate buoyancy at great depths. Others believe that the melon is used for echolocation (the use of sound to determine the location of objects such as prey).

A number of different sounds have been recorded for the northern bottlenose whale, and it may be that the melon is involved in sound production or directional focusing of sounds.

Northern bottlenose whales are found from the Arctic ice pack to about 40 degrees latitude on the east and west of the Atlantic Ocean. They are usually seen in small groups of between 5 and 15 individuals. These groups are almost always found far out at sea, away from the coast in deep waters. In spring they are frequently found near the Arctic ice pack, but in fall they tend to move south into warmer waters.

These whales are known to dive for long periods and to great depths, sometimes below 3,000 feet (900 meters). Bottlenose whales regularly stay underwater for over half an hour, and unsubstantiated reports suggest that they may hold the cetacean dive record of two hours below the surface. The northern bottlenose whale feeds primarily on squid, as well as on fish and starfish. These prey are hunted, caught, and eaten during deep dives.

While the melon of the northern bottlenose whale is undoubtedly a useful structure, it has also been a primary reason for this cetacean's downfall. A large northern bottlenose whale can hold up to 440 pounds (200 kilograms) of oil in its melon. Whale oil was once the principal source of fuel for lamps, which led the whaling industry to concentrate heavily on this species—especially after other whales became scarce from overhunting.

The tendency of bottlenose whales to approach boats and remain near injured group members made killing them easier than other whales. Over 50,000 northern bottlenose whales were taken in northern Europe during the 40 years of whaling from 1881 to 1920. While the main purpose of hunting these whales was for the large amounts of oil each whale provided, the meat was not wasted. It was used in

Norway on fur farms and in England as pet food.

After pressure was exerted on the northern bottlenose whale during those 40 years of hunting, the population declined so that commercial whalers no longer concentrated on this species. Over the next few decades, the population began to recover, but because of the enormous profit gained from even a single individual, commercial whalers again began to hunt the northern bottlenose whale. Caught in a vicious cycle, the population again crashed, and by the 1960s it was no longer profitable to concentrate on hunting this species.

Unknown numbers

Because of the combination of its relatively small size and its vast open-water habitat, it is not known today how many of these whales remain. It is known that a fraction of the perhaps 100,000 previously calculated northern bottlenose whales still survive, for although modern whaling equipment became quite efficient, whalers consistently killed fewer animals over the years until the catch became almost nothing.

It is hoped that with the ban on whaling now in effect, the northern bottlenose population will begin to make a recovery. But until the difficult task of monitoring the population of these unusual two-toothed whales is

completed, scientists will not know the true status of this whale for certain.

Bowhead Whale
(Balaena mysticetus)

ESA: Endangered

IUCN: Lower risk

Weight: Up to 110 tons (100 metric tons)
Length: 40–65 ft. (12–20 m)
Diet: Zooplankton
Gestation: 365–420 days
Habitat: Open oceans
Range: Oceans and seas of the arctic Northern Hemisphere

THE BOWHEAD WHALE may well be one of the most bizarrely shaped mammals in the world, and it is certainly the oddest-looking of the cetaceans. This whale is mostly head: its skull takes up almost 40 percent of its entire body. The bowhead whale's enormous mouth has a curved S shape when viewed from the side. The thin upper jaw ends in a sharp bony point, while the huge lower jaw is shaped like

The bowhead whale is frequently found in areas of broken ocean ice and is considered a creature of the pack ice edge. It follows the ice as it retreats and spreads with the seasons.

a giant scoop. The 300 or so baleen plates that are suspended from the upper jaw are longer than those of any other whale.

The bowhead whale's unusual appearance is further enhanced by its eyes, which, by their position near the end of the mouth, appear to be set near the halfway point of the body horizontally and below the midpoint vertically. The front of the lower jaw is usually bleached white, while the rest of the whale is black or gray.

The bowhead whale has an unusual method of feeding, which it shares with its close relatives the right whales.

Like other baleen whales, the bowhead whale feeds on small animals such as krill by filtering water through its bristlelike baleen plates.

However, unlike most other baleen whales, the bowhead whale usually feeds on the surface, skimming along the top and taking in mouthfuls of prey.

This is the only large whale to spend its entire life above 50 degrees latitude, or in polar Arctic water. Because of this range, the bowhead whale has a thicker cover of blubber on its body than other whales in order to protect it from these cold waters.

Although the bowhead whale remains in cold northern waters all year round, it still performs a limited migration in the spring and fall, apparently keeping close to the edge of the pack ice.

Little is known about the bowhead whale's social system. Although this whale is thought to usually travel alone or in small groups, much larger groups are sometimes seen, especially during their migration. These occasionally appear to be single-sex groups. What seem to be small feeding groups have also been observed, in which the whales move in a V-formation. Like other whales, the bowhead whale does not appear to feed during the breeding season, relying instead on stored reserves of fat.

Tons of uses

Bowhead whales belong to the group of whales called right whales, which includes the northern and southern right whales. These species were all named right whales because whalers considered them to be the right whales to hunt, given the enormous amount of oil and baleen that a single whale could produce. These whales are slower than most other whales, averaging only about 5 miles (8 kilometers) per hour, compared to speeds of up to 30 miles (50 kilometers) per hour for some of the faster species. Right whales were often found in large groups close to shore, and, because of their percentage of blubber, they had a greater tendency to float once they were killed. All these features were an immeasurable help when hunters attempted to capture, kill, and handle creatures that could weigh up to 110 tons (100 metric tons).

The bowhead whale was an important part of the life of northern coastal people during historical times, so much so that some groups had different names for whales of different ages. For people hunting whales in small boats or kayaks, the peaceful, slow-moving bowhead whale was a bonanza of meat, blubber, oil, baleen, and bone.

During the great whaling period that stretched from the 1600s to the early 1900s, the bowhead whale was one of the most important animals in the economy of Europe. After the destruction of the more coastal northern right whale populations, the whaling industry concentrated on a northern cousin known as the Greenland whale. This bowhead's oil was used to light the lamps in homes throughout much of Europe. A single bowhead whale could produce up to 30 tons (27 metric tons) of oil and one ton (0.9 metric tons) of baleen. The bowhead whale was slaughtered wherever it was encountered. While its remote northern home provided some protection, so great was the economic boon of a single whale that hunters were willing to risk their lives on the pack ice in search of it.

The result of this intensive demand and heavy hunting pressure was predictable. The bowhead whale was eliminated from one area after another, and whalers were quick to locate new groups once a known population was destroyed. By the early 1900s, few bowhead whales remained. In the 1930s, a moratorium on commercial bowhead whale hunting was effected. However, this and future regulations protecting the bowhead may have come too late for up to three of the four major populations, and perhaps for the species as a whole.

While today there may be anywhere from 4,000 to 8,000 bowhead whales in the Alaskan population, distinct populations found along the Siberian coast, eastern Canadian coast, and western European coast have declined to a few hundred each. Inuit communities are still allowed a few bowhead whale kills every year, but they are closely monitored and it is not believed that this practice will have a serious impact on the remaining population.

Oil spill risk

A more serious potential danger lies in the destruction of the few remaining bowhead whales breeding and foraging grounds by pollution. Many Arctic coastal areas that the bowhead whale uses are being or will be explored for oil—both offshore and along the coast. A major oil spill, such as the one in Prince William Sound in 1989, could easily damage the coastal ecosystem upon which the bowhead whale depends. Decisions concerning oil exploration in the Arctic must take into consideration the remaining populations of bowhead whales if this whale is to have any chance of recovering its numbers.

The fin whale is found only in deep ocean waters, near the edge of the continental shelf. It travels singly or in groups of between 3 and 100 or more.

Fin Whale
(Balaenoptera physalus)

ESA: Endangered
IUCN: Endangered

Weight: Up to 77 tons (70 metric tons)
Length: 55–88 ft. (17–27 m)
Diet: Krill and other small crustaceans, fish and cephalopods (squid)
Gestation: 330–345 days
Longevity: Up to 100 years
Habitat: Open oceans
Range: Temperate oceans of the Northern and Southern Hemispheres

THE FIN WHALE is a somewhat smaller version of the largest animal ever known, the blue whale (family Balaenopteridae). Although the fin whale is the second longest whale in the world, it is much lighter than many other whale species. Like the blue whale, its body is long, but it is actually slimmer than the blue whale. This allows the fin whale to move through water with a minimum of drag and therefore travel at high speeds.

The fin whale is notable for its fairly large dorsal or top fin, which can be up to 24 inches (61 centimeters) long. This fin, which is larger than that of the the blue whale, varies subtly from individual to individual and allows whale researchers to identify and study specific fin whales.

Baleen plates

Like all members of the cetacean suborder Mysticeti, the fin whale has plates of baleen suspended from the roof of the mouth instead of teeth. These keratin plates act as strainers, trapping small animals such as shrimplike krill and small fish such as sand eels and herring, while allowing water to pass through.

The fin whale has a series of grooves along the underside of the mouth and throat that allow the mouth to expand greatly. It shares this trait with other rorquals. Rorquals are the group of baleen whales that includes the blue whale, sei whale, and humpback whale. These grooves allow a fin whale to take in much larger quantities of water than whales

that do not have them, and therefore it can take in more of the tiny prey items it feeds upon.

Two-toned face

Perhaps the oddest thing about the fin whale is its coloration. Most of the fin whale's head and body is patterned in a dark gray. However, the right side of the head, including the right side of the tongue and baleen plates, is much lighter in color or almost white. Many theories have been offered for this asymmetrical (uneven) coloration, and most concern feeding. One theory is that this light color helps the whale sneak up on its prey, while another says that the light area acts to scare and herd prey into a tighter clump for easier feeding. What is known is that when feeding, a fin whale frequently lies on its right side, so that the pale area is facing down. Exactly why this is done, however, is still a subject of debate.

Migration

The fin whale is one of the fastest whales, and it frequently dives to great depths. It is also a migratory species. In the spring, groups of fin whales move into colder, more productive water near the poles to feed. This whale spends an average of about 120 days in its northern feeding grounds, when it manages to eat enough food for the rest of the year. It has been estimated that a fin whale may eat as much as 7,000 pounds (3,200 kilograms) of krill and small fish every day while in its feeding grounds.

In the fall, fin whale groups move back to warmer tropical waters to breed. During the breeding period, the fin whale eats very little, or it may not eat anything at all.

Due to migration patterns, all rorqual whales have distinct Northern and Southern Hemisphere populations that may never meet. All fin whales move north in April and May. However, for the northern population, this is springtime. The move, therefore, takes them into the colder waters of their feeding grounds. For the southern population, the northward move takes them into warmer water where breeding occurs. A few months later the reverse occurs, with the southern population moving south toward the pole and the northern population moving toward the equator to breed.

Hunting victims

Because of the speed of this whale and its habit of remaining far out to sea, the fin whale was not heavily hunted during the early years of the whaling industry. However, as technology caught up with large, self-sufficient whaling ships, the fin whale—due to its large size and relative abundance—became a valued species to commercial whalers.

In fact, it became the main whale taken in southern waters during the middle of the 20th century. By the time the practice of whaling was suspended, the population of fin whales was probably only one-quarter of its original number. While some data suggests that this whale may now be increasing in number, because of its slow rate of reproduction, even in the best of situations it will be many years before the fin whale can be said to be no longer in danger.

Gray Whale

(Eschrichtius robustus)

ESA: Endangered

IUCN: Lower risk

Weight: 22–40 tons
(20–36 metric tons)
Length: 35–50 ft. (11–15 m)
Diet: Small crustaceans
Gestation period: 405 days
Longevity: Up to 70 years
Habitat: Coastal ocean waters
Range: Coastal north
Pacific Ocean

THE GRAY WHALE may be one of conservation biology's great success stories. Like the peregrine falcon or the bald eagle, the gray whale has gone from a species once threatened with extinction to one whose numbers have increased to the point where it appears to no longer be in danger. However, as with any large animal that is easily disturbed, has a slow birth rate, and whose habits lead it into conflict with humans, the gray whale may never again be completely safe.

Skin features

The gray whale (family Eschrichtidae) tends to be dark gray or even black. The skin is often patchy-looking, with whitish skin spots or groups of white barnacles to reinforce this appearance. An adult gray whale can have up to a few hundred pounds of barnacles clinging to its body. The gray whale is one of the few cetaceans that does not have a dorsal fin, sharing this feature with, among others, the bowhead whale.

The gray whale belongs to the group of whales called the Mysticeti, or baleen whales. Like other Mysticeti, the gray whale has no teeth. Instead, it has around 150 plates of brushlike baleen that hang from the upper jaw and are used to strain out small animals from the water.

Coastal Pacific migrant

The gray whale is a coastal whale, rarely found far out at sea. It can be found on both the eastern Pacific and western Pacific coasts. A few hundred years ago it was found on both coasts of the Atlantic Ocean, from North Africa and Florida to the near Arctic. However, both Atlantic populations are now extinct, with the last Atlantic gray whale disappearing during the 1700s.

The eastern Pacific gray whale is still the most common whale seen off the coasts of California, Oregon, and Washington. This population performs a yearly migration of over 11,000 miles (18,000 kilometers). During the spring and summer, they travel to the Bering Sea and coastal waters near Alaska, although a few always remain behind in their southern range. In the fall, the northern population of whales moves south along the Canadian coast and the western United States to the northern coast of Mexico. There, near the Gulf of California off the coast of Baja California, these whales spend the winter months. This warm tropical area also has a number of bays, and it is in only five of these bays that the eastern population of the gray whale gives birth.

Population change

The western population of the gray whale also spends the spring and summer in the northern Pacific, mainly in the Sea of Okhotsk near the Russian coast. In the fall, this population travels south past Japan and winters near the coast in the Sea of Japan and along the coast of Korea.

The gray whale tends to be found either alone or in small groups.

Normal migration in the gray whale is performed by either solitary individuals or groups of up to 15 animals. In the summer and winter grounds, however, larger groups may be seen—especially near good feeding grounds or in the breeding bays. The gray whale appears to do most or all of its feeding in the northern summer regions. There, unlike other baleen whales, the gray whale feeds by digging or plowing along the sand and mud of the shallow bottom of coastal areas, sucking up sediment and straining organisms through its baleen plates. Long gouges are regularly found along the bottom of the Bering Sea during sonar mapping or exploration, showing areas where the gray whale concentrates during feeding.

The gray whale has been important to the coastal people

of western North America and eastern Asia for at least 2,000 years. The regular migration of this whale allowed people to prepare to hunt it during specific times of the year. These whales would sometimes travel within view of shore and rarely more than a few miles out to sea, so the effort involved in capturing this species was comparatively small. Its frequent active surface behavior—including surfacing to blow every four to five minutes, lifting its head above water (spy hopping) and leaping or breaching—made locating and following this whale fairly easy.

Jeopardy

Because the gray whale was such an easy target, when its breeding bays were finally discovered in the mid-1800s, the gray whale's survival became seriously jeopardized.

Pre-whaling estimates placed the eastern gray whale population at around 20,000 but during a 20-year period, more than 10,000 gray whales were taken from the breeding grounds alone.

This intense hunting pressure meant that the gray whale population dropped down to perhaps only a few hundred during the early 1900s.

Hunting pressure

Similar hunting pressures affected the western gray whale population, which had the additional problem of breeding in an area having a high human population.

This meant more disturbances from fishing and development happening during the important calving period.

Since this whale population was always fairly small, probably numbering only a few thousand before commercial whaling began, it was quickly driven to the brink of extinction.

Today there may be less than 100 western gray whales left. Some scientists argue that this population is already extinct, and that all sightings are of eastern gray whales that are off course. The eastern population has fared much better.

Special protection

The International Whaling Convention proposed protection of these whales in 1946, excluding regulated subsistence hunting in the north. Since then the population has rebounded, with estimates placing the population at pre-whaling numbers, around 20,000. This has led the United States to consider removing the eastern population of the gray whale from the endangered species list.

While the gray whale is a success for the conservation movement, it is only a partial success. Two or perhaps three out of the four major populations of this whale are now extinct.

Development

Although the eastern Pacific gray whale is now out of immediate danger of extinction, it still faces many other threats. These include the following: the development of coastal areas and future offshore oil development along the migratory path and near feeding and breeding grounds—not to mention harassment from the vastly increasing number of boats that use the same waters as the gray whales.

Humpback Whale

(Megaptera novaeangliae)

ESA: Endangered

IUCN: Vulnerable

Weight: Up to 34 tons (31 metric tons)
Length: 35–59 ft. (11–18 m)
Diet: Small fish and crustaceans
Gestation period: 330–345 days
Longevity: Up to 48 years
Habitat: Open and coastal ocean waters
Range: Oceans and seas of the Northern and Southern Hemispheres

THE HUMPBACK WHALE is one of the better-known whales in the world due to the regularity with which it enters shallow coastal waters, where it can frequently be observed by boaters. An entire whale-watching industry has arisen around the humpback whale's preference for living along the coast.

Another reason for the humpback whale's familiarity and popularity is its acrobatic behavior. The term *humpback* refers to this whale's habit of bending its back at the point of its small dorsal fin before diving, so that the fin is raised high above the surface of the water. It frequently breaches, or leaps out of the water, sometimes entirely clearing the surface. Few people who have observed a 30-ton (27-metric-ton) humpback leaving the water and crashing down with a sound that can carry for miles will ever forget the sight or sound. Other common behaviors

regularly seen include lob-tailing, or waving the tail out of the water; flipper waving or slapping, where the enormous pectoral flippers are raised out of the water; and spyhopping, where the whale raises its head so that the body is vertical and the eyes are above the water's surface, supposedly to enable the whale to look around.

The humpback whale belongs to the group of whales called baleen whales (family Balaenopteridae). Like all the members of this group, the humpback whale has baleen plates in its mouth instead of teeth, and it uses these plates to strain out the small organisms on which it feeds. The humpback whale belongs to a smaller classification called rorquals, which includes the blue whale. All rorquals have deep grooves along their lower jaw and throat that allow the throat area to greatly expand when feeding.

Bubble feeder

Perhaps the most unusual behavior observed in the humpback whale involves its feeding. Like all baleen whales, a humpback can feed simply by opening its mouth, taking in water filled with small animals such as krill and fish, and straining the water out through the baleen plates. However, the humpback whale has a peculiar method of localizing its prey in order to maximize its feeding efforts. When a school of krill or small fish such as sand eels is located, a humpback whale will frequently swim below the school and emit a stream of bubbles. This stream is often released while the whale is swimming in a spiral, which has the effect of

The humpback whale tends to migrate from colder northern waters to warmer tropical oceans to breed.

causing the bubbles to encircle the school and forcing the small animals closer together. At that point the whale moves in and sweeps through the school with its mouth open, scooping up huge numbers of its prey. Some humpback whales are also known to use their long pectoral fins or tail to force schools of prey into tight groups, and it appears that some humpback whales will feed together, perhaps working as a team to herd prey.

The most obvious difference between the humpback whale and all other whales lies in the humpback whale's pectoral fins, or flippers. These are huge—far longer than those of any other whale, even those of the blue whale. The flippers on a humpback whale can be more than 13 feet (4 meters) long. They are also oddly notched along the front edge, giving a scalloped or spiked look. These fins can be much lighter in color than the rest of the dark gray body. The tail flukes of this species tend to have large whitish or pale gray patches. The position and size of these patches are specific to each whale and allow researchers to identify individual whales by their markings. The researcher's job is made even easier when the humpback whale raises its tail above the surface, which it does often, giving a clear view of the color pattern on the flukes.

A humpback whale has a rather small dorsal fin set well back toward its tail. Like all baleen whales, the humpback whale has a pair of blowholes through which it breathes. The water spout or blow of the humpback whale has a distinctive bushy appearance. This whale also has a series of bumps on the face and head, each with a large hair growing from the middle. These hairs may have some sensory application and perhaps are used to sense current changes.

During the breeding season, little or no feeding occurs. Unfortunately, this fasting puts an enormous drain on the reserves of blubber that a whale has accumulated during the rest of the year. The female, who must produce over 100 pounds (45 kilograms) of milk a day to feed her calf, suffers especially.

Coastal troubles
Because of the humpback whale's coastal habitat and acrobatic habits, the northern

population of this whale has been a prime target of the commercial whaling industry since the 1600s. In the early 1900s, commercial whalers turned their attention to the population in the Southern Hemisphere, due in part to the rapidly declining population in the north. Over the next 60 years, more than 200,000 humpback whales were taken by the whaling industry. From a preindustrial world population estimated at more than 125,000, the humpback whale was reduced to less than 10,000 individuals.

Since 1962, the International Whaling Commission has banned commercial hunting of these whales. However, because of the concentration of these whales in some of the most productive fishing areas in the world, the humpback whale is continually facing disturbance from humans. Every year many humpback whales get tangled, trapped, and suffocated in fishing nets. While obviously a disaster to the whale, this problem is also a disaster to fishers, who must spend thousands of dollars to replace gear, and whose fishing season—often only a few weeks or months long—can be completely ruined by a whale running afoul of a net.

As overfishing has depleted much of the fish stock even in these productive waters, whales and fishing boats tend to be found in closer and closer proximity wherever large schools of fish are found. This increases the likelihood of a tragedy for both. Unlike tourists who pay whale-watching cruise boats for the opportunity to view one of these creatures, many fishers consider the humpback whale to be a pest and have little sympathy for an

animal that can so easily bring them economic ruin. Efforts must be made to educate fishers about the economic gains brought to their communities through whale-watching tourist revenue, and to put into place a system for rescuing netted whales. Guidelines for reimbursement after netting accidents and stricter controls over fishing will allow the recovery of the depleted stocks of fish that both whales and fishers depend on.

Northern Right Whale
(Eubalaena glacialis)

ESA: Endangered

IUCN: Endangered

Weight: Up to 200 tons (180 metric tons)
Length: 42–60 ft. (13–18 m)
Diet: Copepods and other small animals
Gestation period: Approximately 365 days
Habitat: Coastal ocean waters
Range: Temperate oceans and seas of the Northern Hemisphere

THE NORTHERN RIGHT whale earned its name during the whaling years of the late 1800s. It was considered by whalers to be the best whale to find and kill because of its enormous reserves of oily fat, used during that era as fuel. This fat reserve was so plentiful that the right whale would not sink in the water after death, making the carcass much easier for whalers to maneuver and process. The right whale was often found near the coast and was not a very fast swimmer, which allowed the boats of that time to overtake the whale easily. Even the genus name reflects the attitude of the early whalers, as the word *Eubalaena* literally means "true whale."

Massive shape

The northern right whale is a medium-sized whale, averaging about 45 feet (14 meters) in length. However, it is much chunkier than the sleeker whales in the rorqual family, such as the blue whale.

Like the other members of the family Balaenidae, the northern right whale is, at best, an un-gainly-looking creature. It has a huge head with an enormous, curved mouth that ends near a relatively tiny pair of eyes. A dark whale, the northern right whale is frequently covered with lighter patches, some of them caused by the growth of barnacles on its skin. As well as light patches, the northern right whale has a series of light-colored bumpy areas on the head called callosities. These callosities differ in placement from whale to whale and help whale researchers to identify individual northern right whales. A pair of blowholes on the top of the head gives rise to a distinctive V-shaped blow, or exhalation.

The northern right whale is one of the few cetaceans that does not have a dorsal or top fin. The only other whales that share this lack of a dorsal fin and occur within the range of the northern right whale are the gray whale and the bowhead whale. The northern right whale's pectoral fins are fairly small and help to contribute to its squat, chunky appearance.

When a whale prepares to go underwater for a long dive, it engages in sounding, a type of deep breathing exercise that enables it to hold its breath for a long time. During sounding, the right whale begins to breathe five or six times a minute for several minutes, then dives straight down into the water for up to 20 minutes.

Giant filter feeder

The northern right whale has a series of more than 200 long, brushlike plates called baleen that hang from the upper jaw. This trait is shared with 11 other whale species. The northern right

A large right whale may weigh as much as a large blue whale, even though a blue whale may be more than twice as long as a right whale.

whale uses these baleen plates to capture small organisms such as copepods.

During the early whaling years, one of the by-products was baleen. The baleen plates were once heavily used in the production of such objects as hoop skirts, umbrellas, and whips.

It is thought that when this whale was common, it frequently traveled in large groups. Even today, the northern right whale can be found in pairs or small groups of up to 10 animals. However, the social structure of these groups is unclear, and it appears that individuals may move from group to group.

The northern right whale makes yearly migrations, heading into cooler northern waters during the summer to feed, then returning to warmer southern waters in the fall. In the south, the northern right whale finds sheltered bays where they can safely give birth and rear their young.

This whale is rarely found in areas of pack ice in the Arctic, nor is it found much below about 20 degrees in latitude; in general, this is a temperate ocean whale.

Human interaction

The northern right whale's use of bays and other coastal areas, especially during migrations and during the breeding season, brings it in close proximity to some of the larger human population centers.

It was once the most commonly sighted whale over most of its range, and it was also one of the first whales to be regularly hunted by humans. Because it was a slow swimmer and did not

sink after dying, it was eagerly sought by whale hunters. The northern right whale produces a vast amount of useable products, such as oil, meat, and baleen.

Oil and baleen

While whale oil was the principal driving force behind the whaling industry, for the right whale hunters, baleen was a close second in importance. This material has the property of coming ready-made in long, thin strips, and its tensile strength combined with its elasticity gives it similar properties to plastic.

The northern right whale was such a profitable and easy target that many populations were wiped out as early as the 1500s, well before whalers had developed the technology to hunt more northerly or more open-water species. It may well have been the destruction of easily accessible populations of the northern right whales that drove whalers farther out to sea in search of more whales, leading to the discovery of other species. By the 1700s, the northern right whale's numbers were so depressed that the European whaling community found it was no longer worth hunting, and the same occurred in American waters 100 years later.

Despite the complete protection that was given to this species in 1937, the northern right whale has not recovered its former population numbers, and recent estimates place the population at only a few hundred in the Pacific and Atlantic Oceans combined. Sadly, it may only be a matter of time before the northern right whale totally declines and becomes extinct.

Southern Right Whale
(Eubalaena australis)

ESA: Endangered

IUCN: Lower risk

Weight: Up to 200 tons (180 tonnes)
Length: 42–60 ft. (13–18 m)
Diet: Copepods and other small animals
Gestation period: Approximately 365 days
Habitat: Coastal ocean waters
Range: Temperate oceans and seas of the Southern Hemisphere

THE SOUTHERN right whale's claim to being a separate species has been debated by scientists for many years. Even today, the question of whether the southern right whale is a species separate from its close relative the northern right whale has not been answered to everyone's satisfaction. While scientists were discussing the merits of this whale, its numbers were dwindling down to the point where the argument has almost become an abstract one.

The southern right whale is virtually indistinguishable from the northern right whale (*Eubalaena glacialis*). Both species look like they are mostly head and jaw, with a huge, curved mouth that ends just below the tiny eyes. This enormous mouth is filled not with teeth but with plates of baleen that the whale uses to strain small planktonic crustaceans and other tiny marine animals from the water. The plates of baleen in a right whale's mouth are some of the largest of any cetacean. Strange whitish bumpy areas called callosities are found on the head area, and these are frequently covered with barnacles.

Distinctive features

In the open ocean, a southern right whale can be distinguished from other whales that share the same range by two obvious features. The first is the complete lack of a dorsal or top fin, making it the only baleen whale in the Southern Hemisphere to lack this feature. The second feature concerns its blowholes, which are farther apart than in most other whales. This creates a distinctive double blow or spout when the whale exhales, and makes identification fairly easy.

This whale apparently made regular migrations from warmer, temperate waters in the winter to the colder waters of the Antarctic in the summer.

Most, if not all, feeding occurs in the colder southern regions, where the upwelling currents and well-oxygenated waters create a bloom of life. There, the whales feed close to the surface, filtering enormous amounts of tiny organisms from the water with their baleen plates.

Groups of southern right whales move north to coastal areas off South America, Australia, New Zealand, and southern Africa to breed.

Late discovery

The southern right whale is a slow-moving coastal whale. During the time when its population levels were still high, it appeared as if this species was fairly social because large groups were seen regularly. This behavior also meant that the southern right whale was an excellent whale to hunt. The fact that the right whale has more oil in its body than any other species of baleen whale, and that it will not sink when killed, led whalers to declare that this was the right whale to hunt, and hence the common name, right whale.

The northern right whale was the first target of the commercial whale hunters. It was hunted almost to extinction by the time the southern right whale was discovered in the early 1800s. The industry then quickly focused its attention on this new species, and within only a few decades the southern right whale had also become extremely rare.

Today it is thought that there may be as few as 3,000 southern right whales left in the world. Certain parts of the population appear to be recovering slowly, as indicated by a mild increase in numbers, but the population as a whole is still low enough that a series of disasters could easily wipe out the entire species. As the southern right whale tends to produce on average only a single calf once every three years, the ability of this whale to increase its numbers is limited. Therefore, if the population is depressed below a certain level, it may be impossible for the southern right whale to recover. This may have already happened with the northern right whale, whose population numbers are probably well under 1,000 throughout the entire Northern Hemisphere.

Another problem facing the southern right whale is the development of coastal areas near this species' breeding grounds. This is especially true along the coast of Argentina, where commercial fishing, coastal development, and offshore oil exploration are rapidly increasing. New activity in the Antarctic region also poses a threat. Oil spills and other forms of water pollution already threaten to cause irreparable damage to the productive but fragile subpolar ecosystem that the southern right whale depends on for survival.

Arguments over development and mineral rights of the Antarctic region continue, and it may well be that the fate of many Southern Hemisphere species, including the southern right whale, hangs in the balance.

Sei Whale
(Balaenoptera borealis)

ESA: Endangered

IUCN: Endangered

Weight: 22–23 tons
(20–21 metric tons)
Length: 40–66 ft. (12–20 m)
Diet: Copepods and other small crustaceans; small schooling fish
Gestation period: 315–365 days
Longevity: Up to 60 years
Habitat: Open ocean
Range: Temperate oceans and seas of the Northern and Southern Hemispheres

THE SEI WHALE belongs to the group of whales called rorquals (family Balaenopteridae). These include the blue whale, the fin whale, the minke whale, Bryde's whale, and the humpback whale. Except for the aberrant humpback whale, all rorquals look quite similar to each other. They all have a graceful, elongated shape that is built for speed and the open ocean.

Rorquals have plates of baleen in their mouths instead of teeth. This is made of keratin, the same material that makes up human nails and hair. It is possible that the baleen plates have evolved from simple horny ridges. The rorquals are identified and separated from other baleen whales by deep grooves that run along the lower jaw and throat. These grooves allow the throat area to expand greatly, enabling the whales to take huge amounts of water—and therefore, food—into their mouths.

Skim feeder

The sei whale, however, is not restricted to the rorqual method of feeding. It habitually swims along the surface with its mouth open, traveling through large concentrations of prey animals such as small copepods, krill, and fish, filtering them out as it swims. This feeding method is more similar to that of the right whale than to that of rorquals such as the blue or fin whale.

The sei whale also has more finely bristled baleen than any other whale, which may enable it to feed in this way. A sei whale will eat most small marine animals, from planktonic crustaceans to squid and small fish. Most feeding is done near the surface of deep, open water far from shore. This whale is most often seen in small groups of up

to half a dozen individuals, although occasionally much larger groups will gather in response to good feeding grounds.

The sei whale is a fast swimmer, like other members of the rorqual family: it has been recorded swimming at a speed of over 30 miles (50 kilometers) an hour.

The seasonal movements of the sei whale are not well understood, as is the case with many whales, but it seems to wander widely, appearing in an area one year but not necessarily returning the next. It does migrate from colder water in the summer to warmer tropical water in winter, where it appears to stop feeding, and where females give birth. Its summer range does not appear to reach as close to the poles as the other rorqual species, but it may occasionally be seen near the edge of the polar ice packs.

When a sei whale dives, it usually stays under for no more than 10 or 15 minutes. However, seis have been known to stay underwater for up to half an hour.

Whaling's poor relative

The sei whale almost escaped the attention of the commercial whaling industry. It was considered to be a poor substitute for the larger, slower, more massive whales that shared the sei whale's range. Unfortunately, the whaling industry managed to decimate the population of virtually every other kind of whale during the mid-1900s, leaving the sei whale as one of the only alternatives. By the second half of that century, sei whales were also being slaughtered in large numbers, with more than 100,000 being taken in the Southern

Hemisphere alone during one 12-year period, and more than 25,000 being taken in one year. This massive and sudden hunting pressure appears to have seriously damaged the populations of sei whales throughout the world. Subsequent harvests were much lower and continued to decrease until all commercial hunting of the sei whale was halted in 1985.

The present population of sei whales left in the world is feared to be much reduced, and is certainly fewer than 60,000.

The predicament of the sei whale is a good example of some of the dilemmas facing conservationists when dealing with a species in danger.

Complex situation

While numerically the sei whale population may seem on the mend, the situation is much more complex than a simple single population figure can describe. The total number of sei whales can be divided into at least three distinct populations that probably rarely or never meet. This fact makes the continued survival of the sei whale much less likely, as breeding opportunities are available only between the sexually mature members of each population (which may number only a few thousand each). It also means that major disturbances can affect the mortality of this whale, from natural causes such as El Niño and disease to human-related effects such as pollution. Since these whales are fast-swimming, deep-water animals, it is extremely costly and difficult to produce an accurate estimate of any one of the populations, much less all three. Therefore, it is not easy to determine whether the sei whale populations are increasing or decreasing.

Sperm Whale

(Physeter catodon)

ESA: Endangered

IUCN: Vulnerable

Weight: 11–55 tons (10–50 metric tons)
Length: 25–60 ft. (8–18 m)
Diet: Squid, fish, sharks
Gestation period: 420–450 days
Longevity: Up to 60 years or more
Habitat: Open oceans
Range: Oceans and seas of the Northern and Southern Hemispheres

THE SPERM WHALE (family Physeteridae) is perhaps the best known and most recognizable of the marine mammals. Immortalized as Moby Dick in 1851 in the novel of the same name, this huge, strangely shaped whale has shared a history with humans that far precedes Herman Melville's literary classic.

The sperm whale is unmistakable when seen. Its huge body appears to be composed of almost entirely head, and in fact this can constitute one-third of the body length. The upper portion of the head is enormous, while the lower jaw is comparatively slim, making the whale appear to have an overbite. The single blowhole is situated at the top front of the blunt, almost rectangular head. This results in a blow, or exhalation, that extends forward rather than upward as in other whales. This is an infallible way to identify a sperm whale—even when no part of the whale is visible above the water. A sperm whale has fairly short, stumpy-looking pectoral fins. The dorsal or top fin is reduced to a fairly small hump far down the back that is followed by a series of smaller bumps that end near the tail. The eye of a sperm whale is set low on the head, near the end of the mouth, creating an even greater sense of misproportion.

Toothed squid hunter

The sperm whale belongs to the group of whales in the suborder Odontoceti. These are the toothed whales, and the sperm whale is the largest toothed whale in the world. Many of the sperm whale's teeth can be over 8 inches (20 centimeters) long. These teeth, found only in the lower jaw, have long been valued by coastal people for use in carvings, in the same way as elephant tusks were valued in Africa and Asia. Finished sperm whale tooth carvings are called scrimshaw.

The sperm whale uses its impressive teeth to hunt for its favorite food, squid. Large squid are usually found in deep ocean waters, and for this reason, the sperm whale is rarely found anywhere near the coast.

To hunt for squid, a sperm whale may spend over an hour underwater at depths of up to 1,200 feet (365 meters). However, the whale is capable of diving much deeper: when one sperm whale was tracked it dived to a depth of 8,000 feet (2,438 meters).

Unlike baleen whales, sperm whales appear to feed in both their northern and southern ranges. They frequently travel in large groups of 10 to 40, although adult males are often found alone. During the breeding season in the tropical part of the range, male sperm whales join up with larger groups of females and young. Fighting over females apparently keeps some males from gaining access to the breeding groups. Perhaps as a result of this mating system, males tend to grow much larger than females.

Sperm whales produce a wide variety of sounds, some of which can travel for long distances underwater. Many of these may be used for communication between whales. It also appears that some of them may be used for echolocation, perhaps to locate prey in the dark of deep ocean waters.

Living oil tanks

The sperm whale's enormous head contains not only the largest brain of any animal in the world, but also an unusual structure known as the spermaceti organ. This is a huge, hollow, convoluted structure of bone that is entwined with nasal passages filled with liquid wax.

The spermaceti organ has long been a center of controversy among scientists who have attempted to determine its function. There are two main hypotheses. The first theory states that the spermaceti organ helps to regulate buoyancy during the sperm whale's deep dives. It appears that a sperm whale, while deep under water, may spend part or all of its time in one spot. The ability to maintain neutral buoyancy—that is, to neither sink nor float—would greatly enhance this ability. By somehow regulating the temperature of the wax in the spermaceti organ, a sperm whale could more easily maintain neutral buoyancy.

The second hypothesis is that the spermaceti organ is involved in producing, enhancing, and directing the sound used in communication and echolocation, and even for emitting sounds used to stun prey when hunting. It is possible that the spermaceti organ plays a role in both buoyancy and the production of sound.

While the sperm whale's strange spermaceti organ has recently attracted the interest of scientists, it has long held the interest of whalers, who have coveted the huge quantities of wax found in the organ. This wax had a variety of uses, with much

of it going toward use as lamp fuel and the production of candles. Other attractions were the teeth, valued for jewelry and carvings; and a substance known as ambergris, from the intestines of sperm whales and used in perfume production as a fixative.

The sperm whale industry truly began in the 1700s. During its peak, only a few thousand sperm whales were taken every year. However, hunting for sperm whales became less intense during the 1800s and early 1900s, when the whaling industry began to concentrate on other species of whales. Then, as most other species of whales were in a general decline because of overhunting, the spotlight was firmly brought back to the sperm whale. By the 1950s, more than 20,000 of these magnificent animals were taken by whalers every year, and this state of affairs continued

for the next 20 years. It was not until the mid-1970s that concern for the decrease in sperm whales led to restrictions on hunting.

By 1985, all hunting for the species was halted. The sperm whale, which was once considered to be the most common whale in the world, is now struggling to survive. Marine biologists hope that the hunting ban has come in time for any remaining animals to regenerate their populations. However, it is now a matter of time before it will be known whether this ocean beast has recovered from its rapid decline toward extinction.

Peter Zahler

Like other whales, including the distantly related baleen whales, sperm whales live in both the Northern and Southern Hemispheres. They make yearly migrations from the colder subpolar waters to the tropical part of their range, where they breed.

White Birds-in-a-nest

(Macbridea alba)

ESA: Threatened

IUCN: Vulnerable

Class: Magnoliopsida
Family: Labiatae
Height: 12–16 in. (30–41 cm)
Leaves: Up to 4 in. (10 cm)
long, ⅖–⅘ in. (1–2 cm) wide
Flowering season: May to July
Habitat: Pineland swamps and
sandy soil
Range: Northern Florida

WHITE BIRDS-IN-A-NEST is a perennial with thick opposite leaves that are broadest at their tips and have winged petioles (leaf stalks). The white flowers are clustered at the top of the plant in short spikes surrounded by prominent bracts. They are two-lipped, with the upper petals forming a hood and the lower petals divided into three different lobes. The corolla is 1 inch (2.5 centimeters) long. The calyxes are also two-lipped: the upper calyx lip is narrow and undivided, and the lower is split into two different lobes.

Breeding system

Little is known about the breeding system or pollination of this species. It could possibly spread through vegetative reproduction, since it can form populations of many stems, and it is not easy to tell if the stems are connected underground. There are no reports of insects visiting the flowers of white birds-in-a-nest, though the flowers are not small

and are held in a prominent position at the top of the plant. It would seem likely that insects do visit the flowers and that cross-pollination occurs. There are no reports that indicate whether this species is self-fertile, and this data may be useful for conserving the species by indicating how it will be affected by populations' becoming smaller and more fragmented.

Distribution

White birds-in-a-nest occurs in Bay, Gulf, Franklin, and Liberty Counties in Florida. The Post Office Bay area of the Apalachicola National Forest has the largest and strongest populations. The Florida National Areas Inventory show that 41 of the 63 known occurrences of this plant are in the Apalachicola National Forest. Most of these sites are within 15 miles (24 kilometers) of each other. Ten of thirteen

This longleaf pineland swamp, in the Apalachicola National Forest, Florida, is one of the natural habitats of white birds-in-a-nest.

sites with more than 100 stems occur within the national forest, including the largest site with an estimated 1,500 plants. This indicates a serious decline of the plant outside the national forest, because it is unlikely that there was any particularly large con-

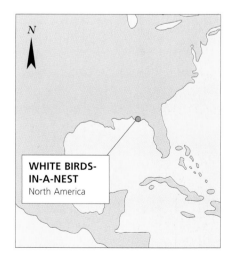

N

**WHITE BIRDS-
IN-A-NEST**
North America

centration of white birds-in-a-nest in the park originally.

This plant inhabits grassy vegetation on poorly drained, infertile sandy soil. It can also be found in seepage bogs and somewhat drier savanna. It generally prefers wet locations and is frequently associated with longleaf pine and runner oaks, which make up flatwoods vegetation that requires a lot of moisture. Fire is important for keeping vegetation open and for lowering competition in these habitats, and it has been documented to trigger synchronized flowering in some species of plants, including white birds-in-a-nest. It is not yet clear, however, whether this plant depends on growing-season or dormant-season fires.

Threats

Many populations of white birds-in-a-nest occur near the town of Port St. Joe, and expansion of the town would affect them. This species is also threatened by developments of cattle pasture and the silviculture practices of the forest service and the forest product industry. The preparation of land for tree planting kills off white birds-in-a-nest, though the plant may recover and grow in young stands of trees. However, as trees mature, white birds-in-a-nest is shaded out and cannot survive. Controlled burns are now being carried out on some managed land, which should benefit white birds-in-a-nest. This burning is done in the dormant season, but there is a possibility that white birds-in-a-nest would benefit more from growing-season fires. Power line rights-of-way provide a habitat for this plant. The use of herbicides rather than mowing for weed control, however, could adversely affect populations.

Christina Oliver

WHITE-EYES

Class: Aves
Order: Passeriformes
Family: Zosteropidae

White-eyes are usually small birds dressed in shades of olive, yellow-green, gray, and brown. All these colors usually do not mix on one species. In size and color, the white-eyes immediately suggest the vireos (*Vireo* sp.) of the Americas. In behavior, they suggest siskins or goldfinches (*Carduelis* sp.). White-eyes often form small groups of 5 to 20 individuals that move together as they feed. Sometimes they even mingle with other species.

The white-eyes are an Old World group of approximately 85 species. All species occur in Africa south of the Sahara Desert, southern Asia, the East Indies, Australia, and many of the Pacific islands. Many island species have suffered from the activities of people, and for some of these birds the changes may be too harsh to endure.

Guam Bridled White-eye

(Zosterops conspicillata conspicillata)

ESA: Endangered

Length: 4 in. (10 cm)
Weight: Unknown
Clutch size: 2 eggs (seen in 1 nest)
Incubation: Probably 10–13 days, as in related species
Diet: Insects
Habitat: Forest, woodland, shrub land, prairie, swamp, coastal strand
Range: Guam, Mariana Islands

GUAM IS THE LARGEST and southernmost island in the Mariana Islands system. The Mariana Islands stretch southward from the general direction of Japan. The bridled white-eye inhabits several of the larger Mariana Islands. Traditionally, the white-eye on Yap and in the Caroline Islands was considered part of the same species. The relationship of these white-eyes in the Mariana and Caroline Islands, however, has recently been challenged. A total of six white-eye subspecies was formerly recognized, but now the Mariana birds are believed to represent one species and the Caroline birds a second. Of the Mariana bridled white-eyes, there are three separate subspecies: one each on Guam and Rota, and the third on Saipan and Tinian. All of them have declined to some extent, but the Guam bridled white-eye has slipped close to extinction.

Appearance

The Guam bridled white-eye has an olive back and tail and an unmarked wing that looks slightly darker olive. Its chin and throat are white, becoming increasingly yellow on the breast and belly to a bright yellow undertail. The bird's crown, nape, and cheek are medium gray with only a slight hint of green. A white mask surrounds the eye and extends through the lore onto the forehead. A thin gray line separates the white lore from the white jawline.

A tiny bird with a stubby tail, the bridled white-eye could be easily overlooked except that it gathers in flocks.

Observers in the early decades of the 1900s reported flocks of up to 20. By the 1980s, flocks of even five or six were rare. The bridled white-eye has been found in all the plant communities on Guam, including secondary growth, but the bird now survives only in the northernmost portion of the island.

Ornithologists have agonized over the dramatic decline of birds on Guam. From the 1960s through the 1980s, Guam's birds just vanished. No single explanation satisfactorily accounts for such rapid decline, but several different factors together very likely provide an explanation.

Lethal pesticide

Immediately after World War II, the American military forces liberally used the pesticide known as DDT to control mosquitoes and other potentially disease-carrying insects. DDT disrupts calcium use, so when animals such as birds lay eggs, they do not have enough calcium to harden the shells. Thin eggshells break easily and lose vital moisture. The result is a failure to reproduce.

Birds that eat insects are generally more susceptible to the effects of DDT. The native fruit-eating birds on Guam did not decline as rapidly or as much as did the insectivorous birds. Without young birds coming into the population to replace old birds

that die, a species declines. But the pesticide was just one of several factors that destroyed or degraded Guam's native plant and animal communities.

Exotic species are found on Guam. Some were brought intentionally and others were transported to the island unintentionally. Several birds, notably the black drongo (*Dicrurus macrocercus*), now outnumber the native birds and are the most commonly seen species on Guam. They may compete with the native birds for food and nesting space, or they may simply be more able to accept modified habitats. Rats, house cats, dogs, and monitor lizards (*Varanus indicus*) were all brought to Guam. All these species eat birds. Some of them are also very good at finding nests and taking eggs and nestlings. None of them, however, is as efficient a predator as the brown tree snake (*Boiga irregularis*).

The brown tree snake first appeared on Guam at the end of World War II. It may have arrived as a stowaway in military cargo, or it may have been brought in as a pet by soldiers. At first people accepted the snake as a way to control the rats that seemed to overrun the island. In just 20 years, however, the brown tree snake had exhausted its welcome. It became as much of a nuisance as the rats. Native to Southeast Asia, the snake prowls by night and is an expert bird predator. It takes eggs, nestlings, and adult birds. The drastic decline of Guam's birds began as the brown tree snake population reached incredible numbers in the 1960s.

While pesticides, including herbicides and insecticides, were

being sprayed across the island, and while exotic species were populating the island, people were expanding their developments. Guam covers only 209 square miles (541 square kilometers), but it supports more than 100,000 people. Some bird species have simply run out of space to live on Guam. The only native forest grows as a thin strip along the limestone cliffs of the island's northern shore. Forest species have nowhere else to live.

Chemicals, exotic species, plows, and bulldozers have made Guam uninhabitable for many of its birds. Because they are unique to Guam, they have no other populations in the world. If lost on Guam, they are lost forever.

Mauritius Olive White-eye

(Zosterops chloronothos)

IUCN: Critically endangered

Length: Unknown
Weight: 7.7–9 g
Clutch size: 2 eggs, rarely 3
Incubation: Unknown
Diet: Nectar, insects
Habitat: Native wet forests
Range: Mauritius Island in the Indian Ocean

THE MAURITIUS OLIVE white-eye originally inhabited Mauritius's rain forests. Specifically, it occupied those forests that received 158 inches (400 centimeters) of rain each year. Very few such forests survive on Mauritius.

Dull olive green above and paler green or greenish yellow

below, the Mauritius olive white-eye has only a white lore and eye ring to distinguish it. It has a longer beak than any other white-eye, and it uses this slender beak to probe into flowers for nectar, which is a major part of its diet. The Mauritius olive white-eye wanders widely in search of enough flowers to provide all the nectar it needs. It probably supplements its sweet diet with insects.

The decline of habitat

Most of the primary forests on Mauritius have been cut. By the mid-1970s, only 4,555 acres (1,843 hectares) or roughly 7 square miles (18 square kilometers) of native, primary forest remained intact. This represents only 1 percent of Mauritius' historical forest area. The primary forest has been cleared for timber production, to plant crops and graze livestock, and to develop plantations of exotic trees. Only a small area in southwestern Mauritius retains any native rain forest, and it is jeopardized by development plans.

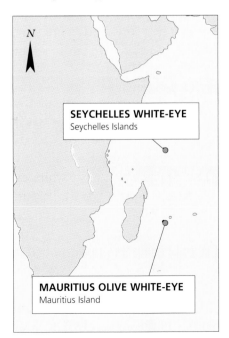

SEYCHELLES WHITE-EYE
Seychelles Islands

MAURITIUS OLIVE WHITE-EYE
Mauritius Island

Besides habitat loss, many of Mauritius' birds have been victimized by exotic species. Such animals as pigs, cattle, goats, Timor deer, rats, and crab-eating macaques cause enormous survival problems for island birds by damaging the native plant communities, overgrazing, and preying on eggs and nestlings. The collective effect of so many stresses has been population decline and extinction. Perhaps as many as 30 bird species have already been lost from all the Mascarene Islands combined. Other species are critically near extinction, with populations numbering only in the low dozens or less. The immediate threat to such low populations is catastrophic natural events. Mauritius is regularly struck by severe cyclones driven by high winds. Small bird populations that exist in fragments of habitat are exceptionally vulnerable.

Falling population

The Mauritius olive white-eye had declined by the mid-1970s to just 350 pairs, or probably 800 to 900 individuals. Through the 1980s, that figure dwindled to maybe 275 pairs—possibly 600 to 650 individual birds. But this estimate has been challenged as being too high. Although the olive white-eye seems better able to endure catastrophic storms than other birds, it is not immune to their effects, nor to the loss of habitat and the predation by rats and monkeys.

Some groups have suggested that flowering shrubs and trees ought to be planted around Mauritius to help the olive white-eye. Such an effort could yield good results, or it could worsen the already grave situation. If native flowering plants were used and planted in appropriate places, the benefits would be worthwhile. The history of such projects, however, has been to select exotic plants. More exotic species, be they plant or animal, is the last thing Mauritius needs. Protection for this bird's remaining habitat would be the best action.

Pohnpei Greater White-eye

(Rukia longirostra)

ESA: Endangered	
IUCN: Lower risk	

Length: 6 in. (15 cm)
Weight: Unknown
Clutch size: Probably 2 eggs, as in related species
Incubation: Unknown
Diet: Probably insects
Habitat: Forest
Range: Pohnpei in the Caroline Islands of the western Pacific Ocean

A TROUPE OF SMALL birds flits twig to twig in the forest undergrowth. They look evenly olive brown above. Their chins are a whitish buff deepening to buff on the throat, and tannish buff on the breast. Toward the belly and undertail they look golden rufous. Their tails are short and their beaks are long and thin. Only the slimmest of white rings circles each eye.

Pohnpei lies at the eastern end of the Caroline Islands in the western Pacific Ocean. Enewetak and Bikini, where the United

As their name suggests, the white-eyes are recognizable by their white eye ring. Forty species are currently listed by IUCN–The World Conservation Union.

States tested nuclear bombs for decades, lie just a few hundred miles to the north and east. Formerly spelled Ponape, Pohnpei covers 129 square miles (334 square kilometers). The island's mountainous interior still holds some primary forest. Enough forest remains to support a fair population of Pohnpei greater white-eyes. This bird, also known as the long-billed white-eye, is unique to Pohnpei. Its status is currently a source of confusion.

Ornithologists, bird collectors, and birders who have visited Pohnpei have generally agreed that the Pohnpei greater white-eye is a rare bird. Ten specimens have been collected since 1931. In 1975, observers conducting bird surveys on the island found the white-eye more than once. Additional survey work in 1983 located the bird in both lowland and montane forest. No direct evidence indicates the species is declining. Some ornithologists suspect this species has always been hard to detect rather than rare. But indirect evidence seems to indicate otherwise.

Non-native species

Black rats and Polynesian rats have both become established on Pohnpei. Both are known predators of birds. They can climb trees and take eggs, nestlings, and even adult birds. On some islands, rats have destroyed entire populations of some bird species. But rats are not the only exotic species on Pohnpei, and not the only exotic species that affect birds. Exotic plants can outcompete native plants and slowly change the character of entire plant communities. Insect populations plus fruit and seed supplies can be strongly affected by exotic plants. These are the basic foods of small island songbirds. If the food supplies decrease, the birds will too.

Several bird species on Pohnpei have shown at least small population declines. Ornithologists are not sure why. The potential combination of habitat loss, exotic predators, exotic competitors, exotic diseases, being shot and collected, exotic plants degrading natural habitat, and decreased food supplies would seem enough to put any species in jeopardy. The Caroline Islands are part of the U.S. Trust Territories, so they come under United States law. The U.S. Fish and Wildlife Service has listed the Pohnpei greater white-eye as an endangered species. This designation extends some legal protection to the bird against shooting, trapping, and habitat destruction.

Seychelles White-eye
(Zosterops modestus)

ESA: Endangered

IUCN: Critically endangered

Length: Probably 5–6 in. (13–15 cm), as in related species
Diet: Insects, possibly nectar
Habitat: Forest
Range: Mahé in the Seychelles Islands

A GREAT FIRE swept over Mahé Island one year in the 1850s, but enough native forest escaped the blaze that the island's bird life survived. The Seychelles white-eye endured the flames, but 120 years later the little songbird began a quick decline from which it may not recover.

To the north and northeast of Madagascar, a great freckling of islands speckle the Indian Ocean over an area of 16,000 square miles (41,600 square kilometers). The islands are remnants of a great plateau now submerged beneath the sea. Several island clusters in this area form the Seychelles Archipelago. Mahé is the largest of 28 islands in the Seychelles Islands group.

Approximately 25,000 people live on Mahé. They have cleared

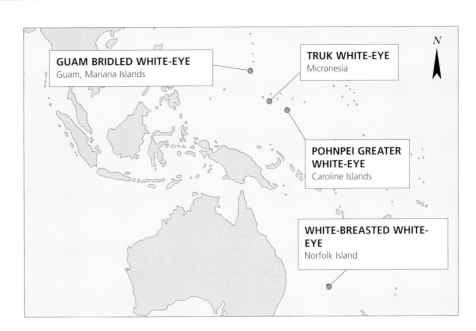

the mangrove swamps along the coast and built cities and homes along the seashore. The lower slopes are densely grown with cinnamon, which was brought to the island by French colonists and subsequently escaped cultivation. It now grows wild. Much of Mahé is planted with tea and other crops. As of 1990, only three small patches of forest suitable for the Seychelles white-eye remained.

The Seychelles white-eye was once considered fairly common in the small amount of habitat available on Mahé. It was seen by various observers but at irregular intervals. A plain bird, it has a gray head and back, brownish rump, and dark tail. The underparts are white with a tannish rufous side. A thin white eye ring continues as a white line through the lore and onto the forehead. It is not considered to be particularly beautiful, but its rarity has made it of interest to birders. As recreational birding became more popular worldwide, and as the Seychelles entered the tourism market, observations and reports of the white-eye increased.

Ornithologists estimated that perhaps 100 white-eyes survived on Mahé in the late 1970s, and they believed that figure was basically stable. The population began a quick decline in the late 1970s or early 1980s. Quite probably the true status of the species was miscalculated in earlier years, and it had already been declining slowly but steadily. The status of the Seychelles white-eye in the early 1990s was unknown. The bird may be extinct. If not, it is surviving in perilously low numbers.

Truk White-eye

(Rukia ruki)

IUCN: Endangered

Length: 5½ in. (14 cm)
Diet: Insects
Habitat: Montane forest
Range: Truk in the Caroline Islands of the western Pacific Ocean

TRUK, OR CHUUK, is a cluster of atolls and islets. Tourism figures prominently in the economy there. People visit Truk to escape their homelands for a while, but the Truk white-eye lives there year-round. The Truk white-eye is also found on some islets such as Polle and Pata, but Tol Island is its stronghold.

Tol is the largest island in the Truk group, but it covers only 13 square miles (34 square kilometers). Much of the lowland forest on Tol has been cleared for commercial crops and plantations. Coconuts and copra, the processed coconut meat, are important export products. Pri-

mary forest still exists high on the mountain slopes, and that is where the Truk white-eye lives.

Oddly colored for a white-eye, the Truk white-eye has chocolate brown plumage. In some light it shows a faint olive sheen. The only special characteristics on the bird are the orange feet and toes and a short, curved white line beneath each eye like an eyelid. Some field guides describe it as a teardrop. No other Micronesian songbird resembles it.

The Truk white-eye spends its time in the outer fringes of the forest canopy. An observer on the forest floor, looking up through the foliage of the canopy, would see only a dark bird against a bright sky. A brown bird in the shadows or silhouetted in the canopy can be overlooked.

Only so many insect-eating birds can live on an island the size of Tol. Quite typically, island birds that evolve in the absence of predators lay fewer eggs than their continental relatives, and they nest only once each breeding season. These behaviors help keep their population levels low in proportion with the resources available to them. Consequently, the Truk white-eye population will naturally be quite small. With such small populations, the birds can suffer dramatic consequences as a result of relatively minor disturbances.

The greatest threat to the Truk white-eye appears to be habitat destruction. It lives only in a small area of the total habitat seemingly available. Ornithologists do not yet understand why the bird is so scarce. Its habitat is vulnerable to global demand for tropical woods and for products that can be grown on plantations on mountainous islands. The best protection for the Truk white-eye is to preserve the amount and quality of its habitat.

White-breasted White-eye

(Zosterops albogularis)

ESA: Endangered

IUCN: Critically endangered

Length: 5½ in. (14 cm)
Clutch size: 2 eggs
Habitat: Forest
Range: Norfolk Island in the Tasman Sea

NORFOLK ISLAND PINES grow as houseplants in half the living rooms in America. They are the most famous thing about Norfolk Island, except possibly for the mutineers of the H.M.S. *Bounty*. Now a bird has again brought attention to Norfolk Island. The white-breasted white-eye may have succumbed to extinction.

Exploration of the southern Pacific Ocean in the 1700s led to the discovery of breadfruit (*Artocarpus altilis*). Polynesians had eaten the starchy fruit for centuries, but it was new to Europeans. Finding that sailors actually liked eating the breadfruit, it followed that growing breadfruit in the British West Indies would provide a cheap source of food for slaves working the sugar plantations. The quest was on to transport breadfruit from the South Pacific to the Caribbean Sea.

Mutiny on the *Bounty*

One breadfruit voyage was led by Captain William Bligh of the H.M.S. *Bounty*, who sailed for Tahiti in 1787. After nearly five months in the South Seas paradise, the crew reboarded their ship in April 1789 for the journey back to the West Indies. Just a few weeks out, Fletcher Christian led a mutiny that left Bligh and 14 crewmen adrift in a longboat. Bligh and all his men survived. The mutineers ended up on uninhabited Pitcairn Island with women and supplies taken from Tahiti. In 1831 the mutineers and their families returned to Tahiti. They left Tahiti in 1856 and settled on Norfolk Island in the triangle between Australia, New Caledonia, and New Zealand.

The first settlers found Norfolk's 13 square miles (34 square kilometers) entirely covered with dense, well developed forest. Unique Norfolk Island pines towered above the shorter canopy-forming trees. The white-breasted white-eye probably inhabited the entire forest on Norfolk. Because the island is so

small, the white-breasted white-eye could never have populated Norfolk in great numbers.

As the 20th century dawned, the white-eye was common enough that collectors found it easy to take. A quiet, solitary bird, the white-breasted white-eye has an olive-brown back, wings, and tail. The underparts from chin to undertail are clear white except for a tannish rufous hue that colors the side and shoulder. The head, including cheek, nape, crown, and forehead, are pale gray relieved by a thin white eye ring that extends slightly forward onto the lore.

Is it extinct?

Probably less than one percent of the original native forest on Norfolk Island survived into the 1990s. By 1962, the white-eye population had declined to 50 birds at best. The last live white-breasted white-eye was seen in 1980. The Royal Australian Ornithologists' Union and the Australian National Parks and Wildlife Service cooperated on a search for the white-eye in 1985, but none was found. The extreme habitat loss, combined with exotic predators (such as rats) and competition from another white-eye species (*Zosterops lateralis*), probably stressed the white-breasted white-eye beyond survival. Without the breadfruit voyages and the mutiny on the *Bounty*, the human presence on Norfolk Island might never have occurred. Had the great forests of Norfolk Island pines survived on the island instead of just in American living rooms, the white-breasted white-eye would probably not be a bird of history.

Kevin Cook

WHITEFISH (NORTH AMERICAN)

Class: Actinopterygii

Order: Salmoniformes

Family: Salmonidae

Whitefish, a taxonomic group that includes ciscoes, live in the icy waters of North America and prefer large lakes and coastal areas with undisturbed and pristine conditions. For centuries, large lakes such as Lake Superior, Lake Huron, and the other Great Lakes, and Canada's Great Slave and Great Bear Lakes, were relatively untouched by humans. Fish populations, including the whitefish, flourished in clean water and were not threatened by non-native species. With the explosion of the human population on the continent and the expansion of industry, however, came pollution, overfishing, introduction of foreign predators, and an ever-increasing influence by people on the biological balance of lakes, streams, and estuaries.

Whitefish and ciscoes are related to salmon, trout, and grayling (Salmonidae). They have an interesting background and long history of controversy about their classification and naming. During their heyday as food fish, ciscoes were marketed as chubs or herring. The true whitefish could be found in rela- chubs that we know today are very different from the chubs of yesterday and, indeed, are classified as cyprinids, not salmonids. This kind of regional naming of fish is fairly common and not entirely surprising. However, there is much disagreement when it comes to naming these deep-water dwellers. Eighteen North American species of whitefish and ciscoes are included in the subfamily Coregoninae.

Some experts argue that this group should be given family status. Others claim it is a subfamily under the family Salmonidae.

Atlantic Whitefish

(Coregonus huntsmani)

IUCN: Vulnerable

Length: 16 in. (41 cm)
Reproduction: Egg layer
Habitat: Lakes, streams, estuaries, coastal ocean
Range: Southern Nova Scotia, Canada

ALSO CALLED THE Acadian whitefish, the threatened Atlantic whitefish is found only along the southwestern coast of Nova Scotia and nearby lakes and streams. This fish leads a borderline existence. Prior to 1929, the Atlantic

Whitefish and ciscoes used to be considered delicacies in the United States as a smoked product (and in certain locations they still are). Fishers went out of their way to find new and better equipment to catch these prized fish.

tive abundance. However, after the completion of a hydroelectric dam on the Tusket River, numbers began to fall dramatically. This species is anadromous (some populations breed in fresh water and feed in salt water), and the construction of the dam—a barrier to migration—dealt a severe blow to the Atlantic whitefish. Fish ladders were installed around the dam to help the fish migrate, but they were improperly designed and monitored. Many fish perished as they tried to swim past the dam's turbine blades. Fishers who illegally captured this fish during its upstream spawning migration compounded the losses by removing fish before they had an opportunity to reproduce.

This salmonid has a typical whitefish shape and pattern of coloration. The body is somewhat compressed from side to side, but it is generally long and torpedo-like. The Atlantic whitefish has a small head with a pointed snout, somewhat triangular body fins, and a moderately forked tail fin; the tail fin lobes are fairly pointed. Just like all

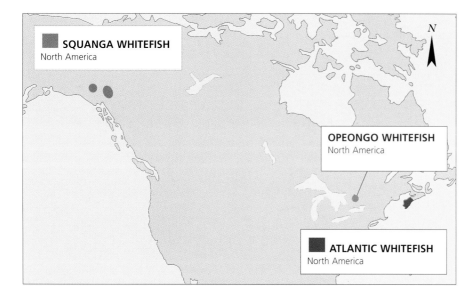

SQUANGA WHITEFISH
North America

OPEONGO WHITEFISH
North America

ATLANTIC WHITEFISH
North America

N

salmonids, this fish has a fleshy adipose fin between the dorsal fin and the tail fin. Overall, this species is silvery, with dark blue-green pigmentation on the back, lighter sides, and a silvery white belly. Fin colors match the body at their point of attachment.

During the month of October, the Atlantic whitefish moves from coastal and estuarine waters into rivers for its upstream spawning migration; fish that remain in a lake year-round move into adjoining streams. Adults consume amphipods, periwinkles, and marine worms when they occupy marine environments; they seek a variety of insect larvae and other aquatic invertebrates in lakes and streams.

While barriers to migration and overfishing began this species' downhill slide, acid rain and snow maybe bringing it closer to extinction—particularly those Atlantic whitefish populations that live their entire lives in fresh water. Over the past 50 years or more, acid levels in lakes and streams that support the Atlantic whitefish have increased to a point where these waters can no longer support this species or many other forms of aquatic life. Unless steps are taken to reverse these trends or to move Atlantic whitefish to more appropriate and secure environs, this fish will fall into extinction.

Opeongo Whitefish

(Coregonus sp.)

Length: 12 in. (30 cm)
Reproduction: Egg layer
Habitat: Open water
Range: Lake Opeongo, Ontario, Canada

ONE OF THE JEWELS of eastern Ontario's Algonquin Provincial Park is Lake Opeongo. The lake is the centerpiece of this popular park, the largest within its borders, and has been studied for decades as the structure of its fish community has changed and been altered by introductions of native and non-native fish. While these introductions were made with the intent of improving the lake, they have had a disastrous effect on one native species in particular, the Opeongo whitefish.

During the late 1920s, the stocking of sport fishes began in Lake Opeongo. The lake was already a popular destination for fishers interested in catching various species, including the native lake trout (*Salvelinus namaycush*) and brook trout (*Salvelinus fontinalis*). Management officials sought to broaden the range of fishing experience by introducing smallmouth bass (*Micropterus dolomieu*). The impact of smallmouth bass on the Opeongo whitefish is unclear.

Not ready to leave well enough alone, a decision was made to stock another non-native fish, the cisco (*Coregonus artedi*), as a food item for the large lake trout. While this introduction may have had a positive effect on the lake trout as well as the native burbot (*Lota lota*) populations, it probably had a devastating effect on the Opeongo whitefish.

By 1960, the cisco became one of the most abundant species in the lake at the expense of less opportunistic feeders like the Opeongo whitefish, the lake whitefish (*Coregonus clupeaformis*), and the yellow perch (*Perca flavescens*); all of these fish consume plankton.

It is most likely that the cisco is a competitor for breeding habitat as well.

Appearance
The Opeongo whitefish has a small and scaleless head, large eyes to find and capture prey, a pointed snout, and an overall appearance that is very similar to other species within the genus *Coregonus*. It has a fairly slender, well-scaled, and streamlined

body that is moderately compressed from side to side. The body fins are swept back, and the tail fin is deeply forked with lobes that are quite pointed. The overall coloration of the Opeongo whitefish is silvery with a green-blue cast to the back, silvery sides, and a white belly; fin coloration tends to match the body or is slightly darker.

This fish breeds annually by broadcasting its eggs over clean sand and gravel. They are fertilized by the male as they sink to the bottom. Some breeding pairs spawn near the mouths of inlet streams as a way to ensure adequate water movement and oxygenation of the incubating eggs; however, this behavior does not appear to be a requirement for successful reproduction. For food, the Opeongo whitefish has a preference for microscopic plankton as well as other aquatic invertebrates that can be found on the bottom, in the water column, and at the surface.

In addition to competition for food and space, the Opeongo whitefish faces other perils. Given its popularity, Lake Opeongo is experiencing more development on its shores and the associated deterioration of overall environmental quality that follows. While these impacts are important, they probably do not pose a long-term threat to this species. For the most part, these impacts can be controlled. The real threat to the Opeongo whitefish remains the introduction of non-native fish, and, clearly, it simply is not technically or politically feasible to remove all ciscoes from Lake Opeongo. As a result, the Opeongo whitefish faces a bleak future within its native range. Currently this fish is not evaluated by the IUCN–The World Conservation Union.

Squanga Whitefish

(Coregonus sp.)

Length: 12 in. (30 cm)
Reproduction: Egg layer
Habitat: Open water
Range: Yukon Territory, Canada

THE SQUANGA WHITEFISH lives in one of the most remote places on earth—northwest Canada's Yukon Territory. With few people and not many miles of roadway, most aquatic environments there are free from impacts imposed by people and, indeed, the four lakes occupied by this species are nearly untouched by human activity. The four lakes are Dezadeash, Squanga, Teenah, and Little Teslin.

Somewhat surprisingly, people have little to do with the current predicament of the Squanga whitefish. Instead, natural forces have worked to restrict this fish's range. The Squanga whitefish can survive only in lakes that do not contain the more aggressive least cisco *(Coregonus sardinella)*.

Apparently, the least cisco competes for food and space and effectively dominates to the point where the Squanga whitefish cannot survive.

Assuming that the four lakes inhabited by the Squanga whitefish remain free of the least cisco, the Squanga whitefish should manage to survive and thrive indefinitely.

Despite the remoteness of these lakes, however, the opportunity for either accidental or intentional introduction of the least cisco into these lakes by people does exist. Clearly, a priority for Canadian organizations interested in saving this whitefish must be the exclusion of the least cisco from lakes holding the Squanga whitefish.

The squanga whitefish is currently not evaluated by the IUCN–The World Conservation Union, and controversy exists regarding its classification. Based on physical characteristics, the Squanga whitefish is very similar to another whitefish, the lake whitefish *(Coregonus clupeaformis)*, which has a much larger range but shares the four lakes inhabited by its relative. Only small differences in the structure of the gills have been identified. This has led some fisheries biologists to consider these two species as one and the same.

However, others argue that behavioral differences separate the lake whitefish from the Squanga whitefish during the breeding season, making them two distinct species.

Like the lake whitefish, the Squanga whitefish has a small head and pointed snout. It has a mild hump just behind the head, but otherwise the body is fairly slender and streamlined. The body fins are swept back and the tail fin is deeply forked. The overall coloration of this salmonid is silvery with a green-blue cast to the back and a white belly; fin coloration tends to match the body or is slightly darker.

This fish breeds annually by spreading its eggs over clean sand and gravel. Some breeding pairs spawn near the mouths of inlet streams for the water movement and oxygenation provided there. This behavior, however, does not appear to be a requirement for successful reproduction. The Squanga whitefish uses its large eyes to find and capture its favorite foods, which include microscopic plankton and insect larvae that can be found in the water column and at the surface.

Cape Whitefish

(Barbus andrewi)

IUCN: Vulnerable

Class: Actinopterygii
Order: Cypriniformes
Family: Cyprinidae
Length: 2 ft. (61 cm)
Reproduction: Egg layer
Habitat: Stream pools and rapids
Range: Bree and Berg Rivers, South Africa

THE CAPE WHITEFISH, a large freshwater species of southwestern South Africa, has a common name that is misleading. Unlike the North American whitefish (family Salmonidae), the Cape whitefish is more correctly called a barb, although the flesh is white and probably was the inspiration for the common name. Barbs are part of the large fish family Cyprinidae.

The Cape whitefish can reach up to 2 feet (61 centimeters) in length. The body is well scaled and typical in shape and proportion to other barbs. It has a long, sloping head; protrusible (extendable) mouth; large body

fins; and a moderately forked tail fin. The favorite foods of this fish are aquatic invertebrates.

Most of the barbs have two fleshy barbels on each side of the mouth, but some members of this genus have only one—and some have none at all. Because of their small size, bright colors, and prolific reproduction in captivity, many barbs are favorites of aquarium enthusiasts. Males are often brilliantly colored during spawning and have elaborate courting behavior. Barbs have no teeth in the mouth, but in the back of the throat they have comblike teeth (pharyngeal teeth) that perform the same function as typical teeth.

Troubles in South Africa

The Berg and Bree River basins in southwestern South Africa are the last remaining refuges of the Cape whitefish. This species is waging a losing battle with the forces of human activities in these basins. Agricultural development in the region has placed a strong demand on local water resources. Because this region has uneven rainfall and steep mountain valleys, farmers are forced to depend on stream and river diversions to irrigate their crops, causing some tributaries to become completely dry at certain times of the year.

Habitat destruction also occurs in the form of stream siltation—the runoff of loose soil into local waters because of deforestation and other agricultural activity. The seemingly insatiable appetite of predatory non-native fish like the smallmouth bass (*Micropterus dolomieu*) has taken its toll on this species, too.

Another destructive human activity in these rivers is stream channelization, where banks are reworked to minimize flooding. In the process, habitat that is historically used by river fish for feeding and reproduction is wiped out. Water diversion dams both block the movement of fish and change seasonal water flow patterns that the fish use as a cue for migration and breeding.

In an effort to save the Cape whitefish from extinction, fish biologists have begun investigating the feasibility of raising this large minnow on fish farms. Aquaculture (the production of aquatic organisms in a controlled environment) could bring the Cape whitefish back from the brink. Researchers have succeeded in spawning this species in artificial ponds. Injections of hormones have been used to try to start the release of eggs and sperm; this technique is in the process of being perfected. Ultimately, the success or failure of these efforts must be tested in secure habitats in the wild. Only with the restoration of proper habitat can the Cape whitefish once again live undisturbed within its natural range.

William E. Manci

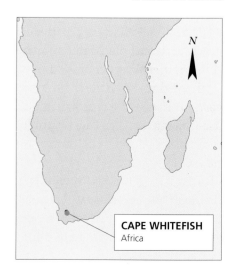

CAPE WHITEFISH
Africa

Texas Wild Rice
(Zizania texana)

IUCN: Endangered

Class: Monocotyledonae
Family: Poaceae (Gramineae)
Stems: Individual stems or culms bend in the current and root at the lower leaf nodes. Culms eventually rise above the water to produce a terminal flowering spike
Leaves: Ribbon-like submerged leaves, mostly ½–1½ inches (1–4 centimeters) broad and 3–5½ feet (1–1.7 m) long
Inflorescences: A loosely branched cluster of flowers called a panicle. Each panicle is around 8–12 in. (20–30 cm) long with spreading lower branches bearing dangling male flowers that produce pollen. The stiffly erect upper branches bear female flowers that produce seeds
Spreading mechanism: By vegetative tillers
Pollination: By wind
Habitat: Headwaters of cool, fast-flowing rivers
Range: San Marcos River, San Marcos, Texas

AT THE BASE OF limestone cliffs, which separate blackland prairie to the east and rocky, eroded hills of the Edwards Plateau to the west, a river arises from large, fast-flowing springs that bubble up through cracks and fissures in the earth. For ten thousand years humans and animals alike were drawn to the clear, flowing water for fish, waterfowl, pure clean water to drink, and solace from the summer heat. The river was lined with bald cypress and sycamore and occasionally widened to form wetlands. All year, in the crystal clear, thermally constant water, bright green ribbonlike leaves of Texas wild rice waved gracefully in the current. During spring, summer, and fall, seeds formed on emergent stems, providing nutritious food for waterfowl and humans.

Settlers arrived at the springs in 1848 and built a city along the riverbank. Farming to the east and cattle ranching to the west occurred in the watershed. Historic photographs of the San Marcos River show Texas wild rice stands approximately 16½ feet (5 meters) in diameter growing in swiftly flowing water and in nearby irrigation ditches.

Altered habitat

The river remained essentially the same until the late 19th and early 20th centuries when technological advances allowed humans to modify their environment in ways unimaginable to previous generations. Flood control dams in the watershed altered the magnitude and occurrence of floods, and three dams within the range of Texas wild rice altered natural hydrologic regimes and sedimentation patterns. The river was channelized and stabilized, and portions were covered with cement screens to withdraw water for industrial purposes. Farming and urbanization increased the amount of sediments and chemical pollutants deposited in the San Marcos River.

In the early 1900s, attempts were made to remove Texas wild rice from the river because it was considered a nuisance. Many mature stands were destroyed and the establishment of new stands was prevented. Although no longer practiced, plant collectors for the aquarium trade routinely removed Texas wild rice and replaced it with more economically valuable aquarium plant species.

The degree of impact of each modification to Texas wild rice is uncertain; however, all these activities and modifications have resulted in a river very different from that in which Texas wild rice evolved and is adapted to. Between 1940 and 1967, Texas wild rice experienced a dramatic population decline attributed in part to habitat modification, bottom dredging, plant collecting, and drifting mats of floating vegetation fragments that interfered with flower emergence. Today the distribution of Texas wild rice is limited to the first 1½ miles (2.4 kilometers) of the San Marcos River, typically in flowing water between about 20 inches (50 centimeters) and 40 inches (100 centimeters) in depth. Seed production is rare in the wild today.

A number of activities continue to threaten Texas wild rice. First, spring flow has been lost due to overpumping of the underground source aquifer. Use of aquifer water in the region for municipal, industrial, and agricultural purposes decreases spring flow. Water usage from the aquifer is projected to increase well into the 21st century as human population in the area increases by an estimated 37 to 47 percent. In dry summers, pumping from the aquifer increases, spring flow decreases, and the river channel narrows

into a new course. Texas wild rice is rooted in the bottom and cannot move, so some is left high and dry and dies.

Today, many non-native species compete with Texas wild rice for space, light, and nutrients. A particularly aggressive non-native species, Hydrilla (*Hydrilla verticillata*) tends to colonize disturbed sites and choke out other species, precluding colonization by Texas wild rice or other native species.

River activities

The cool, clear flowing water of the San Marcos River is desirable not only for plant and animal life but for humans also. People come to the river to wade, swim, and boat during most of the year. These activities disturb the river bottom, increase streamside erosion, and contribute litter and pollution from parking lots and other facilities. Some fear the river is being "loved to death."

Since Texas wild rice was classified as endangered by the U.S. Fish and Wildlife Service in 1978, a number of programs have been initiated to save it from extinction. Texas wild rice plants were collected from the wild and are now grown in captivity, where the plants produce seed and new generations of plants are used for research to learn as much as possible about its life history.

North American relatives

Texas wild rice is one of three wild rice species found in North America: Northern wild rice and Southern wild rice are the other

A canoe rests among a stand of wild rice growing in the Bowstring River, Leech Lake Indian Reservation, Minnesota.

TEXAS WILD RICE
North America

two. Unlike Texas wild rice, these are both annuals that produce submerged ribbonlike leaves only during an early stage of development. Northern and Southern wild rice are common in lakes and are an integral part of Native American culture in the Lake District of the United States and Canada. As a marketable grain product, they have substantial economic importance.

A team of researchers is unraveling the story that DNA tells about the genetic diversity of Texas wild rice and how closely related it is to Northern and Southern wild rice. Researchers are also learning the special conditions required to store Texas wild rice seeds for up to 100 years. The seeds can later be used for propagation, research, or restoration. Genes from Texas wild rice may have the potential

to improve resistance to disease and other pests in domestic wild rice stocks. Based on what is now known through research, observation, and trial and error, a restoration project is under way for Texas wild rice. Whether this project is successful or not will depend not only on whether new plants can become established, but to a greater extent on the region's commitment to preserve and maintain spring flow for the San Marcos River and to control and manage other activities that damage or destroy Texas wild rice. The greatest challenge will be to change the way people think about water use and conservation. Only then will the cool, clear water of the San Marcos River continue to flow over the graceful, vibrant green, ribbonlike leaves of Texas wild rice.

Paula Power and Kathryn Kennedy

Wolverine
(Gulo gulo)

IUCN: Vulnerable

Class: Mammalia
Order: Carnivora
Family: Mustelidae
Weight: 15–68 lb. (7–31 kg)
Head-body length: 26–41 in.
(66–104 cm)
Tail length: 6¾–10 in. (17–25
cm)
Diet: Carrion, birds' eggs,
lemmings, rabbits, berries, fish,
deer, wild sheep, moose
Gestation period: Up to 272
days
Longevity: Up to 17 years in
captivity
Habitat: Tundra and taiga
zones, deep northern forests
Range: Northernmost regions
of the United States; isolated
populations in California;
Canada, Estonia, Finland,
Mongolia, Norway, Russia, and
Sweden

KNOWN AS THE devil beast of the tundra and boreal forest, the wolverine is a fierce and strong carnivore. It is also known as the glutton. The wolverine looks like a giant marten (or weasel), and, indeed, they are both in the same family. But it also looks like a scaled-down bear, a creature with which it often shares more than just a prodigious appetite. Like the bear, the wolverine is inclined to lumber and waddle rather than run all out. With the help of its sharp claws, it too can easily climb trees. Also like a bear, it is an excellent swimmer. As a predator, the wolverine makes up in endurance what it lacks in speed. A wolverine can lope along for exceptionally long distances and is known to be capable of traveling as far as 28 miles (45 kilometers) in a single day. Another similarity to the bear is the wolverine's rather poor vision and hearing. But it has an excellent sense of smell.

Not even the grizzly or the black bear, however, has been more resented by trappers and hunters. As an expert scavenger, the wolverine is known to trigger traps and eat the bait left on them, it will devour the animals caught in those traps before they can be claimed by the trapper.

The wolverine is a tireless scavenger. It will use its teeth and claws to gain access to cached (stored) food, then it will emit a noxious smell to contaminate whatever stored food it does not immediately consume.

A disappearing range

In the past the wolverine ranged throughout Scandinavia and northern Germany. In North America, it was known to frequent the forests of the Pacific Northwest southward to central California. These days its range is much reduced. In Europe it is now found only in parts of Scandinavia and the northernmost regions of the former Soviet Union. It has disappeared from most of southeastern and south-central Canada and has been all but eliminated from the lower 48 states since the beginning of the 20th century.

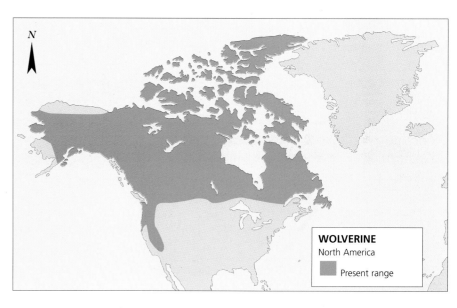

From time to time there are reports that the animal has been seen in Washington, Oregon, Idaho, Wyoming, and Colorado. For the most part, however, the wolverine is concentrated in thinly populated northern areas, places where it can live in relative peace from humans. Today it is found primarily in taiga and northern tundra zones, but also in the deep forests of northwestern and north-central Canada.

Appearance

The wolverine has long, thick fur, which is generally dark brown or blackish with a lighter patch along the sides and over the

In the far north where day or night is often extended, the wolverine alternates between four-hour periods of rest and activity. During the summer, it is generally nocturnal.

rump. The muzzle is usually darker than the head and neck, and it often has a light bow-tie-shaped patch on its throat. Its teeth are strong and razor sharp.

During the warmer months the wolverine feeds on carrion, squirrels and other small mammals, campground leftovers, berries, and roots. It is not a swift runner, so during the warmer months it has few opportunities to dine on deer, elk, moose, or larger animals. In winter, however, the animal's light weight, together with its broad paws, enables it to travel quickly over thin icy crusts of snow. At such times it may pursue and attack the largest foraging animals in its territory. It does not hesitate to attack and kill an adult moose that may outweigh it by a thousand pounds or more. In fact, the

wolverine is known to scavenge on the kills of cougars and bears.

Like the gray wolf, with which it shares some remote hunting territories, and like northern carnivores in general, the wolverine tends to require a large range. Unlike the gray wolf, it does not hunt in packs. It is a decidedly solitary creature. Members of the same sex do not share territory. Territories are marked with an anal scent and also with urine.

For shelter the wolverine may construct a rough bed of leaves in a cave or rock crevice. It may take up residence under a fallen tree or in a burrow made by another animal. Most maternal dens in Finland have been found under the snow. One to five young are born between January and April. At birth the young nurse for 8 to 10 weeks, leave their mother after six months, and attain adult size after a year. They reach sexual maturity in the second or third year of life.

The wolverine has been hunted for its fur, which, while neither soft nor particularly beautiful, is warm, waterproof, and accumulates less frost than other kinds of fur. For these reasons it is highly valued by northern people.

As recently as the late 1970s, as many as 2,000 wolverine pelts a year sold for an average of about U.S.$180 each.

Although trapping for fur has contributed to the decline of the wolverine, this has probably not been as significant as persecution for its reputation as a nuisance.

This animal has been hunted, poisoned, trapped, and otherwise persecuted for its tendency to prey on reindeer and livestock.

Renardo Barden

WOLVES

Class: Mammalia

Order: Carnivora

Family: Canidae

Once wolves enjoyed a range greater than any other mammal except *Homo sapiens*. Now they live in greatly reduced numbers, mostly in remote regions of the world that are of marginal importance to people.

Regarded as a menace to livestock and a danger to humans, the wolf long ago was effectively exterminated from western Europe. It has fared little better on the other side of the Atlantic. During the last 300 years in North America, the wolf has been systematically hunted, trapped, shot, and poisoned to the brink of extinction.

Although it posed only a relatively minor threat to livestock, and attacks against human beings were all but unheard of, the wolf was targeted because it was inconvenient. It was killed not necessarily for what it did, but because of fears of what it might do. Interestingly, as wolf populations dwindled in North America, coyote populations seem to have expanded greatly.

The wolf evokes strong feelings. Farmers and ranchers and traditional outdoor enthusiasts regard it as a treacherous enemy. Zookeepers, conservationists, and other knowledgeable people have more positive feelings about the wolf's important habitat role.

A wolf looks like a big coyote, or perhaps a German shepherd or husky—especially the latter. They are superb communicators. Not only do they howl and use their voices in a variety of ways, but they also depend on their tails to keep them in harmony with their associates. Like the dog, the wolf uses its tail to claim and acknowledge its place in existing social orders. Communication with the tail is a visual, one-on-one form of communication.

Howling is a nonvisual form of wolf communication. There are many ideas about why wolves howl. Some say that howling is a fanciful kind of martial music intended to inspire enthusiasm for a coming hunt. Others suggest that howling is a summons to assemble, a call to action. Still others maintain that a howl is a kind of warning to other wolves to keep their distance. Of course, a howl may be all those things and more.

Territory marking is a routine part of any patrol. Experts have observed that as a pack moves through its territory, some form of marker is left regularly at a rate of about once every 787 feet (240 meters).

Since not all wolves live in packs, territory marking is perhaps even more important to the solitary wolf. Scent marking often seems to include information about an animal's gender and reproductive cycle. These can be important considerations to a wolf looking for a mate.

Wolves are adaptable and can flourish in a variety of habitats. However, they do need space and suitable prey. For all their intense social organization, wolves are not among the world's most successful hunters. Experts who have observed them in action estimate that only about 10 percent of all wolf hunts meet with success, which is rather surprising.

Protected by legislation and conservation groups over the last 20 years, North American wolves that were formerly close to extinction are now beginning to rebound.

Indeed, there are plans to reintroduce protected wolves to some of the lands where they once were able to wander freely.

Gray Wolf

(Canis lupus)

ESA: Endangered

IUCN: Lower risk to extinct in the wild

Weight: 45–176 lb. (20–80 kg)

Head-body length: 40–63 in. (100–160 cm)

Tail length: 14–22 in. (36–56 cm)

Diet: Carnivorous

Gestation period: 60–63 days

Longevity: 8–16 years

Habitat: Deep forests, mountains, tundra, taiga

Range: Alaska, Canada, and portions of western Montana; also isolated areas of Wyoming, Idaho, Minnesota, and Michigan; remote regions of Europe and Asia

EXCEPT FOR THE most arid deserts and the most tropical of forests, the original habitat of the gray wolf was spread throughout the Northern Hemisphere. However, thousands of years of persecution by people all over the world have reduced the numbers of this species and radically limited its range. Today, there are small gray wolf populations in the Balkans, Portugal, Spain, Italy, parts of eastern Europe, Scandinavia, and south-central Asia. In the first half of the 20th century, the gray wolf was plentiful in much of Eurasia. But after World War II and continuing until 1962, the former Soviet Union systematically killed as many as 40,000 to 50,000 animals a year. In some ways, the former Soviet Union was just catching up with similar eradication efforts undertaken by American settlers beginning in the 17th century. By the beginning of the 20th century, the gray wolf had been virtually eliminated from the Midwest and western United States (although a few animals hung on in remote areas of Minnesota, Wisconsin, and Michigan).

Today, thanks in part to its protected status, the gray wolf seems to be making something of a comeback in North America. It is now solidly established in northern Minnesota, where it is protected by federal law (although wolves preying on livestock may be killed by federal agents there). Small numbers of gray wolves have also reappeared in Montana and Idaho, and perhaps remote regions of Wyoming.

Of intense interest to gray wolf enthusiasts is whether the animal will migrate naturally back to Yellowstone National Park in Wyoming. Should the animal arrive in the park on its own, it will automatically come under the protection of the Endangered Species Act of 1973, which will severely restrict attempts to kill or remove it from the park for any reason whatsoever. If, on the other hand, the gray wolf is reintroduced in the park, its status will be considered provisional. That means it will be susceptible to destruction or removal should its presence in the park become troublesome.

Some wolf experts believe that the gray wolf's reappearance in Yellowstone would reduce populations of deer and elk, which would almost certainly mean fewer winter starvation deaths for the park's foraging animals.

Appearance

Characteristically, the gray wolf's fur is gray with brownish gray patches and some grizzling. In some populations, all-white or entirely black specimens are sighted. The fur on the back and on the tail tends to be darker than the rest of the animal; underparts and legs are yellowish to white. The outer hairs are coarse and bristly, and the underfur is so dense that the gray wolf can sleep on the snow in temperatures well below freezing.

The gray wolf feeds mostly on mammals larger than itself, including deer, elk, caribou, bison, moose, and musk ox. It hunts these animals in groups known as packs.

Packs usually consist of between five and eight members, although they have been seen with as many as 30 animals or

The gray wolf is the largest of the wolf species. Although there is considerable variation in its size, in general the largest specimens tend to be found in the northernmost reaches of its range.

GRAY WOLF
North America

Former range

Current range

(males are on average about 10 to 15 percent larger than females). The alpha male tends to initiate pack activity, lead the pack on hunts, guide its movements, make decisions, and assume control at critical moments during a hunt. He remains in charge of the pack as long as he is strong enough to control and dominate other members. Sometimes the alpha male is challenged by younger wolves or new pack members. If beaten in combat, the formerly dominant alpha wolf will either accept a diminished status or leave the pack and become a lone wolf.

Behavior

There are also alpha females, usually mated to the alpha males. Males and females tend to have separate dominance systems or hierarchies. These ranks are reinforced and regularly tested by aggressive behavior and submission displays. Generally, only the most dominant wolves in the pack mate. Some scientists think that the dominant female arouses fear in other females, triggering hormones that may interfere with the ovulation of less dominant females. Without ovulation, the females are not fertile. Although reproduction belongs only to the strong and the dominant wolves, pup rearing—particularly the feeding of the meat-hungry pups—is shared by all pack members.

Hunting range

The hunting range of a pack varies with the availability of game. It can be from more than 5,000 square miles (13,000 square kilometers) in Alaska during the winter to just 7 square

more. In general, there seems to be some relationship between pack size and the size of prey being hunted. For example, large packs of wolves may be more successful at preying on moose, musk oxen, and caribou, while

smaller packs may be better suited for hunting deer and elk.

A wolf pack is like a family unit, generally consisting of an adult pair and their mostly grown offspring. It is usually dominated by a male called an alpha male

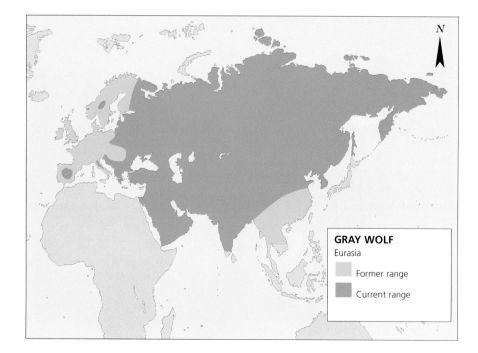

GRAY WOLF
Eurasia

Former range

Current range

miles (18 square kilometers) in southeastern Ontario. The hunting range is basically the same area as the defended territory. There is generally little or no overlap between ranges of different wolf packs. Sometimes, when conditions warrant it, larger packs split up into smaller packs. The reverse may also happen.

Nocturnal hunters

Gray wolves are essentially nocturnal animals. During the summer, the pack usually sets off on a hunt in the early evening and returns to its den about dawn. The pack tends to travel in single file and patrol known areas, roads, streams, or frozen lakes. In winter, daylight activity tends to increase; the animals wander farther and do not necessarily return to any fixed location. Prey is located by chance encounter, direct scenting, or following fresh tracks. Odors can be detected as far as 1¼ miles away (2 kilometers).

Long-distance travelers

In the far north, gray wolf packs have been known to travel as far as 124 miles (200 kilometers) during a single day's hunt. Northern packs that depend on caribou meat make seasonal migrations with their prey. The pursuit of prey is a team effort, particularly in the open. While one wolf closely pursues the quarry, other pack members fall back and fan out laterally. In this way, however the pursued animal may alter its course, it is always converging on another pack member.

During prolonged chases, a relay takes place with the lead wolf frequently falling back to rest while other, fresher wolves press the pace in the hope of exhausting the hunted animal.

A dangerous predator?

While gray wolves do hunt livestock, experts and ranchers rarely seem to agree about the extent of predation. In Michigan, for example, wolves are estimated to kill about one in every 2,000 head of cattle and one in every 1,000 sheep annually.

While the hunting, trapping, and killing of wolves is illegal in every state but Alaska, the U.S. Department of Agriculture in Michigan continues to eliminate about 100 wolves per year for killing or menacing livestock.

The gray wolf is often seen as a threat to human safety. While fatal attacks have apparently occurred in Eurasia, in North America there appears to be only two documented cases of attacks on humans. In 1982, a Minnesota deer hunter was kicked and clawed but not bitten by a wolf near Duluth; and in 1987, a young girl was bitten after shining a bright light in a wolf's eyes. In other, older incidences of wolf attacks in North America, domestic dogs have usually been involved; gray wolves have attacked these pets and then turned on the human beings in their company.

And what of the prospect of wolves returning to Yellowstone? Recently polled Yellowstone visitors have favored bringing back the wolf by a 6-to-1 margin. Of Wyoming residents living near Yellowstone, 44 percent have expressed approval of bringing the gray wolf back to Wyoming, while 34 percent opposed its reintroduction.

Maned Wolf
(Chrysocyon brachyurus)

ESA: Endangered

IUCN: Lower risk

Weight: 44–51 lb. (20–23 kg)
Head-body length: 47–51 in. (120–130 cm)
Tail length: 11–15¾ in. (28–40 cm)
Diet: Small mammals, birds, eggs, insects, reptiles, and occasional roots and fruit
Gestation period: 62–66 days
Longevity: Up to 13 years
Habitat: Grasslands, savannas, swampy areas
Range: Central and eastern Brazil, eastern Bolivia, Paraguay, northern Argentina, and Uruguay

THE MANED WOLF IS the smallest wolflike wild canid and has the longest legs relative to its body size. This animal looks something like a giant red fox and may in fact have more in common with the red fox than with known species of wolves.

The maned wolf's long, soft fur is yellowish red or russet to mahogany and is generally darker along the back of the neck and back. The muzzle and lower legs are also dark and may be completely black. In contrast, the throat and tail tuft are usually white but may be light tan. The animal is known for its mane of long, shaggy reddish fur that it deliberately erects when angry or frightened. The maned wolf has a rather long skull with a pointed muzzle, rounded eyes, and large ears.

Hunting technique

Even with its long legs, the maned wolf is not a particularly fast runner. It is more probable that its legs evolved to allow this animal to peer over high grass and shrubbery that has traditionally covered much of its range. In any case, the maned wolf rarely pursues its prey and, whenever possible, seems to prefer a careful stalk and then a foxlike pounce. The maned wolf leaps high in the air, pins its intended prey with its front paws, and tries to bite a vital area.

The maned wolf is a nocturnal creature but sometimes becomes active in the late afternoon, perhaps in response to a scarcity of prey animals. Its diet is omnivorous and includes carrion.

A loner

Unlike the gray wolf, the maned wolf does not live in a pack. In fact, it seems to be the most solitary of wolves, seeking out companionship only during the

Some scientists have proposed that the maned wolf has developed long legs to enable it to pounce on its prey.

breeding season and otherwise hunting or living on its own. But, unlike many other solitary creatures, maned wolves do reasonably well in captivity and can usually be persuaded to tolerate the company of other maned wolves—following an initial period of fighting to establish dominance.

Vocalizations

While the gray and red wolves of the Northern Hemisphere are inclined to howl, the maned wolf prefers a more foxlike yapping and barking. The closest it comes to howling is a kind of deep-throated, single bark that it emits mainly after sundown. Sometimes it makes a high-pitched whine. A growl is associated with aggressive behavior.

Struggle for survival

The maned wolf is not hunted for its fur, but ranchers routinely shoot and trap it in the mistaken belief that it preys on livestock. It is now belatedly protected by law in Argentina, Brazil, and throughout much of the rest of its dwindling South American

MANED WOLF
South America
Present range

range. It has virtually disappeared from Uruguay, however, and struggles to survive in other parts of South America. Part of the problem is that the maned wolf is native to an area that farmers and ranchers find easier to clear by burning than by plowing. Grazing animals that are hunted by the maned wolf are unable to find any forage after a large-scale burn, and their populations decline. Deprived of prey, the maned wolf in turn ceases to reproduce and eventually starves or succumbs to disease.

The maned wolf is also vulnerable to a form of illness called cystinuria. This is an inherited metabolic defect that is sometimes fatal.

Red Wolf

(Canis rufus)

ESA: Endangered

IUCN: Critically endangered

Weight: 44–88 lb. (20–40 kg)
Head-body length: 40–52 in. (100–132 cm)
Tail length: 12–16½ in. (30–42 cm)
Diet: Rodents, rabbits, deer, wild pigs, birds, birds' eggs, and carrion
Gestation period: 60–63 days
Longevity: Up to 14 years in captivity
Habitat: Upland and lowland forests, swamps, and coastal prairies
Range: Southern Texas; western Louisiana; released into Cape Romain Wildlife Refuge on Bull Island, South Carolina, and Alligator River Wildlife Refuge in North Carolina

ONCE THE RED WOLF roamed the southeast and south-central United States from Florida to Texas and north to Missouri. But like most carnivores, the red wolf was traditionally treated as a threat to livestock and people. It has been intensively bountied, hunted, trapped, and poisoned to the edge of extinction. Driving the red wolf from its habitat seems to have had unexpected results: it stimulated coyote populations. In fact, the red wolf has interbred with coyotes, a development that has contributed to controversy about what is—and what is not—a purebred red wolf. Indeed, there is evidence that the red wolf is itself a hybrid, born of the union between the gray wolf and the coyote.

The red wolf is generally grayish with a buff or reddish tinge on its back. This is often overlaid with black and whitish hair. The tail is usually tipped with black. The underparts are a whitish to pinkish buff. The red wolf's fur is shorter and thinner than that of the gray wolf.

The red wolf actually looks more like a coyote than a gray wolf. The red wolf is lighter and smaller than the gray wolf and its legs and ears are longer. It favors smaller prey and has smaller ranges with milder climates.

Traditionally it is found in a wide variety of habitats, including forests, prairies, and wetlands.

Unlike the gray wolf, the red wolf does not form packs. In fact, the basic social unit is a mated pair (more like the coyote), although sometimes larger groups have been reported. These groups consist of nearly grown offspring with their parents. Litters of four to seven pups are born in the spring after a gestation period of about two months.

Hybrid howl?

Vocalizations are similar to those of the coyote and the gray wolf, but the red wolf has a distinctive howl. It builds slowly, hits a melodic high, then trails off evenly after about six seconds. Red wolves are said to have the most melodic howls of all.

The red wolf is usually nocturnal. It makes its den in rocks, hollow trees, and natural stone slopes. It preys on rodents, rabbits, pigs, snakes, birds and their eggs, and small deer. Like other wolves, the red wolf will eat carrion when it is available.

The red wolf is indigenous only to North America. Once it ranged widely through the southeastern United States, but by 1980 it was regarded as effectively extinct in the wild.

Fortunately the red wolf's predicament was well known to wildlife experts. Concerned that interbreeding with coyotes was bringing about the genetic

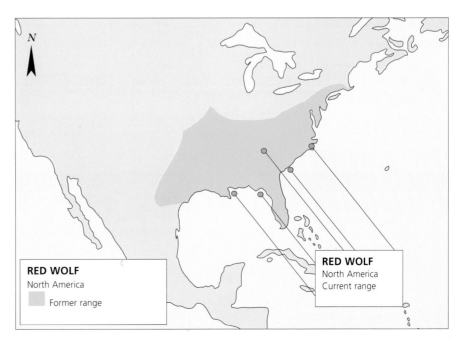

RED WOLF
North America
Former range

RED WOLF
North America
Current range

The red wolf has suffered the fate of virtually all large North American carnivores: relentless human persecution and progressive habitat destruction.

destruction of this species, experts captured 17 red wolves (thought to be purebred) living near the Louisiana-Texas border. Following the passage of the Endangered Species Act in 1973, they began a captive breeding program to save the red wolf from breeding itself into extinction. By October 1990, 131 red wolves existed in captivity.

Controlled breeding of red wolves was not enough; naturalists wanted them returned to the wild. In 1977, a small number of red wolves were released in Cape Romain National Wildlife Refuge on Bull Island in South Carolina. In 1987 four pairs of captive-bred red wolves were released into the Alligator River National Wildlife Refuge in northeastern

North Carolina. As of 1993 there were at least 30 red wolves living in this refuge.

Three islands off the shores of South Carolina, Florida, and Mississippi are also currently home to captive-bred wolves. The hope is that once the wolves have learned to survive in these environments, they can gradually be reintroduced into other mainland areas. In 1991, red wolves were also released into Smoky Mountains National Park in eastern Tennessee. By 1997 this population held as many as 37 individuals.

Still, the red wolf, like all wolves, has a natural public relations problem. Ranchers and farmers do not easily think well of wolves. The U.S. Fish and Wildlife Service has begun several reeducation programs designed to persuade locals that red wolves do not pose significant dangers to people, and pose only marginal—and manageable—risks to livestock.

The program seems to be a success. Already the newly settled wolves are proving to be significant tourist attractions. The changing circumstances of the gray and red wolves in North America may yet be cause for optimism in the fight to protect endangered wildlife.

Renardo Barden

Northern Hairy-nosed Wombat

(Lasiorhinus krefftii)

ESA: Endangered

IUCN: Critically endangered

Class: Mammalia
Order: Diprotodontia
Family: Vombatidae
Weight: 42–68 lb. (19–31 kg)
Head-body length: 40 in. (100 cm)
Tail length: 2 in. (5 cm)
Diet: Grasses
Gestation period: Unknown
Longevity: Unknown
Habitat: Forest grassland
Range: Queensland, Australia

EARLY SETTLERS TO Australia often mistook the wombat for a small bear. Because of its burrowing ability, and because it emerges from holes in the ground, it was also mistaken for some kind of badger.

The wombat is neither a bear nor a badger. It is a member of the marsupial family, members of which, like the kangaroo, nurse their young in abdominal pouches. The female wombat has two mammary glands within the pouch that provide milk for the young to nurse.

The wombat is a shy and nocturnal animal that makes its home underground, burrowing large networks of tunnels for nesting and storing food. It is similar to many rodents in that it creates escape tunnels in case it is pursued by a predator. Like rabbits, each individual wombat family nest is linked to many others, forming a warren. Despite these behaviors, extensive observation of wombats, in the wild and in captivity, shows that they have little if any organized social structure.

Unusual diggers

Wombats dig in a unique way. Unlike cats or dogs, which alternate front paws while digging, the wombat first makes five to seven swipes with one claw, then changes to the other for another series of swipes. When enough dirt has been loosened, the wombat pushes the dirt under itself with its front claws, shoving it backward out of the tunnel with its rump. This activity contributes to the hardening of the wombat's skin (the backside of a wombat is often as hard as a wooden plank). Once thought to be relatively unintelligent, according to recent studies, the wombat may be the most intelligent of the marsupials.

The hairy-nosed wombat has a thick coat of fine, silky fur to protect itself from the elements.

Aggressive behavior between two wombats is rare. Even males tend to avoid each other rather than do battle.

The fur is either brown-gray or gray streaked with pale brown or black. Its ears are small and rounded, and the eyes are small, suited to life underground.

The wombat lives in a relatively dry habitat, preferring savanna, woodland, and grassland with low shrubs. It is territorial and will defend its home. Despite the interconnection of wombat tunnels into warrens, the wombat prefers to

NORTHERN HAIRY-NOSED WOMBAT
Australia

remain solitary and not share its feeding space. Aggressive behavior is rare, but when two males get in each other's way, the conflict is resolved in a sort of shouting match amounting to a series of grunts and shoving. Two wombats will rarely bite each other.

Wombats are born in the spring and remain in the mother's pouch for six or seven months. They usually have only one young per season, but twins have occasionally been reported.

Habitat loss

Wombats have been hunted for food by aborigines and settlers alike. But the primary reason for their decline is attributed to the loss of habitat caused by over-grazing cattle and sheep and by urban sprawl. This species is now found only in Epping Forest National Park, near Clermont, central Queensland.

In 1971, most of this area was designated a national park by the state government of Queensland and the Australian government.

The hairy-nosed wombat's population numbers were estimated in 1996 at about 67 individuals.

George H. Jenkins

WOODPECKERS

Class: Aves

Order: Piciformes

Family: Picidae

Subfamily: Picinae

Woodpeckers are very active birds. They are able to excavate holes in wood-sided buildings and can also damage plantations, fruit orchards, and ornamental trees. Noise and damage give the woodpeckers a bad reputation, but they are not pests. In fact, woodpeckers are extremely helpful.

Cavities that woodpeckers excavate and then abandon are quickly taken over by a great many other birds. Known as secondary cavity nesters, these birds nest in holes but cannot excavate their own. Woodpeckers help speed the recycling of nutrients in an ecosystem. By shredding dead wood they increase the rate of decay, and decay makes nutrients locked in dead plant tissues available to other plants and animals.

Woodpeckers depend on forests, woodlands, and swamps. How people use or abuse trees determines what happens to different woodpecker species. Many have already declined and several are now endangered.

Helmeted Woodpecker

(Dryocopus galeatus)

IUCN: Endangered

Length: 11 in. (28 cm)

Weight: Unknown

Clutch size: Unknown

Incubation: Unknown

Diet: Probably insects

Habitat: Lowland forest

Range: Southeastern Paraguay, extreme northeastern Argentina, southern Brazil

A TAPPING HIGH in a tree of southern Brazil betrays the presence of a woodpecker. It slides around the trunk into view. A bright red crest sweeps back from the crown and nape, and a red whisker marks its jawline. Its forehead, face, and throat are a tannish buff. A white rump interrupts the uniformly black back, wings, and tail. Alternating bars of pale brown and black pattern the underparts. It is a helmeted woodpecker.

Often described as the least known woodpecker in the world, the helmeted woodpecker escaped several attempts to locate it until the 1980s. Historically it was found in the region where three nations meet. It was recorded in Paraguay, across the border in Misiones, Argentina, and through portions of four Brazilian states: Rio Grande Do Sul, Santa Catarina, Paraná, and São Paulo.

The helmeted woodpecker inhabited the forest long before there were countries. It vanished from Rio Grande Do Sul in the 1920s, from Santa Catarina in the 1940s, and Paraná in the 1950s. Ornithologists believed it was entirely gone from Brazil, until a sighting in western São Paulo in the mid-1980s renewed hope that the bird still survived there. No reports have come out of Paraguay in decades, but a small population of helmeted woodpeckers has been found in

HELMETED WOODPECKER
South America

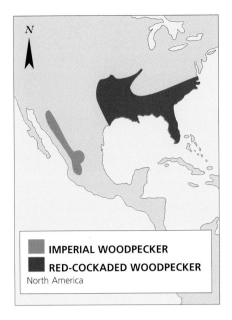

IMPERIAL WOODPECKER

RED-COCKADED WOODPECKER

North America

Iguazu National Park in Misiones, Argentina. Misiones is a small appendage of land that separates Paraguay from Rio Grande Do Sul in Brazil.

The helmeted woodpecker disappeared from Brazil because of a random but deliberate dismembering of its great southern forest. People working independently but motivated by the same goals cut and cleared the forest. They removed the trees in order to plant crops and grow grass. Cattle were fattened on the grass, and their beef was shipped to many foreign markets. Bit by bit, parcel by parcel, the forest was nibbled away until only isolated fragments remained. The helmeted woodpecker may yet survive in some of them, but so far none has been found.

Before ornithologists could learn the details of its life, the helmeted woodpecker disappeared. The lack of natural history information prevents ornithologists from preparing any kind of meaningful recovery plan. The best that can be done is to protect the remaining tracts of lowland forest where the species

used to occur. Study of the surviving population in Argentina may eventually provide the information needed to help preserve the helmeted woodpecker.

Imperial Woodpecker
(Campephilus imperialis)

ESA: Endangered

IUCN: Critically endangered

Length: 21½–23 in. (55–58 cm)
Weight: Unknown
Clutch size: Unknown
Incubation: Unknown
Diet: Insects
Habitat; Primary forests
Range: Northern and western Mexico

A GREAT, BLACK BIRD sails on 3-foot (90-centimeter) wings through the shadows of the forest. It alights not on a branch, but on a vertical trunk. Almost immediately it takes a couple of quick hops up the trunk and disappears around the back side. This is its habit. If anything had been following it—a hawk perhaps—the quick move around the trunk could make the difference between life and death. Such a defensive move comes naturally to the imperial woodpecker.

Dressed tuxedo-style in black, white, and a touch of red, the imperial woodpecker makes a striking figure. The bird is mostly black. Its head, neck, upper back, shoulders, and breast are faintly glossy with a greenish or bluish

sheen. The belly, sides, and tail are not glossy but are sootier, not so deep black. The outer flight feathers are likewise sooty black, but the inner flight feathers are pure white. When the woodpecker sits with wings folded, the inner flight feathers form two large white patches over the back. Thin white lines run along the seam where each wing joins the body. Together they form a white vee across the back. A fine crest on the bird's head is scarlet on the male and black on the female. Her crest is curled noticeably forward, which is quite different from any other woodpecker. The eye is dull yellow, almost whitish; and the beak is pale. Unlike most smaller woodpeckers, the imperial does not look compact. Smaller woodpeckers have short necks that look appropriate for their physique and size. The imperial has a long, slender neck that adds to its elegance.

Each pair of imperial woodpeckers can claim and defend territories up to 10 square miles (26 square kilometers). Large territories prevent very many woodpeckers from occurring in any given area. Consequently, the imperial woodpecker probably never occurred in high densities anywhere in its range. The imperial woodpecker has never been studied in detail, and some ornithologists fear it may have slipped into extinction.

Some expanses of pine-oak woodland yet survive in the species' old haunts. The total clearing of great woodland tracts no longer occurs on the same scale as it once did. Much tree cutting now targets selected trees. Without being able to study the bird, no one knows what effect such a tree cutting policy has on the imperial woodpecker.

The last verified sighting of an imperial woodpecker was in 1958. In the 1990s, however, there were claims of sightings in three different areas, giving hope that this species may yet exist.

Ivory-billed Woodpecker

(Campephilus principalis)

ESA: Endangered

IUCN: Extinct

Length: 19–20 in.
(48–51 cm)
Weight: Unknown
Clutch size: 1–4 eggs, rarely 5
Incubation: Probably 20–22 days
Diet: Insects, fruits
Habitat: Forests, swamps
Range: Southeastern United States, Cuba

BY FAR THE largest woodpecker in the United States, the ivory-billed was a black bird smartly accented with white. A white line originating on the cheek behind and below the eye ran down the neck and onto the back. The pure white inner flight feathers formed a broad white patch over the lower back when the bird folded its wings as it clung to the side of a tree. A conspicuous, pointed crest from the back of the head was black in the female but bright red in the male.

The bird's keenest feature, however, was its nearly white beak. Native Americans killed these large woodpeckers and col-

lected their beaks as baubles.

The ivory-billed woodpecker historically inhabited the ancient forests and swamps of Cuba and the American South. The species preferred the primary forests of river bottoms but did occur in pine woodlands, if only to feed. It ranged from eastern Texas and Oklahoma into Arkansas and southeastern Missouri, southern Illinois, western Kentucky and Tennessee, all of Louisiana and Florida, plus portions of Mississippi, Alabama, Georgia, and the Carolinas.

No one was able to thoroughly study its natural history before it was too scarce to study. Several factors contributed to the species' troubles, but ornithologists have never satisfactorily answered the question of just why the ivory-billed woodpecker vanished.

Human fears and superstitions about swamps, human demand for lumber products, prejudice and ignorance in the emerging profession of forestry, and commercial demand for museum specimens all played some role in the demise of this bird. Because of negative feelings

IVORY-BILLED WOODPECKER
North America, Cuba
▨ Former range

about swamps, people did not challenge the draining, burning, and cutting of this habitat. Swamps also produce valuable trees. Sweet gum (*Liquidambar styraciflua*) produced more hardwood than any other single tree species in the early years of the United States. Bald cypress (*Taxodium distichum*) yielded a valuable rot-resistant wood. Various oaks (*Quercus* sp.) contributed to lumber output as well. Those trees that were not useful were often cut just to get them out of the way. Thus, entire swamps were demolished.

Bad forestry

Early forestry practices encouraged ridding forests, woodlands, and swamps of useless or unproductive species and especially of dead, sick, or damaged trees. It was believed that such trees merely encouraged insects and disease that would infect healthy trees if left standing. Today, ornithologists know that such trees are vital feeding trees for many kinds of birds. Modern forestry practices on public land must consider the full sweep of a forest or woodland as a commu-

The ivory-billed woodpecker has not been seen in the United States since the 1950s.

nity and not simply as a crop of lumber. This modern view came too late to help the ivory-billed woodpecker.

Thoughtless hunting

In the heyday of museum collecting, specimens were to be taken at all cost. Rarity or the possibility of extinction only made the last specimens all the more valuable. One collector paid local hunters for ivory-bills, buying 17 in the years 1892 to 1893. They all came from the Suwanee River area of northern Florida, and none has been seen there since.

A large insect-eating bird with a specialized feeding technique needs a lot of space. From scant evidence, ornithologists believe a pair of ivory-bills needed 3 square miles (7.8 square kilometers) or even more to meet their needs. Small patches of riparian woodland or forest and fragments of swamp could not sustain many ivory-billed woodpeckers for long. Timber cutting was intense and thorough in the southern states during the latter 19th century and early decades of the 20th century. The last known ivory-billed woodpecker in the United States vanished in the 1950s.

A small population survived in Cuba. The bird had not been seen on the island since 1973, but in 1986 a group of ornithologists searching portions of eastern Cuba found three ivory-bills, plus signs of their presence in other areas. The Cuban government immediately responded with appropriate protective measures. Even there, however, there have been no recent sightings, and many ornithologists now consider it to be extinct.

Okinawa Woodpecker

(Sapheopipo noguchii)

> **IUCN:** Critically endangered

Length: 8–8.5 in. (20–21.6 cm)
Weight: Unknown
Clutch size: Unknown
Incubation: Unknown
Diet: Insects
Habitat: Forest
Range: Okinawa, in the Ryukyu Islands of Japan

A FROG, A BEETLE, a rail, and a woodpecker make northern Okinawa a special place. Those particular animals live nowhere else but on this Pacific island. But if current conditions remain unchecked, they may soon live nowhere at all.

The Okinawa woodpecker has a pinkish overall appearance. The forehead is black, and a black whisker mark streaks down its jawline. The crown is dull red. The back is gray with a rose wash that makes it look almost brown. The wings and tail are dark gray brown. The sides and the belly are dull rose. A neutral gray covers the cheek and continues down the side of the neck onto the throat and the breast. The chin is paler.

As a species unique to a single island, the Okinawa woodpecker has never been abundant relative to other birds. It was, however, fairly common in the wooded hills of northern Okinawa a century ago. It declined steadily as human development increased. By 1941, the woodpecker was considered very rare with proba-

bly only 100 birds still alive. Current population estimates vary among different ornithologists. Some range as low as 40 and some as high as 200.

The woodpecker prefers primary forest but does use some secondary forest. Most of the primary forest has been cut. After World War II, the United States held Okinawa. The island was returned to Japan in 1972. The Japanese government quickly began a program of subsidizing tree cutting to produce chipboard, a cheap and largely inferior substitute for plywood. Without government backing, the chipboard industry could not have survived. Okinawa's woodlands and forests were nearly stripped. Only small pockets and patches survived. Cutover areas were not restored or replanted with native trees, but cultivated plantation-style with exotic trees for perpetuating the lumber industry. The Okinawa woodpecker does not use the exotic trees, and if it did, it would likely be treated as a pest. Besides commercial cutting, the remaining patches of primary forest and older secondary forest are cut for firewood by local people.

The Japanese government set aside a 17.5-acre (7-hectare) reserve for the woodpecker, but such a small tract is inadequate for the preservation of an entire species. In 1987 the International Council for Bird Preservation appealed to the Japanese government to act decisively on behalf of the woodpecker. The reasoning in favor of the endangered bird was less persuasive than arguments about soil erosion, siltation, and subsequent damage to fisheries and other resources.

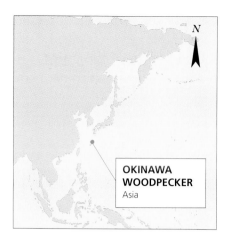

OKINAWA
WOODPECKER
Asia

Before meaningful action is taken, the Okinawa woodpecker could be extinct—leaving only the rail, the frog, and the beetle to save.

Red-cockaded Woodpecker

(Picoides borealis)

ESA: Endangered

IUCN: Vulnerable

Length: 8½ in. (21.6 cm)
Weight: 1½–1¾ oz. (40–48 g)
Clutch size: 3–5 eggs
Incubation: 10 days
Diet: Primarily insects, seasonal fruits
Habitat: Mature pine woodlands
Range: Southeastern United States

THE RED-COCKADED woodpecker dramatically polarized American sentiments in the mid- and latter 1970s. The Endangered Species Act of 1973 was still fresh, and how it was going to work was still uncertain. People held the naive idea that endangered species were only condors and eagles and whales—glamorous animals that lived somewhere else and could be coddled a bit without getting in anyone's way. Then the Endangered Species Act struck home with the snail darter (*Percina tanasi*), involving the Tellico Dam in Tennessee. Suddenly Americans were awakened to the fact that protection was for all endangered species, big or small, glamorous or not.

The red-cockaded woodpecker was a feathered equivalent of the snail darter. Water developers could not believe anyone would seriously object to a dam in favor of a puny fish. Likewise, loggers and others in the timber industry could not believe anyone would go to great lengths to protect a woodpecker. This was considered insanity.

The debate

People in favor of logging argued that woodpeckers destroy trees needed by people, and that cutting trees creates jobs, which in turn puts food on families' tables. Protecting a woodpecker would take food out of children's mouths when loggers lost their jobs. In addition, people with jobs receive paychecks to spend, thereby keeping money moving in the economy. If unemployed loggers have no money to spend, businesses will suffer. Foresters argued that leaving mature pines uncut was bad forestry practice. They argued that it was a waste of vital lumber and that not cutting mature trees would drive up the cost of lumber.

Ornithologists, on the other hand, argued that a species' survival was at stake. Forests were more than trees waiting to be cut. They argued that certain values exceeded human economics: scientific values, ecological values, global values. Bird defenders argued that humans cannot ethically decide which species shall live and which shall become extinct. Other trees in other places might be cut for lumber, it was argued, but the red-cockaded woodpecker had nowhere else to go.

No-win situation

No one won, and no one lost. But the criteria for identifying an endangered species and devising a plan for its recovery matured in a hurry. Endangered species management quickly evolved into a profession that did not always fit in with traditional wildlife management. Soon people had jobs helping endangered species rather than sending them into extinction.

Appearance

A smallish woodpecker, the red-cockaded probably has the least amount of red on its head of any North American woodpecker, except for the three-toed species. A small white fluff runs over the base of the beak, but the forehead is otherwise black, which continues over the crown and down the nape. A black stripe down the jawline separates the white cheek from the white chin and throat. The breast and belly are also white, but the sides are patterned with oblong spots or short streaks. The wings are dull black with rows of white spots. The back is barred with black and white. A small white spot above and behind the eye is separated from the white cheek by a short black line that ends in a small red spot, which gives it its name.

The red-cockaded wood-pecker occurs from eastern Texas and Oklahoma and southeastern Missouri through parts of Kentucky and Tennessee and all the southern states into Virginia. John James Audubon wrote that this woodpecker was common even in New Jersey.

Unique behavior

The species behaves uniquely among American woodpeckers. A breeding pair forms the nucleus for a clan, and offspring from previous seasons remain with the parent birds and act as helpers with new broods of offspring. When the young birds mature and are able to breed, they leave the clan and start one of their own. No clan ever has more than one pair of breeding birds. The clan remains on its territory year-round. The breeding pair selects an area where pines are 60 to 75 years old. They choose trees afflicted with a fungus (*Phellinus*

The red-cockaded woodpecker is one of the many species that brought the plight of endangered species to the attention of the American people.

pini) that causes heartwood rot. The woodpeckers excavate their nesting and roosting cavities in the trunks of live trees. Sticky pine resin oozes from the wounds of the excavations. The dripping forms long streaks. This resin buildup might deter predators or possibly attract insects. The habitat the red-cockaded woodpecker chooses for nesting is usually reported as forest because the term is used by Americans to mean any place where trees grow. From the standpoint of a plant geographer, red-cockaded woodpeckers use mostly pine woodlands. The crowns of the trees where the woodpeckers live do not form a continuous overhead canopy.

Much of the area where they live is open enough to allow good undergrowth, but when the undergrowth develops too fully, the woodpeckers vacate that area and establish themselves in more suitable habitat.

Still declining

The red-cockaded woodpecker ranks among the most thoroughly studied endangered species in the United States. Yet, despite what is known about this bird, and despite deliberate actions to protect it, its population continues to decline. Habitat loss on private land probably accounts for much but not all of the decline.

Other factors such as the size and quality of suitable habitat tracts, the proximity of habitat tracts to each other, and the proximity of land uses that disturb the woodpeckers or otherwise degrade habitat quality also figure into the problem.

Kevin Cook

Red-collared Woodpecker

(Picus rabieri)

IUCN: Vulnerable

Length: About 12 in. (30 cm)
Weight: Probably 8 oz. (227 g)
Clutch size: Unknown
Incubation: Unknown
Diet: Probably mainly ants
Habitat: Primary and secondary forest, up to 2,200 ft. (670 m)
Range: Parts of Laos and Vietnam

THE EURASIAN woodpecker genus *Picus* comprises at least 14 medium to large species that have several features in common: they display a lot of green in their plumage; their bills are straight or very slightly downcurved and more or less pointed; and many feed at least part of the time on the ground, with ants making up a big part of their diet. Seven of this group are found in the forests of Indo-China, with the red-collared woodpecker by far the rarest of them.

Protected areas

This species is known from four protected forest areas in Laos, where it is now considered to be locally common, while in Vietnam it has been recorded in five areas (three of them protected), including southern Annam, which is a southern extension to its known range in that country. Elsewhere, there is just one old record from Yunnan province in China, though it seems likely that areas of Cambodia also provide a home for this attractive bird. Despite being commoner than

RED-COLLARED WOODPECKER
Southeast Asia

was once feared, its fragmented range and the continuing threat of logging mean that a question mark still remains over its long-term future.

Like most members of its family, the plumage of the red-collared woodpecker is very striking. Birds of both sexes display mid-green upperparts, paler green underparts, and a red collar and mustache stripe, though on the female the red is not as conspicuous, and her crown is black in contrast to the bright red of the male's. Most of this bird's family is highly vocal, but although the red-collared woodpecker has been heard drumming on tree trunks, its calls are undescribed.

Sociable species

Seen singly, in pairs, or in small family parties, red-collared woodpeckers regularly join mixed-species flocks—for example, with other woodpeckers and babblers. They often feed low down in trees and, in the same way as other *Picus* woodpeckers, they frequently forage on the ground for ants.

Virtually nothing is known about this species' breeding behavior, but the breeding season is thought to be between January and March. Juvenile birds have been seen in July in Vietnam. More information on breeding requirements would help conservation efforts.

Found in evergreen and semi-evergreen forest at low altitudes, and locally in tall mixed deciduous forest, the red-collared woodpecker is usually scarce or absent from selectively logged and disturbed forest. It can be found in small and degraded patches of forest provided that some large trees remain.

More data needed

Clearly, then, the prime threat to this species is the widespread destruction of its lowland forest habitat. More information is required on its range and on its precise habitat requirements. Armed with this information, a key priority must be to establish a wider network of protected areas.

Tim Harris

WOOD-PIGEONS

Class: Aves

Order: Columbiformes

Family: Columbidae

Wood-pigeons belong to one of the largest bird families in the world: the one that includes pigeons and doves. Pigeons inhabit all the continents except Antarctica. They have even pioneered onto many remote oceanic islands.

A notable behavior of pigeons is that they feed their young on so-called pigeon's milk. The pigeon's milk is not like mammal's milk. It is just a thickened lining of the bird's crop (a pouch in the bird's gullet that is used to hold and soften food before it is digested).

Fairly colorful and medium-sized as pigeons go, the wood-pigeons are closely related to the rock dove (*Columba livia*). This is the wild species that people have domesticated. In many places the rock dove lives wild again, as a feral bird. It is the famed but sometimes disliked pigeon of cities and parks.

Not all members of the genus *Columba* thrive as well as the rock dove. Several wood-pigeons have suffered population losses when people have moved into the birds' homelands. Some of these species now face questionable futures.

Gray Wood-pigeon

(Columba argentina)

IUCN: Vulnerable

Length: Probably 13–14 in. (33–35.6 cm)

Weight: Unknown

Clutch size: 1 egg

Incubation: Unknown

Diet: Unknown

Habitat: Forests

Range: Sumatra and small islands including Banyak, Mentawai, Lingga, Riau, Karimata, Anambas, and North Natuna

THE GRAY WOOD-PIGEON's flight feathers are black, and so is the outer half of its tail, but its overall plumage is a silvery gray accented by a slight green gloss on the nape. Its feet and toes are largely bluish gray, dabbled with faint pink. Its beak is pale green toward the tip and darker purplish brown at the base. The female is slightly darker gray and lacks the shiny quality. Compared to other pigeons, the gray wood-pigeon is rather plain. The silvery gray, however, is unique among the birds of the family.

For many years ornithologists believed this bird did not occur on Sumatra itself. It was known to occupy the Banyak and Mentawai Islands along the Indian Ocean coast, and it appeared as far away as the North Natuna Islands in the South China Sea. Such distribution would seem peculiar if the species did not occur on Sumatra. It was finally found on the great island, but its status is uncertain everywhere.

Lost to progress

Many small islands in Southeast Asia have been completely cleared of all native plant communities. Plantations of coconut, bananas, and other tropical crops have been established in place of natural forests. Losing a small island of habitat here and a part of an island there seems like a very small loss indeed, until all the islands and all the losses are added together. The gray wood-pigeon has disappeared from Burong Island, Malaysia. Doubt-

The gray wood-pigeon inhabits mostly small, forested islands around the island of Sumatra.

less it has declined on other small islands as well. Research is needed to determine the status of the gray wood-pigeon on other islands in its range.

Maroon Wood-pigeon
(Columba thomensis)

IUCN: Vulnerable

Length: 16 in. (41 cm)
Weight: Unknown
Clutch size: Probably 1 egg, as in related species
Incubation: Unknown
Diet: Fruits
Habitat: Forest
Range: São Tomé in the Gulf of Guinea

THE MAROON wood-pigeon grows larger than any other pigeon in West Africa. Its gray head contrasts with the reddish purple or purplish maroon back, shoulders, sides, and breast. The back color fades to dark gray on the rump and a paler gray on the belly and undertail. The wings and tail are slate gray, nearly black. Small white spots pattern the small feathers of the wings and breast. The beak is yellow.

The maroon wood-pigeon sports a long tail proportional to its overall size.

This pigeon is a forest bird that probably wandered over most of its home island of São Tomé. Historically, it was also found on Dove Island. Whether it was a resident there or just a frequent visitor was never determined before it vanished from the island altogether.

São Tomé lies approximately 125 miles (200 kilometers) off the coast of Gabon. Surrounded by the Gulf of Guinea, São Tomé is the remnant of an ancient volcano. The Portuguese settled the uninhabited island in 1471 when

MAROON WOOD-PIGEON
Africa

they sent unwanted people there. For two centuries, São Tomé was the center of the African slave trade. It became independent in 1975. Its 330 square miles (855 square kilometers) now support sugarcane, coffee, and cocoa, among other crops. Much of the island was originally forested, but the primary forests still surviving on São Tomé are limited to the mountainous interior, which rises 6,639 feet (2,024 meters).

Hunting pressure

People on São Tomé have hunted maroon wood-pigeons probably since the island was settled. One written account describes how islanders built fires in forest clearings to attract the wood-pigeons so that they could be shot more easily. Pigeons provide meat to a lot of people around the world. They have been hunted for food, for recreation, and for capture. Pigeon hunting on São Tomé soon exceeded the limit the wood-pigeon could tolerate. In 1955 a law banned pigeon hunting, but it was never

enforced. The plight of the maroon wood-pigeon clearly demonstrates how unrestrained, unregulated hunting can threaten a species' survival.

Arguments that local people need the protein are unrealistic. When a species becomes extraordinarily rare, or even extinct, then local people get no protein at all from that source. Regulated hunting would allow some taking of maroon wood-pigeons but would also protect a core population that could sustain the species. Annual surveys would determine breeding success and current population level. The population status of the maroon wood-pigeon in the early 1990s was not known. Ornithologists expressed some fear, however, that the species needed protection. The last tracts of primary forest on São Tomé need to be preserved, and hunting needs to be regulated. If either is neglected, the maroon wood-pigeon could vanish quickly.

Nilgiri Wood-pigeon
(Columba elphinstonii)

IUCN: Lower risk

Length: 16½ in. (42 cm)
Weight: 13½ oz. (383 g)
Clutch size: 1 egg
Incubation: Unknown
Diet: Fruits, buds, snails
Habitat: Evergreen and deciduous forest
Range: India, from southern Bombay through western Madras, Mysore, and the state of Kerala

A STRING OF hills runs north to south along the western edge of the great Indian peninsula. In India they are known as the Western Ghats. There, in the hills above 2,000 feet (610 meters), lives the Nilgiri wood-pigeon. A deeply colored bird, it has a dark brown back with a strong purplish maroon sheen. Its rump is less shiny and its tail is grayer, nearly black. The chin is pale, dingy gray. The color continues onto the throat and darkens as a bluish gray on the breast, then quickly fades to dirty gray on the lower breast, belly, and undertail. The head is a light blue-gray that yields to a black patch with white spots on the nape. It is a handsome pigeon that has become hard to find.

Ornithologists do not know much about this particular pigeon. Many details of its natural history have yet to be discovered. They do know, however, that it inhabits all the primary woodlands (evergreen, deciduous, and mixed) and prefers small fruits and buds as its main diet. Some have been seen eating small snails. The Nilgiri wood-pigeon spends much of its time alone, but observers report seeing this bird in pairs and small groups.

Much hill country in India has been cleared to open it for agriculture, livestock grazing, hay production, and other uses. The growing human population of India has placed enormous demands on the land to produce food. No one has determined whether the Nilgiri wood-pigeon can adapt to secondary woodlands and artificial habitats. The growing infrequency of reports suggests it cannot.

Sri Lanka Wood-pigeon

(Columba torringtoni)

IUCN: Vulnerable

Length: Probably 12–13 in. (30–33 cm)
Weight: Unknown
Clutch size: 1 egg
Incubation: Unknown
Diet: Fruits
Habitat: Evergreen and deciduous montane forests
Range: Sri Lanka

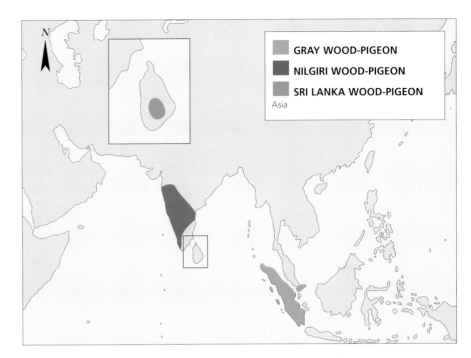

GRAY WOOD-PIGEON
NILGIRI WOOD-PIGEON
SRI LANKA WOOD-PIGEON
Asia

A DOZEN DIFFERENT pigeons have been found on Sri Lanka. Two of them are rare stragglers, and ten of them are native. Of these ten, the Sri Lanka wood-pigeon is the only one unique to the island. This wood-pigeon is an elegant bird. Its shoulders, back, and tail are slate gray with a bluish sheen. The rump is a paler gray. The flight feathers are sooty, not so slaty or black. The chin and throat are white, but the breast and belly are dull rose or grayish purple-pink. The sides are slightly darker. The bird's entire head is pale gray with a faint pink wash.

This wood-pigeon has unusual plumage on the lower nape and extreme upper back. It is black and white, variously described by different observers as "spotted" or as a "chessboard." Some paintings illustrate it as more zebra-striped. Handsome as the wood-pigeon is, few people see it. The species haunts montane forests, particularly the wet forests in the southwest, usually above 3,000 feet (914 meters). Native forests are becoming ever more scarce on Sri Lanka as people replace them with plantations.

Small country

Sri Lanka covers 25,332 square miles (65,610 square kilometers), an area slightly less than half the size of Alabama. Shaped like a teardrop, the island is mostly flat along the coasts and in the northern three-quarters. Low mountains texture the island's southern quarter. Monsoons from May to September sweep across the Indian Ocean and blow across the southwest portion of the island. The moisture-burdened air reaches the mountains and dumps up to 200 inches (508 centimeters) of rain a year. The northern and eastern sections of Sri Lanka receive only 25 to 75 inches (63 to 190 centimeters) each year. The mountains are mined for iron and for limestone, which is processed into cement and other products. The forests are cut for tropical woods and then replaced with plantations of tea, coconuts, cocoa, pine, and eucalyptus. Monterey pine (*Pinus radiata*) from North America and eucalyptus (*Eucalyptus* sp.) from Australia have also been widely planted as lumber crops.

The Sri Lanka wood-pigeon does not use the tree plantations. It is an arboreal bird of primary forests. It eats small fruits that it collects from the forest canopy. This wood-pigeon does not gather in great flocks but usually lives in pairs. It does wander, however, in search of adequate food supplies. The seeds of pine cones do not attract the wood-pigeon. The crowns of pines probably do not offer enough cover for a forest canopy bird such as the Sri Lanka wood-pigeon. Some preservation attention has been turned to the last patches of primary forest, but illegal firewood cutting, tree poaching, and other problems continued through the 1980s. If the forests are not preserved, the Sri Lanka wood-pigeon will continue to decline.

Kevin Cook

Woundfin

(Plagopterus argentissimus)

ESA: Endangered

IUCN: Vulnerable

Class: Actinopterygii
Order: Cypriniformes
Family: Cyprinidae
Length: 3½ in. (9 cm)
Reproduction: Egg layer
Habitat: Swift, murky, and warm streams over sand
Range: Virgin River in Utah, Arizona, and Nevada

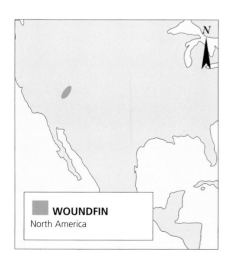

WOUNDFIN
North America

LIKE SO MANY other fish that are native to the Colorado River system, the woundfin has succumbed to the onslaught of human development and destruction of habitat that has changed the nature of this once undisturbed waterway. While the woundfin is still found in the Virgin River, a tributary of the Colorado River in Utah, Arizona, and Nevada, this fish has not been found in tributaries of Arizona's Salt River (Gila River basin) since 1915. Dams (the scourge of most native fish), predation, and competition from introduced predatory fish like the red shiner (*Cyprinella lutrensis*) quickly eliminated the woundfin from the Gila River basin.

This fish depends on warm and murky river water for its survival. It is left with just the opposite when dams and their associated reservoirs completely alter streams. Dams cause sediments and other suspended matter to settle out, leaving only clear, cooler water. They also change seasonal downstream water flow. Fish like the woundfin have evolved to respond to seasonal cues such as water flow rate and temperature. Without these cues, the woundfin is incapable of properly controlling its reproductive cycle.

The woundfin has survived in the Virgin River above the dams and reservoirs that spelled the downfall of other woundfin populations. It is a free-flowing stream that is somewhat removed from larger cities and still retains its historical characteristics. Water flow in this river varies greatly, from torrents during periods of heavy seasonal rain to a trickle during the long, dry

The woundfin is small but well suited to life in the rivers of the Colorado River basin. It has a flattened and wedge-shaped head, pointed snout, and streamlined body.

periods. Water temperatures soar over 90 degrees Fahrenheit (32 degrees Centigrade) during droughts, but the woundfin has adapted to take all of this environmental variability in stride.

Battling habitat change

Despite the relative remoteness of the Virgin River and the toughness of the woundfin, the fish must still contend with environmental assault. To many people, the Virgin River represents opportunity—opportunity to use the water for agriculture, for the production of energy, and for potable (drinkable) water. Agricultural pollution has significantly degraded many miles of the river. Projects designed to desalinate water from springs that feed the river, and the construction of a power plant cooling reservoir, could unleash similar havoc on the remaining woundfin habitat.

Unlike most other river fish, the woundfin has no protective scales over its body; but, as a result, it spends less energy on swimming because of reduced drag. All its fins are large relative to its body; they are triangular and swept back, except the tail fin, which is deeply forked. This fish uses spines in its dorsal fin and pelvic fins to defend itself from predators, a physical trait that is unusual for a member of the family Cyprinidae. The woundfin has small eyes that are only of minor help in searching for food in the murky water.

Instead, this fish relies on other sensors, such as taste and smell. Little is known about woundfin reproduction, but during the summer breeding season the females probably deposit eggs over the sandy bottom. Favorite foods of this species include insect larvae and algae covered with aquatic protozoans.

The woundfin has an interesting and distinctive coloration pattern, with tan on the back and silver on the sides and belly. A faint horizontal line can be seen on each side of the fish's tail section.

The future of this species is unclear and will depend on the efforts of a recovery team to restore damaged habitat and prevent further habitat destruction. The expansion of agriculture and proposed business and commercial activities in the fish's range are still threatening. These kinds of uses of the Virgin River are incompatible with the needs of this endangered species and should be avoided or modified. Attempts to relocate and establish the woundfin in other places have failed.

William E. Manci

WRENS

Class: Aves

Order: Passeriformes

Family: Troglodytidae

There are 79 species of wren found mostly in North, Central, and South America. The only representative of the Troglodytidae family outside the New World is the winter wren, which is found across much of Europe, Asia, and North Africa. The greatest diversity of wrens is in Central America.

Most wrens are small or medium-sized birds with short, rounded wings and thin, longish bills. Though not brightly colored, wrens are often strikingly marked in combinations of browns, black, and white. They are usually found singly or in pairs, and attention is often first drawn to them by their loud and musical songs. The largest part of a wren's diet is made up of insects.

Many wren species have already declined, and several are now endangered.

Apolinar's Marsh-wren

(Cistothorus apolinari)

IUCN: Endangered

Length: 5 in. (13 cm)
Weight: Probably ⅓–½ oz. (10–12 g), as in related species
Clutch size: Unknown
Incubation: Unknown
Diet: Insects
Habitat: Marshes
Range: Boyacá and Cundinamarca, Colombia

AMID THE CATTAILS of a South American marsh, a short, cheery song repeats over and over again. Quiet spells followed by harsh, angry scolding—like the buzz of a great insect—punctuate the singing. Here and there, scattered all about the broad expanse of cattails, the singing rises and

The Apolinar's marsh-wren perches on cattails or other marsh plants. It is a wary bird, and will travel through the stems rather than fly over them.

falls, comes and goes. This is the singing of a colony of Apolinar's marsh-wrens.

High in the Colombian Andes lives the Apolinar's marsh-wren. It is a bird of cattail (*Typha* sp.) marshes, although it occasionally inhabits other marsh plant communities. A tiny bird, it is a master at staying out of sight. When curious or annoyed, it often weaves its way through and among the tangled stems rather than flying over them.

A dull gray eye stripe separates the medium brown forehead and crown from the

APOLINAR'S MARSH-WREN
South America

tannish, sand-colored face. The sandy color extends down the sides of the neck and onto the upper breast and sides. The chin, throat, and belly are dingy white. The lower belly and undertail are dull golden tan. Alternating streaks of dark brown and dingy white pattern the upper back. The lower back and rump are the same golden tan as the undertail. The wings and tail are banded dark brown and tan. The slender beak is thin and slightly decurved. The Apolinar's marsh-wren closely resembles the sedge wren (*Cistothorus platensis*). A common but elusive wren of the eastern United States, the sedge wren also inhabits the montane marshes of Colombia.

The Apolinar's marsh-wren is not so widely distributed. It is found only in the states of Boyacá and Cundinamarca. It occurs in a patchy, uneven distribution at elevations of between 8,200 and 13,120 feet (2,500 and 4,000 meters). Where it occurs, it often congregates in loose colonies. Each male defends a territory in the marsh, but many nesting pairs inhabit the marsh. Entire marshes that look suitable for the wren may go uninhabited. What marshes it has historically inhabited are dwindling away. Habitat

loss threatens the Apolinar's marsh-wren. Marshes are grazed by livestock, burned, and drained for farming or improved grazing.

No population estimates have been developed for the Apolinar's marsh-wren, but it did not appear to be critically imperiled as of the late 1980s. It could become further endangered if the rate of marsh destruction continues as it did for most of the 1970s and 1980s.

Colombia has nearly three dozen national parks. The parks include portions of all the major plant communities in the country. In this respect, the Colombian parks excel over the national park system in the United States. Some experts have credited Colombia with having the best parks program in South America. Unfortunately, funding and law enforcement are not always equally available. Still, the park system is in place, and the intent to preserve the nation's flora and fauna is established within the government. Conditions are suitable for the habitat of the Apolinar's marsh-wren to receive the attention it needs.

Kevin Cook

Niceforo's Wren

(Thryothorus nicefori)

IUCN: Critically endangered

Length: 5¾ in. (14.5 cm)
Weight: About 1 oz. (25 g)
Clutch size: Unknown
Incubation: Unknown
Diet: Chiefly insects
Habitat: Acacia scrub
Range: San Gil area, Colombia

SO LITTLE IS KNOWN about the Niceforo's wren that it is still not certain whether it should be considered a separate species or simply a race of the rufous-and-white wren, which is its neighbor in northern Colombia and Venezuela. In fact, Niceforo's wren is known from just one location in the Santander department of Colombia, and there, in the western foothills of the eastern arm of the Andes, its favored acacia scrub is found in the valley of the Río Fonce.

A few specimens of this bird have been collected since it was first described in 1945, and these can be seen in the Museo de la Salle, but no live birds have been sighted since a pair was discovered half a mile (1 kilometer) east of the town of San Gil in 1989.

Subtly attractive

Although not brightly colored, Niceforo's wren is a very attractive little bird. A rich brown crown, black eye stripe, long white eyebrow, and black streaking on the white cheeks lend the bird a very distinctive facial expression. The upperparts are brown, with black bars on the tail, and the underparts are off-white. Its plumage differs only subtly from its close relative: it is

NICEFORO'S WREN
South America

not as reddish above as the rufous-and-white wren, and its flanks are grayish, rather than brown. With a medium-length, slightly decurved bill and a longish tail, Niceforo's wren has the typical shape of all members of its family.

Wrens are renowned songsters, and although the voice of this species is not known, the closely related rufous-and-white wren sings beautifully, delivering a deep, melodious, flutelike liquid whistle. Indeed, the bird's song could be important in deciding whether Niceforo's wren deserves its taxonomic status as a distinct species.

Widespread cultivation, with arable crops, coffee plantations, and clearance for pastureland, has disrupted much of the natural habitats of the San Gil area, though it is not known to what extent this has affected the acacia scrub. Since the birds seen in 1989 were in a remnant of this habitat, the effects of cultivation are clearly important and measures have to be taken to protect this specialized habitat.

Zapata Wren

(Ferminia cerverai)

IUCN: Critically endangered

Length: 6¼ in. (16 cm)
Weight: About 1 oz. (30 g)
Clutch size: 2
Incubation: Unknown
Diet: Insects, spiders, caterpillars, small snails, lizards and berries
Habitat: Saw grass marshes
Range: Zapata Swamp, Cuba

THE ZAPATA WREN must be one of the hardest of all bird species to see. For a start, one would need to travel to a tiny area in the southwest of Cuba within a 12½-mile (20-kilometer) radius of the town of Santo Tomás. In this region is the Zapata Swamp, the location that gave the bird its name. But even in this very localized tract of savanna-type grassland, it is almost impossible to locate this species—which numbers less than 200 pairs—unless you are familiar with its song and are able to track down its point of origin.

The song is high-pitched, strong, and very musical, starting with a low, guttural note and changing into a canary-like warble. It is often repeated three times before the bird falls silent again. In the breeding season, between January and July, the intervals between bouts of singing are shorter than during the rest of the year.

To make viewing even more difficult, singing birds do not announce their presence from exposed perches but from the saw grass thickets and bushes that are their favored habitat. If disturbed, the Zapata wren is

ZAPATA WREN
Cuba

more likely to run away through the undergrowth than to fly, so even views of this bird in flight are difficult to obtain.

It is not surprising, then, that ornithologists did not even know of the species' existence until 1926. Neither is it unexpected that the first nest was not found until as recently as 1986, and only a handful have been located subsequently. From the evidence of those that have been discovered, it appears that the globular nest structure is typically built about 3 feet (1 meter) above the ground in saw grass.

The lucky observer who does get to glimpse a Zapata wren will note its small size, brown upperparts delicately striped with black, and pale grayish underparts; the underside of the long tail is marked in much the same way as the upperparts. The tail is depressed when the bird sings. Typically for a wren, the bill is longish, as are the legs.

Soon after its discovery the bird was thought to be common in the Zapata Swamp, but it does not retain that status today. One of the prime reasons for that is the periodic burning of its specialized habitat during the dry season: fires spread from surrounding sugarcane plantations, and 10 to 25 percent of the swamp grassland is incinerated this way every year. Predation by the introduced mongoose is also considered to be a problem. So what can be done? Of prime importance is conserving the saw grass habitat of Zapata Swamp, limiting dry-season burning, and, though this is easier said than done, controlling mammalian predators.

Tim Harris

Wild Yak

(Bos grunniens)

ESA: Endangered

IUCN: Vulnerable

Class: Mammalia
Order: Artiodactyla
Family: Bovidae
Subfamily: Bovinae
Tribe: Bovini
Weight: 1,800 lb. (820 kg)
Shoulder height: 62–79 in. (157–200 cm)
Diet: Grass, moss, lichens
Gestation period: 258 days
Longevity: Unknown
Habitat: Alpine tundra
Range: Tibetan plateaus

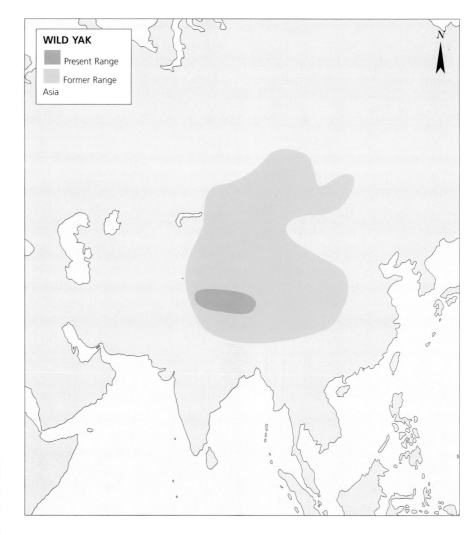

WILD YAK
Present Range
Former Range
Asia

THE WILD YAK was once found from Siberia to Tibet, Nepal, and Kashmir. Now, however, its range is reduced to only the plateaus of Tibet. Except for the kouprey, the yak is probably the least known of all of the wild cattle. Yet the domesticated form of the yak is extremely well known

In many respects, the wild yak is the opposite of the domestic yak in terms of size and temperament.

and is an indispensable animal of the highlands of central Asia.

The wild yak is much larger and much more wary than its domestic counterpart. The domestic yak is a relatively docile beast of burden and is extremely valuable for its hair, milk, and meat, as well as for its carrying capacity. In the high altitudes of south-central Asia, it is an absolute necessity to the local inhabitants. The domestic yak is even used to carry people.

The wild yak, by contrast, is difficult to approach, and the local people have a great respect bordering on fear of the wild yak bull. The wild yak is hunted intensively. Its long fur and skin is prized, as is the meat. This animal inhabits the higher plateaus and plains of Tibet during the summer, often at over 15,000 feet (4,570 meters) in altitude. It descends to the lower elevations during the harsh winter weather.

The yak's natural habitat is sparsely covered with vegetation;

therefore, it must cover a great deal of ground each day to find enough to survive. It moves from grazing site to grazing site, each quickly becoming depleted. It avoids high temperatures, but can easily withstand very low temperatures. Interestingly, it is common for the wild yak to bathe in rivers and streams even in cold weather. It lives primarily on grass when it is available but very often eats mosses and lichens. It has a rough tongue surface that aids in licking lichens off rocks.

Social organization

The wild yak is found in herds consisting of just a few animals or up to 200 individuals. These herds usually consist of cows, calves, and young bulls. Mature bulls are often found in small bachelor groups. These bachelor groups break up from September to October during the breeding season to join the females. Considerable battling goes on between wild yak bulls for dominance. Young yaks are born the following June.

The yak's tail has always been highly valued. The Romans used the tails as fly whisks, and in Turkey they were used as symbols of royalty. In India they were religious symbols, while in China they were dyed various colors (usually red) and used as cap decorations.

The wild yak commonly retreats when it spies humans. Not infrequently, it will—by chance—come into contact with a domestic yak. It is usually hostile and belligerent to the domestic yak, even to the point of attacking and killing it.

Reasons for endangerment

The wild yak is considered an endangered species because its remaining populations are all in remote, isolated areas where enforcement of protection is difficult, if not impossible. Therefore, it continues to be hunted. While there are millions of domestic yaks in Asia, there are probably no more than a few hundred wild yaks still alive. The captive population consists of a handful of animals in some Chinese zoos. There is no existing breeding program, which means that there is currently no plan to help the wild yak to survive.

Warren D. Thomas

ZEBRAS

Class: Mammalia

Order: Perissodactyla

Family: Equidae

Simply put, zebras are black-and-white members of the horse family (Equidae). This fact brings up several commonly asked questions. Are zebras white with black stripes, or black with white stripes? The answer is neither. If the hair is removed, the same striped areas are pigmented in the skin, so they are still black-and-white animals. The next commonly asked question is: are they striped horses or striped donkeys? The answer is neither. They are zebras, a form unto themselves. As a matter of fact, many scientists feel that the striping pattern predates the plain, nonstriped pattern in the evolution of the horse.

All zebra species are found in Africa. However, like other members of the horse family, their origins go back to North America. They are just one surviving form in the 60-million-year evolution of the horse that began with the tiny *Eohippus*. There are many subspecies of zebras, most of them identified by the regions they inhabit and their distinctive stripe pattern.

The most common forms of zebras—subspecies of Burchell's zebra—are found over much of the veld and savanna south of the Sahara Desert. These zebras are usually found in small family groups with a number of mares, foals, and a dominant stallion. Young males are driven from the group toward the end of their first year, and they are often later found in bachelor groups.

Zebras are territorial and defend their identified space violently. They are efficient grazers and will occasionally browse. People think of zebras as being grassland animals, which they are, but some of them are found in arid desert environments, where their efficient food gathering and digestive systems sustain them quite well. There is an old adage about zebras: one never sees a skinny zebra in the wild. There is a great deal of truth to this.

Superficially it would seem that a zebra's coat could never be considered camouflage for protection, or what biologists call cryptic coloration. Their dramatic striping seems to call attention to these animals. However, out on a flat grassy plain, at a distance, the black-and-white stripes appear to merge into gray. This gray blends with the mists of the morning, the heat convection currents of the afternoon, and dusk's waning light—in short, an effective camouflage after all.

Grevy's Zebra

(Equus grevyi)

ESA: Threatened

IUCN: Endangered

Weight: 800–1,000 lb.
(363–454 kg)
Shoulder height: 56–64 in.
(142–163 cm)
Diet: Grass, leaves, shoots
Gestation period: 365–395 days
Longevity: 20–25 years
Habitat: Semi-arid to arid
scrubland
Range: Ethiopia, northern
Kenya, possibly Somalia

THE GREVY'S ZEBRA is the largest, most powerful, and, in some respects, most spectacular of all the zebras. It has the thinnest stripes and the largest ears in proportion to its head size. Its voice is also quite different, sounding much more donkeylike than the voices of other zebras.

The Grevy's zebra is found in North Africa. Its range used to include Somalia, Ethiopia, and northern Kenya, but now its numbers are greatly reduced. Because of concern for the Kenyan population, there have been a number of attempts to translocate this species to other areas in Kenya, but with poor to limited results.

In this species—and in all zebra species—the young are born in what is called a precocious state, fully capable of following their mother within hours after birth. Even so, they are a favorite target for predators of the African veld. Hyenas, leopards, lions, and the Cape hunting dog all prey on the young and occasionally on adults. However, zebras are very alert, and it is difficult for predators to approach a family of them. If a predator manages to pull down a foal, the female will often vigorously defend its young until the predator is driven off.

No security

The future of this animal is in jeopardy because of the political instability of humans within the same home range. Although the Grevy's zebra is afforded official protection, this does not always translate into real protection in the wild. The wild population is estimated at less than 15,000. Fortunately there is a healthy population of Grevy's zebras in

Grevy's zebra lives in small herds with the same typical behavior of other zebras. Scrub thorn and acacia are able to adapt to this hostile environment as well as the zebra.

captivity—some 500 individuals in nearly 100 institutions. The Grevy's zebra is a regal and beautiful animal in any setting. By zebra standards, it is a relatively easy animal to keep; however, it must still be intensely managed. Some males are tolerant of the females and even of their foals, but many are not. Foals must be kept separated from the males to keep the males from injuring or killing them. Often it is possible to put the female with the male only for breeding purposes. They then must be quickly separated to prevent injury to the female.

Mountain Zebras
(Equus zebra)

ESA: Endangered

IUCN: Endangered

Weight: 660–815 lb.
(300–370 kg)
Shoulder height: 45–52 in.
(114–132 cm)
Diet: Grass, leaves, shoots
Gestation period: 365 days
Longevity: 20–25 years
Habitat: Rocky areas; semi-arid, arid scrub brush
Range: Southern Africa

MOUNTAIN ZEBRAS are all found in south and southwestern Africa. There are two forms: the Cape mountain zebra (*Equus zebra zebra*), found only in the Cape Province of South Africa; and the more common Hartmann's mountain zebra (*E. zebra hartmannae*), found in Namibia and Angola.

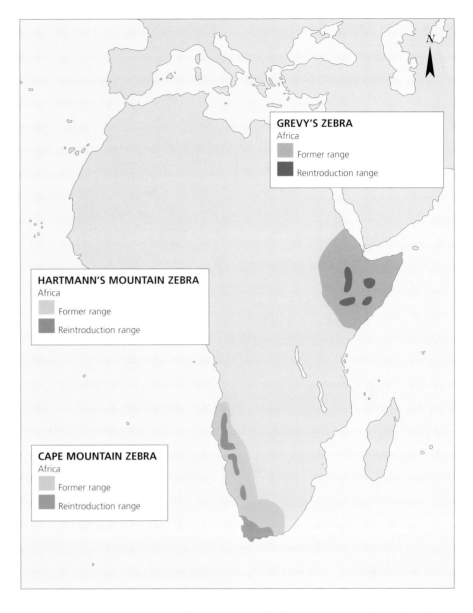

GREVY'S ZEBRA
Africa
Former range
Reintroduction range

HARTMANN'S MOUNTAIN ZEBRA
Africa
Former range
Reintroduction range

CAPE MOUNTAIN ZEBRA
Africa
Former range
Reintroduction range

The mountain zebras have a unique striping pattern: the area over the hips just above the tail forms what is known as a grid-iron pattern unique to this species. They also have a specialized hoof that is more resilient and nonskid than those found on other zebras. This unusual form of hoof also grows 2½ times faster than that of any other member of the horse family. This unusual modification of the hoof has the effect of making these zebras very surefooted in rough terrain. It also ensures that in walking over sharp rocks and ledges, their hooves are not worn down too quickly (which would make them lame).

The Cape mountain zebra was almost totally wiped out in the last century, with only a handful surviving on Table Mountain outside of Capetown, South Africa. With strict protection, this subspecies has bred back to the point that the Capetown Nature Park where it is located has reached its maximum capacity (about 500 individuals). Therefore, the government is now distributing surplus individuals to other areas. The future of the Cape mountain zebra looks encouraging, since it is afforded complete protection and is now being carefully managed.

The other mountain zebra, the Hartmann's mountain zebra, is found over a much larger and more remote area. Unfortunately, hunting pressures are rapidly driving it from threatened to endangered status. In the past it was killed because of competition with domestic animals for food and water.

It was also commercially hunted as a source of cheap leather. This zebra is now completely protected and hopefully its numbers will start to increase. There are probably less than 10,000 in the wild.

Hartmann's mountain zebra's range is at first appearance one of the most unlikely places in which one would expect to find a member of the horse family. It is a tortured land of twisted, rugged rock outcroppings and great sand flats and pans. The vegetation is sparse, and a great deal of it is inedible from the zebra's perspective because it is composed of plants that are heavily armed or toxic. Water holes are few and far between, and it can be difficult to find sufficient water. But somehow through all of this, the zebra finds sufficient food to maintain itself in surprisingly good condition.

Not for domestication

In the early colonial settlement of Africa there were many attempts to domesticate the zebra, but most of them were abandoned. The zebra simply has a high-strung character, and even with domestication it is difficult to handle. In addition, it does not have anywhere near the stamina

and working capability of the domestic horse.

There are no captive populations of Cape mountain zebras outside of Africa. However, there is a healthy population of Hartmann's mountain zebras in European and North American zoos. They can be successfully kept in captivity, but they must be carefully managed.

In a captive setting it is not uncommon for the males to become quite vicious and, if not contained, they have been known

The Hartmann's mountain zebra is found in Namibia and Angola.

to kill foals and even mares. Another problem of captive management is that the animals must be kept on extremely abrasive surfaces to make sure their hooves wear down and grow properly. If their walking surfaces do not do the job, it is not uncommon for zookeepers to have to trim their hooves every three months.

Warren D. Thomas

Small-eared Zorro

(Dusicyon microtis)

IUCN: Data deficient

Class: Mammalia
Order: Carnivora
Family: Canidae
Weight: 20–22 lb.(9–10 kg)
Head-body length: 28–39 in. (71–99 cm)
Tail length: 10–14 in. (25–36 cm)
Diet: Carnivorous
Gestation period: Unknown
Habitat: Tropical rain forest
Range: Amazon Basin

SMALL-EARED ZORRO
South America

THE SMALL-EARED ZORRO is—for the time being—classified as a dog in the family Canidae, and is a carnivore. It is, in fact, a real mystery animal. The zorro appears to be a dog that walks like a cat and has a potent anal gland like a skunk.

Early visitors to the New World seemed to have been similarly confused. *Zorro* is the Spanish word for fox, a mistake of identification by early settlers who observed this rare animal in the jungles of South America. The name was given to several species of small-eared dogs that behaved in a foxlike way, yet the small-eared zorro does not appear to be closely related to the fox, or to any other member of the canine family.

Some modern-day experts have a completely different taxonomic name for this species: *Atelocynus microtis*. The range of

Nothing about the small-eared zorro's appearance is helpful for identification.

the zorro and its nocturnal lifestyle make it difficult to classify. Its range is apparently the Amazon Basin in Brazil, possibly including parts of Colombia, Venezuela, Ecuador, and Peru. The small-eared zorro has not been studied in the wild at all, and only a few have ever been captured. All that is known of these animals is what has been observed of them in captivity.

The zorro has extremely small ears for a canine, which baffles researchers. The closer a canine species' range is to the polar regions, the more likely it is to have small ears. This is because reduced ear size is usually associated with the need to conserve heat in cold climates. Conversely, canine species in hotter, tropical climates generally have larger ears to help cool the animal down. The zorro's ears contradict this general rule.

A male small-eared zorro observed in captivity was reasonably tame, allowing people it recognized to approach it and even pet it. A female, however, in the same institution was less sociable, remaining unfriendly regardless of exposure to humans. No small-eared zorro has ever been born in captivity. Current population figures are nonexistent, and the social order of this species is unknown. All that can be assumed is that the ongoing disruption of rain forest habitat in South America will have detrimental effects on this little animal before scientists have much chance to learn from it.

George H. Jenkins

Saving endangered wildlife

UJUNG KULON NATIONAL Park is the last natural habitat of the Javan rhino, the world's rarest large mammal. Located on the western tip of Java, Indonesia, this isolated emerald peninsula is a grim reminder of the seemingly insurmountable challenges facing conservationists today.

The fact that Ujung Kulon exists at all is remarkable. The island of Java is one of the most densely populated on earth, with more than 90 million people packed into an area about the size of New York state. The need to grow enough food to support this mass of humanity led to the conversion of 99 percent of the island's forests into farmland. As its forest habitat receded, so did the rhino, and it is estimated that less than 60 survive on Java today—all in Ujung Kulon.

Recognizing the importance of this unique species and habitat, the Indonesian government declared Ujung Kulon a national park. However, the creation of a protected area is generally not enough to ensure the survival of wildlife or their habitats. Despite the efforts of the Indonesian government, rhino poaching still occurs in the park. In Asia, rhino horn is prized for its presumed

Because of poaching threats, black rhinoceroses (*Diceros bicornis*) in Zimbabwe travel with armed guards.

medicinal value; and for local people, there is an economic incentive to kill rhinos. A rhino is worth more dead than alive.

Although social and economic factors are working against the Javan rhino, conservationists must also contend with biological realities. The rhino population is so small and isolated that there is a greater chance for inbreeding, raising the risk of disease and extinction. Smaller populations are also more vulnerable to catastrophic events, either natural or human-caused. A disease epidemic could wipe out the entire population in a few months, as could a major fire or storm.

All these problems lead to one inescapable conclusion: the Javan rhino is in serious trouble, and without human intervention, its chances of extinction are high. Unfortunately, this case is not unique. Similar problems exist in a thousand different parks and reserves around the world. So what are some of the steps human beings can take to stop the decline of Earth's wildlife?

Few efforts to save wildlife will be successful unless the numbers of Earth's dominant species—*Homo sapiens*—can be stabilized or reduced. The world's population is now about 6 billion, and even though the average birth rate has begun to decline, most experts believe that the human race will reach 8 to 10 billion by 2050. Much of this growth will take place in developing countries in Asia, Africa, and Central and South America—regions that are rich in biological diversity—and something will have to give. The demand for resources and space will continue to increase, leaving little that can be done to preserve wildlife or wildlife habitats.

Apathy and ignorance are wildlife conservation's most deadly adversaries. If wildlife is to be saved, then people must learn to appreciate the interconnectedness of all life. They need to know how consumer habits contribute to environmental problems and, ultimately, to species' extinction. For example, a person who buys a soft drink in an aluminum can may not be aware that the metal came from Brazil. Aluminum production requires vast amounts of electricity, which has led to the construction of dams in the Amazon Basin. This, in turn, may have contributed to the flooding of thousands of acres of tropical rain forest. If people understand these consequences, they may change their buying habits or do something to compensate for them—such as recycling.

Cost of conservation

Economics are another important factor in wildlife conservation. A case in point is the spotted owl controversy in the United States. The number of northern spotted owls has been declining due to the clear-cutting of old-growth forests in the Pacific Northwest. The species has been classified as endangered by the U.S. Fish and Wildlife Service. Efforts were made to curtail logging on federally controlled lands, but the logging industry has strongly opposed any attempt to reduce cutting. Many people say jobs are more important than the owl. On the other hand, if logging of old-growth forests is allowed to continue at its present rate, the spotted owl could be extinct in a matter of years. How can we decide the right course?

The fate of many species will probably be decided by such cost/benefit analyses. Poor countries pose special challenges to conservationists where impoverished people and their governments have immediate problems. To people engaged in a daily struggle for survival, an endangered animal is nothing more than a source of food or income. As a result, some wildlife and wildlife habitats may have to become self-supporting—a concept called sustainable use.

There are many cases in which the recognition of species as renewable resources may have saved them from extinction. For example, the skins of wild saltwater crocodiles are extremely valuable, and these animals have been hunted almost to extinction. In Papua New Guinea, however, young crocodiles are brought into captivity, raised to optimum commercial size, and then killed humanely. Profits from these farming operations go directly to the local people, giving them a powerful incentive to protect wild breeding stock.

Managing the wilderness

Few habitats left on Earth are unaffected by humans, but measures could be taken to minimize damage and destruction to them.
• *Preventing conflicts between animals and humans.*
Shrinking wildlife habitats and growing human populations have led to an increase in direct conflicts between humans and wildlife. For example, the grizzly bear of North America poses real dangers to hikers. In an attempt to prevent problems, park managers educate visitors about the dangers. They can also reduce chances that bears and humans will come into contact by cleaning up garbage dumps that attract bears and preventing people from feeding the animals.
• *Controlling animal populations.*
When ecosystems become altered, it often becomes impossible for predators and prey to maintain their relationship. In small, fragmented areas, over grazing and trampling by large or

migratory mammals can cause extensive damage to vegetation, ruining it for other species as well as themselves. Fenced reserves, no matter how large, are essentially mega-zoos that require intensive management in order to sustain the wildlife contained within. Culling (selectively killing) elephants is a common practice in African national parks and is used to prevent one species from outcompeting another. Another option would be translocation.

• *Controlling or eliminating exotic species.*

One of the many ways humans alter their environment is by transporting organisms across natural barriers and dispersing them. The introductions are unpredictable and often destructive. For example, Ecuador's Galápagos Islands have long been ravaged by an army of aliens brought there by humans: donkeys, cattle, goats, pets, and rats. These recent invaders are threatening some of the region's unique wildlife. Feral goats on Fernandina Island nearly caused the extinction of the indigenous land iguana. Fortunately, efforts to control or eliminate goats in the Galápagos Islands have been successful, and in some cases the natural ecosystem has been effectively restored.

• *Maintaining genetic diversity.*

Inbreeding, or the mating of close relatives, is a problem in small populations. Highly inbred animals tend to be more susceptible to disease or have higher rates of infant mortality. Genetic variability is the raw material of natural selection, so if there is a reduction of genetic variability within a population, all members of the population will be genetically similar. In a changing environment they may not have the genetic requirements to survive. In a larger gene pool, the similarity between individuals is less, and in a changing environment a small number of the population may have the right requirements to survive. Biologists who design wildlife parks are giving more thought to including wildlife corridors that allow species to move between parks. This helps to avoid having small populations become isolated and thus encourages genetic mixing.

• *Controlling disease.*

Many new conservation techniques involve the movement of animals from one location to another to promote breeding. This increases the risk of spreading disease. Domestic species can infect wild animals and vice versa. Unfortunately, our current knowledge of wildlife diseases is poor. Knowing when or if to treat wild animals is often difficult. In some cases, it may be better to let a naturally occurring disease run its course. Those animals that do survive will have an immunity to the disease and be less affected in the future.

• *Manipulating and restoring habitat.*

The continued existence of wildlife depends on there being sufficient habitat available to provide food, shelter, and other necessities of life. Unfortunately, throughout much of the world, natural habitats have been or are being altered or destroyed at an alarming rate. In some cases, however, wildlife can thrive if habitats are manipulated to enhance certain features. For example, where populations of waterfowl in the midwestern United States and Canada have dwindled, wooden nest boxes have been provided for species that nest in holes.

What is next?

Intensive intervention will be necessary in order to preserve wildlife, especially the larger vertebrates. Any decision to intervene must be made on a case-by-case basis, often with imperfect knowledge. Some conservationists disagree with this view. They argue that the risks of extinction are exaggerated. While accurately estimating the present rate of extinctions may be impossible, there is certainly enough information from national parks in the United States to say that the long-term effects of habitat fragmentation are real. A 1987 survey indicated that 14 national parks in western North America had, since their establishment, lost a total of 42 species of mammals in their boundaries. Even the largest of our parks are apparently not immune.

Others believe that the best way to preserve wildlife is simply to leave it alone. However, doing nothing is a choice that has many consequences as well. Those who argue that species can be saved simply by preserving their habitats are incorrect. There is ample rhino habitat in Africa, but the animals continue to lose ground primarily as a result of poaching. Humans must intervene when it becomes necessary to save individual species in order to maintain and restore whenever possible the balance of nature in heavily altered ecosystems. Of course, all of this costs a great deal of money. If placed in proper perspective, however, it may be worth it.

Endangered wildlife is our planet's early warning system that our environment is becoming degraded. As more species succumb to extinction, we edge closer to ecological disaster. How these changes will affect the human race we can only guess. But despite the enormous challenges ahead, there is hope. Not all cases of endangered species have tragic endings. The peregrine falcon, American alligator, brown pelican, American bald eagle, and bison were on the brink of extinction, but with human assistance they have made a comeback. Public and governmental support for wildlife conservation is increasing.

Michael Hutchins and Nina Fascione

Vanishing amphibians

IN THE STILLNESS OF a primeval swamp in an obscure, remote past some 350 million years ago, a radical evolutionary advance was made. A fishlike amphibian breathing air through primitive lungs struggled onto the land. So began a revolutionary adventure: the rise of the vertebrates or backboned animals onto the planet. It is an adventure that continues today.

Today some 5,000 species of amphibians constitute a mere remnant of what was once a dominant and abundant class of animals. Later amphibian forms gave rise to another terrestrial class of vertebrates, the reptiles.

Present amphibians still form a connecting link between fish and reptiles. However, the great age of amphibians is now past. Modern-day amphibians are not just odd survivors from primeval swamps; they have evolved from ancestral forms that were plentiful some 395 million years ago.

Amphibian species today are threatened by many challenges. Massive ecological changes, such as deforestation and the draining of wetlands, degrade or outright destroy habitats that many amphibians need to survive. Aerial spraying of insecticides throughout many tropical countries poses a serious threat, for it poisons amphibians as well as insects. Although the insecticide DDT has been banned in most Western countries, malathion has now taken its place. The bare, moist skin of amphibians also increases their sensitivity to various pollutants and pesticides, and acid rain has wiped out many aquatic larval populations.

Scientists have been reporting declines in amphibian populations for the past 20 years. Perplexing to many scientists is the loss of some species in what appears to be pristine (or undisturbed) habitat. When this happens for no apparent reason, one can be sure something serious is going wrong somewhere.

A case study

One of the most beautiful amphibian species in the world is the spectacular golden toad (*Bufo periglenes*), found only in a few square miles in the Monte Verde Cloud Forest in the remote Cordillera de Tilaran mountain

This poison frog (*Dendrobates tinctorius*) has a shiny skin and vivid markings. The skin secretions of these frogs are extremely toxic to humans and are used by hunters to poison blowgun darts.

range of Costa Rica. The females are dark with yellow and scarlet splotches. As toads go they are rather attractive, but the females are pale in comparison to the gaudy carrot orange of the males. In the past, during most of the year it was rare to encounter any golden toads in the Mount Verde reserve. They led a secretive life. The best time to spot these toads was early in the spring, when small breeding ponds produced a dazzling array of color and movement as golden toads congregated by the hundreds.

Golden toads are known as explosive breeders, a reproductive strategy of many animal species. With explosive breeding, an entire population of toads is synchronized. That is, they come into the ponds to breed and lay their fertilized eggs, then leave within one week. When the eggs hatch and the tadpoles metamorphose (change) into toadlets, they soon saturate the area with their sheer numbers. With so many about, it does not take long before toad predators are satisfied, allowing a reasonable number of toads to survive and repopulate the area.

In 1987, researchers noticed that the golden toad population had declined. The following year a mere handful was sighted. Every year since then, biologists have been making a pilgrimage to the breeding ponds, hoping to again witness one of nature's grandest spectacles. They have found only empty ponds. It is difficult to find reasons for the loss of the golden toad, since Monte Verde Cloud Forest is considered a pristine habitat. One possible

This colorful amphibian is a red salamander (*Pseudotriton ruber*); it can be found near brooks and springs in central to eastern North America. It needs a moist habitat because it expires through its skin and the lining of its mouth.

reason for the decline in this amphibian species, as well as glass frogs and other species in the area, may be a natural one, since these ponds are near active volcanoes. Poás, some 50 miles away, and Arenal, upwind from Monte Verde, spew sulfur dioxide and sulfas into the reserve.

Environmental sensitivity
As a class, amphibians possess a series of physical characteristics that may make them especially vulnerable to environmental hazards. Amphibians first evolved from freshwater fish some 350 million years ago, and even

though they are considered land vertebrates, they are still associated with wet or damp places. Their thin, moist skins allow them to exchange ions with their surroundings. Permeable skin makes it possible for amphibians to absorb oxygen and moisture from water (amphibians cannot drink). Some amphibians do not use lungs at all and only respire through their skins. Because of their two life stages—one in water and one on land—they are more prone to come into contact with harmful substances.

Amphibians absorb heavy metals, detergents, pesticides, and other industrial contaminants in soil or water that will pass easily through their bodies. They also prey on insects and other invertebrates that may have residues of pesticides and other contaminants in their body tissues. Amphibian eggs are fragile and are often laid in temporary ponds or pools that are subject to air or waterborne pollutants and drought. Often large numbers of eggs are deposited; tens of thousands of eggs laid by one female may be lost to environmental damage.

Because of their sensitivity, amphibians are strong indicator species. They signal humanity that there is an overall deterioration of Earth's ecosystems. In the past, coal miners sent a canary in a cage down the mine shaft to determine whether any deadly, odorless gases were present. If the canary came up alive and well, it was then safe for the miners to enter the mine. Like canaries that die when exposed to gases deep in a coal mine, amphibians may be our miners' canary, indicating through their decline the poisons of an industrialized society.

Amphibians occur from south of the equator to the Arctic Circle. During the 1990 National Academy of Sciences symposium, scientists identified crashing populations in silent ponds, rivers, and mountains, as well as in rain forests. There were dramatic declines in 16 countries, representing all the continents. Alarming declines were reported in eastern and western Canada. There have been heavy losses in the western Rocky Mountains, southeastern United States, Central America (particularly cloud forests in Costa Rica and Guatemala), the Andes of South America, and Australia.

Population declines in the northwestern United States are even more severe than in the southeast, which seems to be faring better. Central and South American declines seem to be related to clear-cutting and burning forests, and to chemicals that are released into the atmosphere as a result. Declines in Europe and Australia are attributable to mining and industrial pollution.

The role of acid rain

As early as 1960, Swedish biologists were investigating a drop in fish populations in many freshwater lakes in Switzerland. During their study, they discovered something unusual about the local rainfall. The pH—the measure of acidity or alkalinity in a liquid—was higher than normal. The rain was abnormally registering a pH of 4.5 when it should have been 6 to 6.5, or nearly neutral. The biologists attributed the high acidic condi-

tion of the rainfall to sulfurous and nitric wastes released into the atmosphere by the burning of fossil fuels such as coal. The acid rain was killing the fish by making the wetlands more acidic.

Similar fish kills were not reported in the United States until 1975, when researchers investigated mysterious die-offs in the Adirondacks and discovered acidic conditions in fresh water. Acidic conditions are not harmful to adult amphibians. In their terrestrial life, amphibians often live amid leaf litter, which is very acidic. But during their aquatic phase, young amphibians are vulnerable to high acidity just as fish are. Acidic conditions prevent embryos from developing properly and hatching.

There are now 12 populations of amphibians in the northeast United States that show range reductions, and seven of these populations suffer from a high acidic rainfall. One example is the mole salamander. Acid snowmelt may release higher concentrations of acid into its breeding ponds. A 1975 population study showed a rapid drop in populations of mole salamanders in Connecticut and Massachusetts in less than a decade.

High-altitude woes

Between 1977 and 1980, Dr. David Bradford of the University of California, Los Angeles, studied the mountain yellow-legged frog (*Rana muscosa*). It lives in lakes at altitudes of 9,840 to 13,125 feet (3,000 to 4,000 meters) in the Sierra Nevada of California. In 1989 he returned to this area to find that the frogs had totally disappeared from 37 of the 38 lakes he had studied.

Amphibian species that live at high altitudes are disappearing at an alarming rate. Recent surveys have indicated that the numbers of Rocky Mountain amphibians have fallen by as much as 90 percent. One of the great mysteries of their disappearance is that most of the habitat in which they occur is pristine and unpolluted.

Some scientists speculate that so-called global warming may have a direct bearing on amphibian losses. Others claim that increases in ultraviolet light created by holes in the atmosphere's ozone layer may be responsible, because excess ultraviolet radiation could damage frog eggs.

Experimentation has demonstrated that fertilized frog eggs exposed to high levels of ultraviolet radiation failed to develop properly. The growth of the embryos was so arrested that the eggs failed to hatch. Adult amphibians have thin skins that may also be especially sensitive to ultraviolet radiation. Species that live at high altitudes would be particularly sensitive to greater exposure to ultraviolet. Some species showing a decline are the corroboree (*Pseudophryne corroboree*) from the snowy mountains of Australia, and Rocky Mountain species such as the red-legged frog (*Rana aurora*), the foothill yellow-legged frog (*Rana boylei*), the Yosemite toad (*Bufo canous*), and the western spadefoot toad (*Scaphiopus hammondi*).

Wetlands loss

A serious threat, particularly to amphibians with small ranges, is the loss of their breeding ponds through human development. An amphibian may arrive at the breeding pond only to be greeted by a new shopping center or housing development.

As a direct result of expansion and development by people, many amphibian populations are being fragmented. Populations that are isolated have little or no opportunity to breed with other populations. As habitat fragmentation continues, these small populations are forced to inbreed among themselves, weakening the gene pool and eventually causing extinction.

Massive deforestation worldwide may be causing subtle global climatic change. Evidence is still, at best, anecdotal, and there is no agreement yet on whether factors such as loss of breeding ponds, and global climate change, have any bearing on amphibian decline. Subtle climate changes may be the cause of the increasing frequency and duration of droughts. Amphibians cannot survive three or four years of drought. Moreover, clear-cutting for timber and the burning of forests for agriculture wastefully destroy much habitat and amphibian life.

Frog legs

Predation by humans, and the exotic predators that people have often introduced into new habitats, have had a negative effect on certain amphibian populations. A taste for frog legs by Europeans and Americans has led to the decline of frogs in America and Asia. Frog legs were once considered delicacies in Europe and America, but with the advent of shopping centers and packaged frozen foods, frog legs are being consumed 10 times more than they were 20 years ago. In 1980,

India began to suffer from increasing swarms of insect plagues. One of the major causes of these plagues was the exporting of tons of native insect controls, in the shape of native frogs, to Europe and America to satisfy gourmet tastes.

India placed a ban on frog leg exports in 1987. However, Asian bullfrog legs are still being exported from neighboring Bangladesh, and to meet the demand, some may be smuggled from India. Frog leg importation by the United States and European markets runs at thousands of tons each year. The United States imported 7,066 tons (6,410 metric tons) in 1982; and Belgium, France, and Italy collectively imported 9,276 tons (8,415 metric tons) that same year. The average weight of a pair of frog legs is 1½ to 1¾ ounces (40 to 50 grams), which is equivalent to 20,000 frogs per ton.

Another practice worldwide is the stocking of ponds with edible game fish, resulting in the devastation of many amphibian breeding ponds. The introduction of game fish into Lake Pátzcuaro in Michoacán, Mexico, and the heavy fishing pressure from local Indians who net them for food and medicinal purposes, has given the Lake Pátzcuaro salamander (*Ambystoma dumerilii*) its endangered status. The large size and edibility of the eastern bullfrog (*Rana catesbeiana*) has resulted in its introduction into a wide variety of localities, both in the United States and abroad, in attempts to farm it for consumption. Being a large predatory species, it usually plays havoc with the resident amphibians when it is introduced into an area. If the earth is losing frogs, toads, and salamanders at an artificially high rate, does it really matter? The answer is an unqualified yes. We cannot destroy large numbers of species in an ecosystem and not expect to see dramatic changes in everything else. Amphibians are critical building blocks in all ecosystems and represent crucial links in the world's food chain, vital to the flow of food energy. Amphibians occur in enormous numbers; the number of salamanders in part of the Appalachian Mountains has a population equal to or greater than all birds and mammals found there. Losses of amphibians worldwide are a result of many factors. One of the likely culprits is high levels of water and airborne toxins from industrialization. Another factor is a reduction in the ozone layer with an associated increase in ultraviolet radiation. To cite another victim, the large chain of harmful carbon compounds released into the air by acid rain, forest burnings, agricultural pesticides, chemical fertilizers, and herbicides has greatly reduced the cricket frog population on Canada's Pelee Island in Lake Erie. Experts estimate that the U.S. Forest Service's clear-cutting timber on federal land kills nearly 14 million salamanders each year in western North Carolina alone. Although the causes of reduction and loss of species appear varied, there seems to be a thread that links them to a global upset of the environment by a heavily industrialized society. Like the miners' canary, the disappearance and decline of our amphibians may be a warning signal of worldwide environmental distress.

In 1998, a five-year study of amphibians in Great Smoky Mountains National Park, which is considered to have the greatest amphibian diversity in North America, was launched by the United States Geological Survey. This was in response to the continuing worldwide decline in amphibians. It is hoped that this monitoring program may help to pinpoint exactly why amphibian populations are declining.

Edward J. Maruska

Captive breeding

IN THE TIME IT takes to read this essay, more than 100 acres (40 hectares) of tropical rain forest will have been destroyed. This progressive loss of wildlife habitat is driving many species closer to the brink of extinction. Yet, in a North American laboratory and veterinary hospital, scientists in white lab coats carefully mix sperm and eggs to create a test-tube tiger. On the Island of Bali in Indonesia, a cage is opened, releasing a small flock of highly endangered Bali mynahs. Bred in captivity, the birds join other members of their kind in nature. Both of these events are part of a cooperative effort by zoos and

A keeper feeds an angonoka (*Geochelone yniphora*) at a captive breeding center in Madagascar. The tortoise is endemic to the island.

aquariums to preserve the world's vanishing species.

The primary goal of conservation is to preserve wildlife in its natural state. However, for some species, the threat of extinction is too great, making direct human intervention necessary. Captive populations are established as an insurance policy against extinction until present threats can be reversed or controlled. For example, although sufficient habitat exists for black rhinos in Africa, populations continue to decline as a result of widespread poaching. Likewise, the Micronesian kingfisher and Guam rail would probably be extinct today if captive breeding populations had not been established. Many other species such as the black-footed ferret, California condor, Asian wild horse, Père David's deer, and Arabian oryx owe their existence solely to captive breeding programs.

Species Survival Plans

In 1980, the American Association of Zoological Parks and Aquariums (AAZPA) declared conservation as its highest priority. The cornerstone of AAZPA's efforts has been the Species Survival Plan, or SSP. Each SSP outlines the ecological problems that are occurring in small populations over long periods of time. Zoos then manage their animals cooperatively to help revive the species. The following are some of the important factors in this effort.

• *Maintaining genetic variation.*
Genetic variation is critical to species survival. In small populations, genetic variation can be lost at a rapid rate. Frequent inbreeding (mating between close relatives) can result in inferior animals with a lower chance of survival. Random, uncontrolled breeding can deplete a population's gene pool. Institutions working together under the SSP share detailed animal records (known as studbooks) and use computer tracking methods to identify genetically appropriate animals for mating.

• *Animal husbandry research.*
While identifying appropriate mates is important for maintaining genetic variation, there are other factors. In fact, if animals fail to survive or breed under captive conditions, any attempt to manage their genetics will be useless. Therefore the first priority of zoo biologists is to ensure that the animals survive and reproduce. Modern genetic techniques such as DNA fingerprinting are used to confirm species or subspecies identity.

A captive breeding herd of Arabian oryx (*Oryx leucoryx*) in Qatar will eventually be reintroduced into the wild.

Depending on how long their populations have been isolated, subspecies may be very similar or very different, either physically or genetically. Asian and African lions, for example, appear to have been separated for a long period of time, and the two are considered different subspecies.

In some cases, zoo researchers have developed solutions to facilitate breeding. Gaur (*Bos gaurus*) are magnificent wild cattle from Asia, but because they weigh more than a ton, they are extremely difficult and dangerous to transport. In fact, it is much easier and cheaper to move semen than a whole animal. Artificial insemination has been successful with a number of endangered species such as gaur, cranes, tigers, clouded leopards, red wolves, and black-footed ferrets. Gaur embryos have even been implanted into a Holstein cow, which gave birth to and raised a gaur calf as her own.

• *Veterinary research.*
Veterinary research is critical for maintaining healthy breeding populations. In order to diagnose and control disease, zoo veterinarians employ modern methods

to diagnose and treat medical problems in both captive and free-ranging animals. Wild mountain gorillas have been vaccinated against measles and treated for injuries by veterinarians with zoo experience.

Space limitations

Species such as the California condor and the black-footed ferret dropped to less than ten reproducing individuals in the wild before they were rescued for captive breeding. Captive breeding is not the preferred course of action for all endangered species, but whatever action is to be taken, it is important to identify species in danger well before they fall to such low numbers. Some critics think that captive breeding should be attempted only as a last resort. However, the sooner recovery efforts are begun, the better a species' chances of survival. The reason that zoos have been so successful with the California condor and black-footed ferret is that zoo personnel knew a lot about two closely related species, the Andean condor and the domestic ferret. Other species may not be as lucky.

If all the space in the world's zoos were combined, it would fit into an area the size of Brooklyn, New York. The amount of space in zoos and aquariums is limited, and tough decisions have to be made regarding which species are allowed to board the "zoo ark." In fact, due to space limitations, no more than about 900 species of vertebrates could be maintained in viable populations by the world's zoos.

To address the issue of limited space, specialists help prioritize which species should be targeted for organized captive breeding programs. For example, there are approximately 500 to 600 manageable spaces for tigers in North America's zoos. If the minimum viable population for a tiger subspecies is 175, then only three of the eight recognized subspecies can be managed effectively in this region.

Since tigers utilize spaces appropriate for other large cats, a decision to maintain three subspecies of tigers may mean that another large cat species cannot be accommodated.

Reintroduction

Reintroduction is the goal of many Species Survival Plans, and species such as the black-footed ferret, California condor, Bali mynah, Arabian oryx, Puerto Rican crested toad, and red wolf have already begun their journey back to viable wild populations. However, success comes only after hard work and planning to overcome the challenges inherent in reintroduction programs.

Before reintroduction efforts can begin, the captive population must be stable and able to produce the additional animals to be released. Hazards that caused the species' decline initially must be corrected, and an appropriate type and amount of habitat secured. Animals selected for reintroduction must be tested and quarantined to make sure that disease is not transmitted or picked up from wild populations.

Captive-bred animals that are released into the wild face competitors, predators, diseases, starvation, and bad weather.

In nature, some animals learn how to cope with these challenges gradually as they encounter them in their lives. Other species, however, do not have to learn certain behaviors and are able to rely on instinct.

Captive-bred animals of species for which learning is important may be at a disadvantage once released. Because they have not experienced life in the wild, they must learn to recognize and escape from predators, locate or capture sufficient amounts of food, and breed with other members of their species. It may be necessary to train some animals prior to their release.

Each species presents new challenges for zoo biologists. Careful monitoring is a must for every reintroduction effort. Without valuable information gained through feedback, the differences between failure and success will remain a mystery and cripple future efforts. However, by experimenting with various release techniques and recording the level of success, the chance for success can be improved.

Multiple strategies

Conservation efforts can take many forms, including habitat protection, control of introduced species, public education, and captive breeding and reintroduction. These measures must be used to their fullest extent and in coordination if endangered wildlife is to survive.

There is no reason why captive breeding and habitat preservation cannot be implemented simultaneously for selected species. Captive breeding will never be the sole solution for today's wildlife, but it can provide a step along the road back to a viable wild population.

Robert J. Wiese and Michael Hutchins

Deserts of the world

NAMIB. DEATH VALLEY. Gobi. Taklimakan. Rub' al-Khali. The Outback. Sahara. These sound like exotic and dangerous places where the sun beats down without mercy. Few humans choose to live in such places, and only the hardiest animals and plants adapt to this region as habitat.

What is a desert?

A region is generally classified as a desert if it has an annual rainfall of 12 inches (30 centimeters) or less. The Sahara, for example, has an average rainfall of 1 inch (2.5 centimeters), although there are areas within this desert where there has been no measurable rainfall for a century or more. For pure aridity, the Atacama Desert of coastal Chile holds the record. In over 40 years of observation, there has never been any measurable precipitation.

On the other hand, the Australian Desert, often called the Outback, records an annual rainfall of 13 inches (33 centimeters); and the Sahara Desert near Algiers, Algeria, receives more than 30 inches (76 centimeters) of rain a year. It is not how much rainfall a region receives, but how much of that rain it retains. A desert may receive a great deal of rain yet lose most of it to runoff, erosion, or evaporation.

Deserts are associated usually with high temperatures. The highest temperature ever recorded was 136 degrees Fahrenheit (57.8 degrees Centigrade in the Libyan Sahara. Death Valley is not far behind, with an all-time mark of 134 degrees Fahrenheit (56.7 degrees Centigrade). Average daytime temperatures in many deserts are well above 100 degrees Fahrenheit (37.8 degrees Centigrade).

The third factor that defines a desert is the quantity of plant and animal life. This is more difficult to measure since there is no specific method for counting the number of species a region contains. In general, the types of plants and animals found in the world's deserts are far less plentiful than the plants and animals living in tropical or even temperate regions of the globe. While biologists estimate there may be as many as 50,000 to 100,000 plant and animal species per acre in the rain forests of Brazil, deserts contain only a fraction of this amount.

Desert types

There are many different types of deserts. There are wet deserts, semi-arid deserts, and dry deserts, as well as hot deserts and cold deserts. There are lowland deserts like Death Valley, which is actually below sea level, and upland deserts like the Taklimakan Desert, which rises up into the Himalayas more than 20,000 feet (6,100 meters) above sea level. All deserts share a sense of sparseness.

Between 10 and 20 percent of Earth is desert. Africa contains the best-known and largest desert in the world, the Sahara—nearly 3 million square miles (7.7 million square kilometers) of the African continent.

Plants of the desert

In a region where there is little shade, little cloud cover, long days of sunshine, extremes of cold and hot, and little consistent moisture, plants have learned to adapt. In fact, deserts are frequently classified according to the kind of plant life they can support and the types of ecosystems that develop.

Cold deserts, such as the interior of Asia and the intermountain zone of North America, provide winter temperatures well below freezing and summer temperatures that often soar above 100 degrees Fahrenheit (37.8 degrees Centigrade). In such a desert, ground-clinging shrubs and large cacti like the Joshua tree thrive. Tropical deserts, like the Sahara and the Australian Desert, provide a home for shrubs like creosote bushes and tumbleweeds. Trees, where they exist at all in these regions, are usually small acacias or low-growing eucalyptus. Under this shrub growth there is often some kind of ground cover, such as tufted grass or short-lived, small flowering plants.

As the desert becomes more arid, the kind of plant life becomes more retentive of moisture. Stem-succulent deserts, like the Sonoran Desert, the Namib, and the southern coast of South America, specialize in a kind of plant life known as succulents.

The giant monolith known as Ayers Rock stands above the desert plain in Uluru National Park in Northern Territory, Australia.

These spongy plants include cacti and euphorbia. Succulents store water in their stems and possess tough outer skins.

Herbaceous deserts are places where shrubs and cacti are less plentiful, and perennial herbs—like wildflowers and grasses—are more common. Many types of drought-resistant trees prosper here, such as the piñon pine. The Kalahari Desert and the Nullarbor Plain in South Australia are two examples.

Finally, there are the sand and salt deserts, where a combination of infertile land and extremely harsh conditions provide little possibility for plant growth. Regions like Death Valley, the central Sahara, and the Rub' al-Khali of Saudi Arabia are deserts where only the toughest plant life

can survive. Lichen, a few mosses, and certain specialized grasses with large, wide-spreading root systems can live in such a hostile climate, gathering what moisture they can from the air.

Of all desert plants, perhaps the best known is the cactus. The cactus generally possesses thick skin that protects the delicate inner cells from heat and dryness. Because leaves are too frail for the harsh desert climate, the cactus has developed spines or thorns to take their place and protect itself from attack by large plant-eaters. Over millions of years, the cactus' stem has grown into a thick, spongy trunk, and its cell structure has evolved to absorb an immense amount of water and let it out in tiny amounts. This means that the

size of a cactus, like the size of most desert-growing plants, changes tremendously according to how much water is available.

While plants in most other regions flower, pollinate, and seed at regular intervals, the saguaro cactus (like most other plants in the desert) reserves these activities for those times when it rains. Rain spurs the cactus to frenzied activity. Within a matter of hours, large yellow and white flowers appear, and bees and ants flock to feed and spread the pollen. The time from rainfall to budding takes only a few days.

Despite its careful lifestyle, the saguaro cactus is a friendly neighbor to many other members of its desert community. Its trunk and arms support the nests of hawks and owls, and the holes

drilled in its green tissue by woodpeckers and flickers become homes for countless birds. Its flowers, buds, and seeds are food for rodents, coyotes, bats, birds, and ants.

Animals of the desert

Desert animals have also learned to adapt to harsh conditions, sometimes in surprising ways. Most desert animals are nocturnal, including reptiles and insects. Although it is widely assumed that cold-blooded reptiles are unaffected by heat, no reptile can survive a temperature over 118 degrees Fahrenheit (47.8 degrees Centigrade). Life in the desert does not begin until nightfall, when it becomes a place of feverish activity.

Most animals live in burrows in the ground to escape the daytime heat. This includes most mammals, such as kangaroo rats, desert foxes, coyotes, and squirrels. Other animals, such as owls and woodpeckers, make their nests in the holes or branches of cacti or desert trees. Like plants, animals must adapt to their environment to survive. The road runner is a prime example. Because it requires fewer muscles and less energy to run than to fly, the road runner and its Saharan cousin the courser (not to mention the ostrich of Australia) have learned how to hunt on foot. They can reach speeds of 25 miles (40 kilometers) per hour or more to catch their prey. Birds that fly, like the peregrine falcon or the black-necked raven, use flight to carry them high above the desert, where the air is cooler.

Most mammals that live in the desert learn to live with very little water. The kangaroo rat can go for months without water of any sort. The camel has a water reservoir on its back in the form of humps—collections of fat cells that store large amounts of water and release it slowly over time.

Another mammal, the addax, is a heavily built antelope with long, curling horns that lives in the desert of northern Africa. Like so many other animals that live in the desert, the addax has splayed, fleshy feet for walking on sandy surfaces and long eyelashes to keep dust and sand out of its eyes.

Many species protect themselves against extreme drought by simply going into hibernation. But at the first rainfall, these animals suddenly revive and within a short time are fully active again. The spadefoot toad tadpole of Arizona and California can live for months—perhaps even years—in a suspended state; but, within hours after a rain, hundreds of them can be observed swimming in waterholes throughout the desert.

What causes a desert?

Deserts are created in two ways. Most deserts are a result of centuries of weather patterns. For example, in regions where wind is rare, clouds cannot protect the earth from the full force of the sun's rays, and rain does not fall. This sets in motion a cycle of arid conditions that starves the soil and prevents plant and animal life from flourishing. Soil that is not covered with plant life is more likely to erode during a cloudburst, creating deep gullies and canyons that carry away fertile soil, rendering the land even less fertile. Where this cycle persists, deserts inevitably form.

Sometimes it is not the prevailing winds but mountains that cause deserts to form. The Andes stop low, rain-bearing clouds from traveling west out of the moist Amazon Basin. These clouds have no more rain to give by the time they cross the mountains, so the slopes on the other side are left barren and scrubby.

Over time the deserts change as weather patterns change. There is evidence that about 20,000 years ago, the Sahara was a temperate region filled with plant and animal life.

The Sahara, then, has developed in fairly recent times. Deserts appear and disappear to be replaced by deserts elsewhere in the world.

Deserts of humanity

Nature is not the only force on this planet that can make a desert. The formation of new desert (called desertification) over the last 3,000 years has been greatly accelerated by a single factor: people. Perhaps 30 percent of all desert in the world today has been caused by the actions of people. Over the last few thousand years, they have stripped huge areas of forest for timber and food. In place of these forests, human beings created farmland or grazing land, most of which became nutritionally exhausted over a relatively short period of time.

Sudan in northeastern Africa was once covered in dense forest. But thousands of years of human habitation have reduced the region to a gravelly desert.

This same pattern can be seen in such diverse places as Greece, Madagascar, and the American Midwest. As the air becomes more polluted and a large array of industrial poisons find their way into our water systems, it is inevitable that still more desertification will take place.

What effect do these artificial deserts have on our planet? An example of desertification is within Sudan and Ethiopia, where mass starvation has occurred. Although environmental conditions such as desertification have been a factor there, years of war and social and political inequalities have contributed to this human suffering.

Fortunately, there are solutions to desertification. Nations can make wiser use of remaining forests and nondesert lands, and they can use modern agricultural techniques that minimize soil damage. Farmers can experiment and develop alternatives to traditional farming. Towns, corporations, and even schools can sponsor and participate in large-scale replanting of trees and other foliage.

All possibilities should be explored, for we will only place the planet and all living creatures—including ourselves—in jeopardy if we continue to take no remedial action.

Jonathan Bliss

The world's forests

FORESTS ARE LARGE expanses where the foliage of trees forms a continuous, or nearly continuous, canopy that shades the area beneath. It is estimated that millions of years ago, 50 to 60 percent of the land surface of the earth was covered by forests. The percentage covered today is estimated at around 30 percent. While there has always been some natural fluctuation in the amount of forest due to long-term climate shifts, human activities have caused the significant drop in forest coverage over the past 5,000 to 10,000 years.

Prior to the rise of humanity, the major factors determining whether an area contained forest were temperature and precipitation. Forests will not develop in an area unless the temperature during the warm season is above 50 degrees Fahrenheit (10 degrees Centigrade) and annual precipitation exceeds eight inches (20 centimeters). The same factors that determine whether there is forest in an area also play a large role in determining the type of forest.

Major forest types
• *Taiga, or boreal forest.*
Taiga, or boreal forest, is found almost exclusively in the Northern Hemisphere, where 10 to 20 inches (25 to 50 centimeters) of precipitation is distributed throughout the year and winter temperatures are far below freezing. There is little land in the Southern Hemisphere at latitudes where the necessary conditions prevail to support this forest type. Trees of the boreal forest are mostly coniferous, or needle-leaf evergreens. These are trees that keep their needlelike leaves year-round and bear cone-like reproductive structures.

There are usually only two layers of vegetation in these forests: the tree canopy and the floor. The canopy is composed of the upper, living branches of the evergreen trees, while the floor is mostly composed of mosses and lichens, with a few herbs.
• *Temperate forest.*
Closer to the equator, in the mid-latitudes, are areas that have a six-month growing season, winters that are not so severe, and more than 20 inches (50 centimeters) of precipitation spread evenly throughout the year. In these places grow extensive areas of temperate evergreen forests; for example, the old-growth forests of the Pacific Northwest of North America. But most temperate forests are composed of hardwood trees with broad flat leaves that are more efficient at capturing light energy and using it for photosynthesis.
• *Tropical forest.*
Occurring primarily on landmasses within 20 degrees latitude of the equator, tropical forests share one important feature: the lack of seasonal temperature changes. Sunlight strikes Earth most directly in the tropical latitudes, and the length of days is uniform. There are no days below freezing, so decomposition goes on year-round. There are tropical areas that experience seasonality, but this is caused by wet-dry periods, not warm-cold ones. Extensive areas of tropical forest experience extremely wet and rainy conditions during part of the year and very dry conditions

during the rest of the year. Many trees drop their leaves during the dry season to reduce water loss. These forests are known as tropical deciduous forest, tropical seasonal forest, and monsoon forest.

Extensive areas of the Tropics do not experience wet and dry seasons and, in fact, receive rain almost daily. It is in these areas—where both temperature and rainfall are relatively high and constant—that the most complex and diverse forests on Earth are found: the tropical rain forests. The average temperature in the rain forest is around 80 degrees Fahrenheit (27 degrees Centigrade) and varies more daily, about 5 to 8 degrees Fahrenheit (2.8 to 4.4 degrees Centigrade), than it does yearly, about 2 degrees Fahrenheit (1 degree Centigrade). Precipitation occurs almost daily, amounting to between 60 and 140 inches (150 to 350 centimeters) per year.

Along with the four layers found in a typical temperate deciduous forest (canopy, shrub, herbaceous, and floor), the rain forest has two additional layers—the emergent layer of tall trees that sticks up above the canopy, and a subcanopy layer. These extra layers allow very little light to reach the forest floor.

Many different animals exhibit their greatest diversity in the tropical rain forest. If the different species of trees and insects are included, the diversity becomes immense. While an area of about 2.5 acres (1 hectare) in the boreal forest would be likely to have two to five species of trees, the same area in the temperate deciduous forest might harbor between 10 and 30 species. In the tropical rain forest, the number of species of trees encountered in an area this size is usually over 100 (often closer to 200). It is the extensive layering that promotes this diversity. Different kinds of food sources in the form of numerous plant species, and different microhabitats taking many

This gray tree boa (*Boa angulata*) basks in a tropical forest in Costa Rica, Central America. It is thought that basking raises the snake's body temperature, which helps it digest its prey.

forms, have played important roles in the barely documented—and as yet poorly understood—richness of insect species found in the tropical rain forests.

Early in the development of human civilizations, people discovered that not only were forest hardwoods good for building and fuel, but deciduous forest soils were fertile and long-lasting when used for agricultural purposes. The quest for fuel and fertile soil, more than anything else, accelerated the historic decline of the extensive deciduous forests. First in China, then in Europe, and finally in North America, growing human populations cleared the deciduous forests to raise crops and livestock. The deforestation, and the reduction of remaining forest into fragments, was detrimental not only to the trees but to the entire community of organisms that made these forests their home. There is little if any old-growth deciduous forest left on the planet. People have now turned their attention to the last great—and probably most vulnerable—forest type remaining: the tropical forest.

While researchers differ somewhat on absolute numbers, it is widely believed that about 1 to 2 percent—or 58,000 to 77,000 square miles (150,000 to 200,000 square kilometers)—of tropical rain forest is either completely destroyed or grossly disrupted each year. Rain forest is disturbed for a number of different reasons. About one-eighth is degraded by nonsustainable fuel wood gathering; that is, harvesting trees for fuel faster than they can grow back. Another one-eighth is lost to the clearing of land for cattle ranching. One-quarter is lost to commercial logging. The remainder—close to one-half—is degraded by small-scale shifting cultivation.

Shifting cultivation, often called slash and burn, involves the clearing of a plot by cutting down the vegetation and burning it in place to prepare for planting crops. Problems arise because rain forest soil is so thin (due to the rapid decomposition and reuse of fallen vegetation) that a plot is fertile for only one or two years. Farmers must continually move on to clear another plot. In addition, when the farmer leaves, the exposed soil easily washes away in heavy rain. Since it is believed that over 200 million people rely on this form of small-scale cultivation, the importance of developing ways to help farm-ers grow crops on the same plot for more than one or two years cannot be overemphasized.

Efforts currently under way to improve methods of growing food crops and trees in the same area will help protect the thin, fragile soil and help it retain groundwater. If successful, farm-ers will be allowed to settle longer in one place rather than continue contributing to forest loss.

Linked extinctions

Reducing the loss of all the world's forests is very important; the life in each forest is so diverse and interwoven that losing even one important species could have a domino effect on many others. For example, a single species of tree could be the sole source of food for several species of insects; or its fruits or seeds could be a major food source for a bird or mammal species. If that tree species were to suffer the loss of its pollinator species—be it insect, bird, bat, or other animal—then that tree species and the many species dependent on it would also be lost.

Since the rain forest contains many species that have tiny populations and limited geographic distribution, these species can be more easily driven to extinction by direct human clearing of their habitat than can the often more numerous and widespread populations of species found in temperate regions. While temperate regions may recover more rapidly to their former state after clearing, thereby allowing species to return, in the tropical forest there is little chance of this happening. Many species that inhabited only a few hundred or thousand acres of cleared land in the Tropics may occur nowhere else on earth. While habitat loss is most devastating to tightly knit communities of organisms typical in tropical forests, it also threatens boreal forests, temperate deciduous forests, mixed forest (where these two blend), and many other ecosystems. Direct degradation of ecosystems by humanity has been going on for several thousand years, although the pace has been more feverish during the past 200 years. Evidence is beginning to mount of other threats to forest ecosystems that may not seem as dramatic as the physical clearing of vegetation, but which, in the long run, may prove equally damaging. One such threat is air pollution.

Pollution stress

During the last half of the 20th century, forested regions in both Europe and in eastern North America have shown signs of reduced productivity and tree death. At first this was puzzling, but eventually many scientists began to notice that areas showing stress experienced highly acidic rainfall, increased concentrations of heavy metals in the soil and water, or an increased concentration in the atmosphere of certain chemicals that react strongly with living tissue. Many affected areas suffered more than one of these conditions. Various types of trees and food crops experienced losses of 15 to 50 percent when exposed to only one of the multitude of chemicals found in Earth's atmosphere.

It is proving difficult to nail down the newest perpetrators of forest damage, because a tight link between damage and any particular chemical agent is difficult to establish. These chemicals are increasingly being used by many industrial and agricultural societies. However, since the cost of possibly irreparable damage to ecosystems is so high, it seems wise to pay the short-term economic cost of reducing the output of pollutants.

Forest fires

In 1997 and 1998, there were devastating forest fires in Southeast Asia. These fires were particularly destructive in Sumatra and Kalimantan in Indonesia, where fires that were started to clear land for commercial agriculture and slash-and-burn farming became uncontrollable. The situation was exacerbated by very dry conditions due to the climatic effects of El Niño. It is estimated that the area of forest destroyed could be as much as 5 million acres (2 million hectares).

Climatic change

Finally, there is the issue of global climate change. While not as immediately threatening as deforestation or air pollution damage, the potential long-term effects of global warming on forests are large. Forests are among the most photosynthetically active ecosystems, and photosynthesis removes carbon dioxide from the air to make plant tissue. Carbon dioxide is one of the gases blamed for the so-called greenhouse effect, where heat is trapped in the atmosphere as the level of carbon dioxide increases. If Earth's atmosphere is indeed heating up, changes will be potentially enormous and unpredictable. As more forests are lost, fewer trees will be pumping moisture back into the atmosphere. How that will affect global climate is still being researched using computer models of climate change.

Problems for forest ecosystems and the species that comprise them are complex and often unpredictable. However, the price will surely be high in loss of species and the lowering of our own species' quality of life if these problems go unaddressed. Humanity must treat seriously all threats to natural habitat and explore all ideas and proposals to lessen the impact of our species on the planet.

Terry Tompkins

Grasslands

APPROXIMATELY 1.5 MILLION YEARS ago on the grasslands and savannas of East Africa, *Homo erectus* was the first big-game hunter to stalk the beasts that roamed the sun-drenched plains. Nearly 200,000 years ago, *Homo erectus* had evolved to become *Homo sapiens*, spreading to Europe and Asia. As far back as 40,000 years ago, these early humans were hunting prey and gathering wild food on the savannas of Africa, India, and Australia. The entire human population has its roots planted in the grasslands of the world.

Great seas of undulating grasses spread across the plains and rolling hills on every continent except Antarctica. They once covered nearly one-third of Earth's land. With the conversion of wild grassland to cultivated farmland, domestic grazing land, and desert wasteland, however, this marvelous resource has been greatly reduced.

Most natural grasslands lie at the center of continents, where the soil is too dry to support a forest yet too moist for a desert. Grasslands are among the most productive ecosystems on the planet, appearing in a variety of forms. From the 25-foot- (7.6-meter-) tall grasslands of Nepal to the short-grass plains of North America, grasslands all have one thing in common: the predominant plant species are long-lived perennial grasses accompanied by grass annuals and broad-leaved flowering plants.

On average, a single acre of grassland will produce 9,000 pounds (4,080 kilograms) of leaves, stalks, and seeds each year. That's six times the average yield per acre of the world's cornfields. Almost 6,000 species of grass can be found around the world, making it the third-largest family of flowering plants on Earth. Grasses are found from Pole to Pole and contain more species that are distributed worldwide than any other flora.

Reasons for the tremendous success of grass species have more to do with how they grow, not where they grow. Grass grows outward from its base instead of expanding from its tip or edges like trees or shrubs. A blade of grass that is ripped, chewed, or burned will quickly grow back. By putting out new growth from its protected base buried beneath the soil, grass can survive a variety of abuse—from being mowed or burned, trampled or grazed. If the roots and base are left intact, the plant will flourish.

Grasslands are known by a number of different names: savannas, steppes, prairies, veld, pampas, and downs. It is not just a difference in language that creates these names, but subtle differences in humidity, soil, and plant life that create unique environments in various locations.

Widely different conditions

The steppes and prairies of the Northern Hemisphere endure extreme temperatures. Hot summers with temperatures climbing above 100 degrees Fahrenheit (38 degrees Centigrade) and freezing winters when the temperature plummets to 0 degrees Fahrenheit (minus 18 degrees Centigrade) test the endurance of both plant and animal life. Most temperate grasslands receive only 12 to 20 inches (30 to 51 centimeters) of rain a year, with most of the rain falling during the summer. Winter brings cold, dry winds and occasional snow.

The temperate grasslands of the Southern Hemisphere lie closer to the world's oceans than their northern counterparts, allowing for milder winters and a more even distribution of rainfall throughout the year. Without trees or mountains to block or slow the moving masses of air, temperate grasslands experience almost constant wind. Grassland winds accelerate the evaporation of water, thereby contributing to an area's dry climate. The wind also aids in the spread of prairie fires, keeping trees and shrubs at a minimum.

Tropical grasslands

Characteristics of tropical grasslands differ in a number of ways from those of temperate grasslands. Savannas are tropical plains or plateaus covered with grass and widely scattered shrubs and trees. Savannas tend to have taller grasses and more trees than temperate grasslands. Most savannas lie north or south of the tropical rain forests that straddle the equator.

The most famous savanna is East Africa's Serengeti Plain, home to more than 100 different species of grass and the largest collection of mixed plains wildlife on Earth. Zebras, gazelles, impalas, lions, hyenas, cheetahs, and leopards are but a few of the mammals that share this plain with numerous species of birds, reptiles, and insects.

Fire

Fire plays an important role in maintaining both temperate and tropical grasslands. Whether started by lightning or humans, grassland fires spread quickly, pushed by winds and fueled by the dense cover of dead stalks. With few rivers or other natural barriers to stop its progress, a grassland fire will race across the plains until it burns itself out.

Grasses are adapted to survive fires, and many varieties actually flourish after a prairie fire. By removing dead plant material that would normally keep the soil shaded, fire opens up the soil to precious sunlight that prompts new growth. Fire also releases nutrients locked within the debris, adding to the fertility level of the soil.

While most animals will run before an advancing wall of flames or burrow underground to escape the searing heat, some animals actually take advantage of grass fire. Insects, rodents, and snakes are flushed from their hiding places to become the next meal for hawks, swallows, storks, and other birds looking for an easy meal. After the fire, vultures and other scavengers arrive to survey the burned-over ground for small dead animals.

Grassland wildlife

Grassland animals share a number of characteristics that help them survive in the grassland environment. Out on the open plains there are few places to hide from predators. Animals of the prairies, steppes, and savannas must either be able to create their own hiding place or run. The preponderance of burrowing animals in almost every grassland environment is proof that creating a hiding place is an effective way to escape predators and fires, and to wait out hot days and freezing winters. About 47 percent of steppe mammals live underground, compared to only 6 percent of forest mammals.

On North American prairies, burrowing owls, ground squirrels, woodchucks, marmots, gophers, and prairie dogs use burrows for survival. On the Eurasian steppes, gerbils, hamsters, mice, and susliks find safety in their underground homes. In Australia, kangaroo rats and a

myriad of small marsupials fill the rodent-like niches.

If an animal is too large to dig a hole and hide, it has to be able to run. The large grazing mammals of the grasslands are among the world's fastest runners, second only to their predators, who have to be fast enough to catch them. In North America, the runners are the bison and pronghorn; in Eurasia it is saiga antelope; and in Africa gazelles, wildebeests, and zebras move at great speed.

Many bird species of the grasslands have found running to be an effective alternative to flight. The road runners, quails, and grouse of North America prefer to run, as do the ostriches of Africa, the emus of Australia, and the rheas of South America. Each of these large birds has lost its ability to fly.

Animals of the temperate and tropical grasslands utilize all edible vegetation. With different animals preferring specific varieties of plants, any single grassland habitat can sustain a large variety of fauna. In some areas, insects are the number one consumers of grass, out-eating all the grazing mammals combined. But then, insects become a prime food source for birds, snakes, rodents, and edentates (anteaters, armadillos, and sloths).

Due to their sheer numbers, size and variety, the most conspicuous residents of the grasslands are herbivores. On the plains of North America, herds of bison and pronghorn once covered the prairies. Today, Africa's Serengeti Plain is still home to millions of large animals that roam in herds as large as one hundred thousand individuals.

A human habitat

Animals are not the only creatures who find the grasslands of the world to be a great source of food. The earliest forms of human beings, *Homo habilis*, survived on wild roots, fruit, and meat scavenged from the kills of carnivores that followed the grassland herds. Stone Age hunters roamed the savannas and

In Kalahari Gemsbok National Park, in Botswana, South Africa, the grasslands are in the form of acacia savanna.

may even have taken steps to bring the animals within range. Anthropologists believe that prehistoric hunters set fires to clear away dead grasses and promote new growth, thereby luring animals to the fresh food source.

On every continent where grasslands once spread across the landscape, native people roamed the land following herds of wild mammals. The nomadic way of life was not limited to the hunter-gatherers. Sheep and cattle herders were in almost constant motion, looking for new pastures for their domestic herds.

In finding grassland soil to be fertile, it didn't take long for humans to start cultivating the land. If there was not enough cropland in a particular area, it was a simple task to convert forest to grassland. As far back as 4,000 years ago, farmers started chopping down trees that covered much of Europe to create pastures. Today, most of Western European grassland is human-made, a result of thousands of years of burning and clearing. In Great Britain, France, and Germany, huge areas of forest have been cleared to cultivate crops and create grasslands for grazing.

Before the arrival of European settlers, the tallgrass prairies of middle America covered over 200,000 square miles (518,000 square kilometers)—from the Allegheny Mountains to the edge of the Great Plains, and from Oklahoma to the Great Lakes. In the state of Missouri, less than half of one percent of the original tallgrass prairie remains. Of the 22 million acres (8.8 million hectares) of natural prairie that existed in Illinois in 1820, less than 2,300 acres (920 hectares) remain.

As global human population increased, grasslands around the world were called upon to feed the masses. Today the temperate grasslands of North and South America, Europe, and Asia literally feed the world. More than one-half the protein and calories consumed by humanity comes from three species of grass: wheat, rice, and maize. The meat, milk, and cheese from domestic grass-eaters such as sheep, goats, and cattle make up a large percentage of the remainder of the human diet. Feeding a planet is a huge task, and grasslands around the world are absorbing the pressure of the rapidly increasing human population. In many cases, constant burning, overgrazing, and intensive cultivation have stripped away native plants and destroyed the delicate balance of natural ecosystems. Without grass cover, wind blows away life-producing topsoil, turning once productive grasslands into lifeless deserts. Replacing native plants with single crops creates a variety of problems, including an increase in pests and weeds. Growing crops without replenishing the soil with fertilizers depletes the soil of life-sustaining nutrients.

Fortunately, many countries are taking positive steps to preserve natural grasslands and restore areas that have suffered from overuse.

• In 1982, Canada set aside 350 square miles (907 square kilometers) of original prairie in Grasslands National Park in the southern province of Saskatchewan.

• Brazil has created Ema National Park to save some of its original pampas grasslands.

• Syrian sheep herders are granted licenses only in limited areas to prevent overgrazing.

• In Nepal, villagers are allowed to harvest grass from neighboring grassland preserves only during one ten-day period each year. This grass is used to build and repair their homes and is an integral part of their lifestyle. With some sound conservation, these people reap their harvest and the grassland is left to flourish for the next generation.

Humanity grew up and came of age on the grasslands of the world. By practicing sensible management of this valuable resource, survival of the diversity of life of both plants and animals will be assured for the future.

Christie Costanzo

Invertebrates

INVERTEBRATES, OR animals without a backbone, have countless different sizes and body forms. They include creatures such as microscopic protozoans and a cornucopia of macroscopic sponges, jellyfish, starfish, sand dollars, corals, planarians, flukes, rotifers, roundworms, clams, snails, octopuses, earthworms, crayfish, spiders, and insects. People are impressed by the size of many vertebrate animals such as the elephant or the giraffe. This is understandable, because 99 percent of all the species on earth are the size of a bumblebee or smaller, and virtually all of them are invertebrates.

A great variety

Together, invertebrates comprise about 95 percent of the world's animal species, 85 percent of which are insects. These species each have special ecological requirements, with different species living anywhere and everywhere on Earth: from the deep oceans to the high mountains, on land and in the air, in salt and fresh water, at the ice-capped poles, in deserts, and in tropical rain forests.

According to theories of the history of animal diversity, the

5 percent of animal species that are vertebrates (including *Homo sapiens*) evolved from invertebrates. So why do so many human beings regard so many invertebrate species as pests? It is true that a relatively small proportion of modern invertebrate species eat plants that are important to people for food, fiber, and building materials. Some carry diseases or cause them in humans, livestock, pets, and garden plants. It has been estimated that insect damage totals U.S.$5 billion annually in the United States alone, in addition to the suffering caused by the diseases they carry.

In general, however, the benefits invertebrates provide to humans and their interests far outweigh the harm they cause. As primary consumers of plants, for example, many invertebrates are important in the food chain because they are themselves eaten by animals that humans use for food. Other invertebrates eat dead plant and animal matter, thereby clearing landscapes of these materials and helping make available to plants the nutrients that otherwise would be lost to the food chain. Some species pollinate the plants people need for food or shelter, or they make useful products such as beeswax or silk. Many people even eat several species of invertebrates such as clams, shrimp, and lobsters.

Thousands of beneficial invertebrate species serve as predators or parasites of the invertebrates that damage our domesticated plants and animals. It has been estimated that beneficial insects are worth about $20 billion annually just in the United States

because of all they do for human interests, especially in their pollination activities.

Despite the benefits provided by almost all of the world invertebrate species, popular concern for their endangerment is usually less than that for endangered vertebrates or for some endangered flowering plants. People tend to empathize with larger animals more like themselves, or they more readily choose to protect conspicuous plants and animals that they consider useful or pleasing to see or hear.

Too little is known

Another reason humans have difficulty in becoming concerned about endangered invertebrate species is lack of knowledge. For most groups of invertebrates, there is only a small number of scientists who can accurately distinguish one species from another. This means that the possibility of protecting a particular species by means of existing state, federal, and international laws is very poor. Even persons wanting to obey wildlife protection laws cannot always honor them, because in not recognizing a particular species, they are completely unaware that a law is being violated.

Many invertebrate species—especially tiny species or those living in tropical regions—are still not known to science; they have never been discovered, described, or named. Some scientists have estimated that there may actually be 30 million species of insects on the planet, meaning that 98 percent of them must still be discovered before it will be possible to determine whether they may be endan-

gered. Indeed, it is likely that many invertebrate species have already become extinct or are now being lost without ever having been discovered.

Even for those species that are identifiable by scientists, their inconspicuousness has limited the amount of research that has been accomplished. There is precious little information about the distribution, life history, and habitat requirements of most invertebrate species. Attempts to accomplish this research are further complicated by the fact that most invertebrate species undergo remarkable changes during their growth and development—changes that render their identification in all but the adult stage (or some other stage on which the taxonomy is based) nearly impossible.

Too few scientists

A related concern is that the number of scientists who are able to identify and study invertebrates is also rapidly decreasing. Students enrolling in science programs in colleges and universities today are more often attracted to currently popular fields such as biotechnology or molecular biology rather than to some of the more traditional subdisciplines, such as plant or animal taxonomy. Every year, therefore, there are fewer young scientists to take the place of retiring taxonomists. Consequently, at the very time in the world's history when the most expertise is needed to describe the earth's wealth of unknown (and rapidly disappearing) biota, that expertise is becoming the most scarce. Scientists believe that every species of plant and

These colorful leaf-hoppers are found in Pantanal, Mato Grosso, Brazil.

animal on Earth has—at the very least—a slightly different habitat or living space requirement or occupation than every other species. Humans have adversely affected many different kinds of habitats on the planet, including the air creatures breathe; the many millions of microhabitats on the land and in fresh water; and in the world's oceans. Some species are more tolerant of these changes than others.

A few species, such as some cockroach and worm species, seem to thrive on them. But the majority of invertebrate species cannot survive these changes. Either they die outright or they become weaker or less capable of reproducing so that their populations gradually decline.

One by one, populations disappear until the species itself is no more. In humanity's conscious efforts to safeguard endangered wildlife, the policy emphasis has been to try to protect and preserve particular species. In fact, in most cases, the decline of one conspicuous species is only a sample of the decline being experienced simultaneously by many other less conspicuous species in the same ecosystem. This is especially true for the nearly invisible invertebrates. Increasing efforts to understand and protect entire ecosystems and their included habitats is certainly the wisest approach. This approach is most likely to save not only the conspicuous species, but also the many others in its environment with which it is interdependent.

Water habitats

It is not possible in one essay to discuss every invertebrate habitat and its microhabitats, all the many invertebrate species that are threatened in those habitats, and some measures that can be taken to stop or reverse present destructive trends. However, one example of invertebrates living in running water may serve to illustrate the overall problem.

Fresh water is of critical importance to all terrestrial organisms, including humans. People need fresh water to drink, to irrigate crops, to transport goods by boat, to provide recreation for fishing and boating, to remove dissolved or suspended wastes, and to drive generators for electrical power. At the same time, a stream is the very lifeline of the countryside that surrounds it. Streams provide a unique habitat for thousands of invertebrate species.

Few streams have been studied intensively to discover all the invertebrate species that live in them. However, there is a small stream in Germany about three feet (1 meter) wide, flowing through pastures and woods, that was studied for nearly 20 years. In that time, 1,044 species of invertebrates were found living in it. About the same time, a stream about 32 feet (10 meters) wide in the sand hills of South Carolina was studied for 15 years; over 650 species of insects were found in that stream (one of the most common species there, a caddis fly, *Cheumatopsyche richardsoni*, is found nowhere else on Earth).

Biologically diverse stream communities are in grave danger. North American rivers once were habitat for the richest freshwater mollusk fauna in the world. These streams were well stocked with species of river snails, mussels, and clams. Today, habitat destruction due to construction of dams and pollution is causing catastrophic losses, such that only a few hardy species are likely to survive much longer.

Some of the major causes for declines in freshwater invertebrate species around the world include engineering projects such as construction of dams, diversion of waterways, artificial channelization of streams to straighten and deepen them, and drainage of wetlands; sedimentation (the clogging of waterways) from roadbuilding and other earthmoving activities, and from runoff over soil exposed by agriculture and deforestation; organic pollution from human and animal sewage; toxic and heavy metal pollution from industries, agricultural fertilizers and pesticides; and cutting of streamside vegetation. Cutting streamside vegetation causes water temperature extremes, wider fluctuations of water levels, and loss of the leaves and branches that fall into streams and provide most of the food energy for their invertebrates (and thus food loss for the fish and other animals that eat them). Because streams have a natural flushing action, it is possible to help streams recover by stopping the source of pollution and by restoring the natural physical habitat. Restoring the physical habitat may include the diversion of water into small wetlands, cutting new stream meanders, adding cobble to revive riffles, and reintroducing stream vegetation. If there are nearby watersheds that still have a diverse community of invertebrates, natural diversity may be at least partly restored in the stream that was damaged.

The future
Invertebrates are an important part of Earth's ecosystems. Much research is needed to find the many invertebrate species that are still unknown and to learn about their requirements. There are still questions about how invertebrates are affected by human activities.

Much remains unknown, but a lot can be done to halt the loss of species (50 to 150 each day). Studies are urgently needed to establish how to change the way we treat our streams and other ecosystems.

John C. Morse

Marine world

MARINE SCIENCE IS still in its infancy; our knowledge of the oceans and their interconnection with the rest of Earth is still growing. While our increasing awareness of the oceans may be reassuring, at the same time we are also learning that the oceans are not as vast as they once seemed. Human activities have had profound effects on the oceans, and we have much to learn about their influence on the rest of the planet.

Artificially segregated on maps and divided by name for human convenience, the world's oceans actually comprise one immense body of water. Much larger than any other single entity on Earth and covering two-thirds of its surface, this great ocean is tied intimately to our lives and the lives of all other animals, plants, and bacteria. When viewed from a coastal beach, the ocean appears to be one uniform body. In fact this marine colossus has distinct zones that provide different habitats for various life-forms. Bathed in life-giving sunlight and atmospheric oxygen, the surface of the ocean is teeming with biological activity. This top layer or zone is only several hundred feet thick; at lower depths, it is dark. Far from being uniformly spread across this zone, plants and animals tend to congregate on the shore, where ocean and land meet. Despite plenty of light, the surface of the ocean far from land is relatively unpopulated because nutrients from landmasses and deep-ocean up- welling currents provide richer, more productive environments along the coasts.

Below the frantic pace of life at the surface, however, the character of the ocean changes. The next zone down is characterized by distinct layers of water that vary slightly in salinity and density. Unlike at the surface, little mixing occurs here.

Fish, mammals, and crustaceans migrate to and from this middle zone on a regular basis. These creatures are well adapted to the near absolute darkness of depths that are measured in thousands of feet. Many species, particularly those that feed on plant material, depend largely on the productivity of surface waters for their sustenance. Deep-swimming, air-breathing mammals such as whales move to and from the surface frequently, but other animals avoid the light and move to the surface only at night.

The ocean's deep trenches and plains (known as abyssal zones) are probably the least well understood zones because they are so hard for human beings to observe. The Mariana Trench in the Pacific reaches a depth of over 36,000 feet (11,000 meters). Modern technology is only now beginning to allow people to explore the ocean floor using deep-sea diving machines.

What scientists have found is somewhat surprising. The ocean floor is less densely populated than the surface, but it is far from lifeless.

Volcanic activity is not confined to landmasses, and it plays a significant role in the patterns of life at the bottom of the sea. Vents that spew not only heat but minerals and other nutrients fuel a wide diversity of life-forms, including bacteria, invertebrates, and bizarre-looking fish.

The surface and coastal zone, mid-level zone, and abyssal zone are loosely linked by ocean currents. Generated by the heating and cooling of water and by Earth's rotation, ocean currents mix and move huge quantities of water.

Ocean productivity

Because of its size, the ocean, along with its resources, might seem inexhaustible. To satisfy some of the food needs of the world, people devised ships, machines, tactics, and gear large enough and efficient enough to bring home the catch. Only human ingenuity—not the availability of the ocean's bounty —could limit the take. Over many generations, fishing gear and techniques improved, as did the catch of finfish, shellfish, and marine mammals such as whales and seals. This trend continued until the 19th and 20th centuries, when fishers and whalers began to see dramatic declines in their catch. They therefore devised better gear and larger boats, not knowing that they were fishing themselves out of jobs. It was discovered that the ocean does have limits on its productivity, and that fishers were exceeding those limits. Fish and mammal stocks were depleted to a point where natural reproduction could not meet the demand. Traditionally, fishers have resisted placing limits on their catch. But in this day of drift nets, purse seines, sonar, and inertial navigation, the odds are heavily stacked in the fisher's favor. Restraint is the only reasonable solution to the maintenance of natural ocean stocks.

While fishing gear and tactics are supposed to be selective, fishers cannot totally eliminate the incidental catch of unwanted fish or marine mammals, known as by-catch. Not only are targeted species threatened by overfishing, but also those species prone to by-catch. The fishing industry is under political pressure to reduce by-catch. One example is the capture of dolphins in tuna nets. Some American companies advertise that their tuna is caught with techniques that do not harm dolphins.

For many fish species, open-water fishing is not the only

The decorator crab (*Macropodia* sp.) is well camouflaged on soft coral.

challenge to their survival. Those species that spend part of their life in fresh or brackish water, such as Pacific and Atlantic salmon and striped bass, also contend with many stresses, including dams that change water quality and block spawning migrations, industrial and municipal pollution, the destruction of streams, and pressure by sport fishers.

The world's refuse dump

The ocean is not inexhaustible. For centuries it has been used as a dumping ground for every form of human refuse. Marine pollution has led to real doubts about the safety of consuming products of the sea or using its other resources. In some cases, marine pollution threatens the survival of entire species. Contaminants and debris found in the ocean, include domestic sewage, agricultural pesticides and other synthetic chemicals, biological waste from hospitals, radioactive materials, garbage dumped from barges, and petroleum from accidental spills and shipwrecks. Most pollution is restricted to the coastal areas where the greatest mass of both humans and sea creatures live, so we poison the very systems that we rely upon most for our continued survival. An "out of sight, out of mind" attitude has existed for too long, and humanity is now seeing the results. Many coastal oyster beds have high bacterial counts. Beaches are frequently closed for the same reason. Lobsters have open wounds, with chemical pollution the suspected cause.

It takes decades to recover from such disasters as the grounding of the *Exxon Valdez* in Alaska, which fouled hundreds of miles of beach with crude oil and killed thousands of birds, fish, and mammals. Less well known are many smaller petroleum-related incidents elsewhere. Strangled gulls and other aquatic birds and mammals wash up on the shore with plastic soda-can rings around their necks. Marine biologists speculate that noise from shipping traffic may adversely affect the ability of whales to communicate over long distances. These problems will worsen unless humanity takes a harder look at its activities.

One more major concern about the marine environment regards world weather patterns and the human factor in global warming. Earth's atmosphere and the ocean are inexorably linked. The ocean has a profound effect on, and indeed controls, weather patterns here on Earth. From hurricanes to blizzards, from hot and dry summers to

Hard and soft corals found in the waters around the Solomon Islands in the South Pacific.

cold and wet winters, the ocean and its cycles play a significant role in influencing global weather daily. An unusually dramatic example is a phenomenon called El Niño. In an unexplained and fairly unpredictable manner, this weather pattern periodically occurs in the Pacific over tropical waters at the equator. Under normal circumstances, an atmospheric low-pressure zone parks itself over the western Pacific near the island of New Guinea. Winds then flow in a westerly direction from South America to fill the low-pressure zone. In the process, these winds drag with them warm surface waters that literally begin to pile up in the western Pacific. Fertile, cold subsurface waters then flow toward the surface along the coast of South America to fill the void. Under the conditions of El Niño, the Pacific low-pressure system moves east to a position much closer to the South American coast. The westerly winds reverse direction to the east and push warm surface water toward Ecuador, Peru, and Colombia. Historically, this dramatic shift has been responsible for disastrous fishing seasons, as well as for flooding in North and South America and drought in places as far-flung as Mexico, Australia, Indonesia, and southern Africa.

Given the relationship between atmosphere and ocean, researchers want to know more about the possible effects of increased carbon dioxide in the atmosphere. Carbon dioxide is a by-product of the burning of wood, natural gas, oil, coal, and other fossil fuels. Each year, millions of tons of carbon dioxide are pumped into the atmosphere as energy products for industry, commerce, and homes are consumed. Airborne carbon dioxide increases the greenhouse effect by trapping the Sun's radiation within our atmosphere. Our atmosphere does this naturally, but whether the oceans are minimizing the greenhouse effect or being overwhelmed by it is not yet possible to determine.

During the late 1900s scientists noticed that coral reefs were becoming bleached. The coral polyps were dying off because they were losing their symbiotic algae, which live within the polyps and provide nutrients. The corals are very sensitive to changes in sea temperatures, and higher-than-normal temperatures, thought to be a symbol of general global warming, is believed to be the cause. The long-term implications for the future health of coral reefs and the animals that depend on them is not known.

There are potentially devastating side effects. Investigators have found that over the 20th century, the concentration of carbon dioxide in Earth's atmosphere rose significantly. This could be responsible for an increase in the average global temperature. If the temperature is rising, some speculate that the polar ice caps could partially melt and release more water into the oceans, thereby raising average sea levels. The threat of flooding to coastal cities and low-lying areas could be severe. Others theorize that ocean currents might slow their rate of movement as warmer ocean waters like the North Atlantic Gulf Stream sink more slowly toward the bottom. The likelihood of this occurrence, or its implications for global weather, is also uncertain.

Carbon dioxide is absorbed by the ocean, and there is debate as to the impact of the greenhouse effect. Scientists do not completely understand the capacity of the ocean to absorb the excess carbon dioxide that humans produce. There is an enormous capacity within the ocean system to absorb and retain carbon dioxide in dissolved form. Researchers want to learn more about how carbon dioxide affects productivity in the oceans. Many variables make it difficult to calculate how the ocean will change if there is an uninterrupted period of global warming.

The future

The marine environment is of such tremendous scope that it will require study for centuries to come. There is doubt as to the eventual outcome of our use and abuse of the ocean system.

Like the sailors of yesteryear, today's explorers seek knowledge. Instead of wooden ships, their tools are deep-water submersibles, tethered robots, automated water sample analyzers, and orbital satellites. The data obtained may provide us with a future that is economically healthy; but more significantly, a detailed understanding of our oceans will allow us to make better informed judgments about the current state of our planet. What is certain is that the ocean will continue to play a role in the life of every organism on this planet. We can only hope that the ocean receives the respect and understanding it deserves.

William E. Manci

Polar regions

THE LANDS AND OCEANS that lie near Earth's poles were not always ice and snow. Millions of years ago they were places of warmth where trees and plants grew. Theory has it that approximately 200 million years ago, a single landmass known as Pangaea began to split apart and drift north and south. These smaller landmasses were spread apart by the formation of new crust deep under the oceans. By 50 million years ago, all of the continents reached their present positions. The lands near the poles began to grow cold because other landmasses blocked the ocean currents that brought warmth. A crust of ice formed over Antarctica five million years ago; another over the Arctic Ocean three million years ago.

The Arctic ice cap spread over what is now North America, Europe, and Siberia, as far south as the present locations of New York and London. Sometimes a warm break in the global climate occurs during an ice age (like the one Earth is currently enjoying) hot enough to melt some of the ice caps. Scientists predict that another ice age will return in a thousand years or so, when the polar ice caps will once again spread toward the equator.

During the year, Earth tilts on its axis in its orbit around the Sun. Six months out of the year, either the North Pole or the South Pole is continually facing the Sun; that is when the sun never sets. As a result, these lands within the Arctic and Antarctic Circles are nicknamed the lands of the midnight sun. Even though the Sun's rays are directed nonstop at the poles during these months, the poles remain forever frozen. The angle at which Earth tilts causes the Sun's rays to cast a weak light, and the atmosphere absorbs much of the Sun's heat. Although there are six months of sunshine, there are also six months of night. The long winter at the poles creates a cold, dry climate, and a habitat suited to only the hardiest wildlife.

The Arctic

The region that circles the North Pole is called the Arctic, but there is no polar continent here. Arctic lands, such as northern Alaska, Canada, Norway, Greenland, Iceland, Siberia, and some small archipelagos, ring the Arctic Ocean, making it nearly landlocked. The smallest and least salty of the world's oceans, the Arctic Ocean dominates this polar basin, covering 5.5 million square miles (14.3 million square kilometers). Most of the Arctic Ocean is perpetually frozen, covered in great sheets of ice. In summer, some of this sea ice melts. Large chunks of land ice (icebergs) break off the mountainous glaciers of Greenland and Spitsbergen and float out to sea; some of these icebergs are remnants of the last Ice Age. When icebergs are spotted on the sea, ships give them wide berth, for as much as 90 percent of an iceberg's mass is underwater. Only the top is visible above the surface. Icebergs have sunk many vessels over the centuries.

Far north in the Arctic zone only mosses, lichens, and grasses can endure the harsh weather. Farther south, on the treeless plains (tundra), plants abound during the short summer. The tundra is the next warmest ecological zone after the Arctic, extending across Alaska, Canada, Greenland, Norway, and Siberia. Even though there are many streams, bogs, and crystalline lakes, it rarely rains there. Cold, dry winds sweep over the plains, making the climate nearly desertlike. A feature of the tundra is its permanently frozen subsoil (permafrost). Frozen all winter, the tundra is boggy in summer. Then the thin top layer above the permafrost thaws, and hundreds of flowers bloom. Many tundra plants such as poppy, heather, dandelion, blue-grass, sage, bluebell, and timothy have relatives in temperate climates.

All Arctic organisms are dependent on other plant life and animals, and although the polar habitat does not have the variety of plant and animal life of a temperate zone, more than nine hundred plant species, three hundred species of moss, and two hundred types of lichen live in the Arctic. Some Arctic animals are vegetarians, like the caribou, lemming, hare, musk-ox, and ground squirrel; others are carnivores, like the fox, wolf, weasel, snowy owl, and polar bear.

Human inhabitants

For thousands of years, the Inuit or Eskimo Indians have lived in the northern parts of Canada,

1718

Alaska, and Greenland. Other nomadic groups such as the Lapps in northern Sweden and Yakuts in northern Siberia hunted reindeer and harpooned sea mammals for food and clothing. Once famous for building igloos, kayaks, and dogsleds, and for making clothes from sealskin, many Inuit today have adopted modern lifestyles. They work in the oil and mining industries, live in houses with electricity, shoot seals from boats, and wear manufactured clothing. Some remember and preserve old customs and hunting skills, but these traditions are rarely practiced.

Antarctica

Antarctica, which means "opposite the Arctic," is a continent at the South Pole that is covered by an ice cap 2 miles (3.2 kilometers) thick. This giant landmass,

This picture shows tundra vegetation in Richardson Mountains, Yukon Territory, Canada, during the summer months.

almost twice as big as Oceania (Australia, New Zealand, Melanesia, Micronesia, Polynesia), remains the most isolated of the continents. It was not discovered until 1820, when an American, Captain Nathaniel B. Palmer, made the first sighting of the Antarctic continent. Its climate prevented exploration until an American named Charles Wilkes went there in 1840. Mountain ranges rivaling the Rockies and Alps, ice shelves, and five volcanos, are some of Antarctica's geographical features, as well as the surrounding frozen oceans. During four winter months of each year, the Sun does not shine on Antarctica. Blizzards and fierce gales of 200 miles (320 kilometers) per hour rage across the central plateau, making Antarctica's climate the harshest on Earth, with the world's lowest recorded temperature of minus 128 degrees Fahrenheit (minus 53 degrees

Centigrade) in July 1983. Antarctica is also the driest place on Earth. Some places in Antarctica have had no rain for two million years. Nevertheless, some wildlife does survive in this harsh environment. Bacteria, moss, lichen, two flowering plant species, and a small, wingless insect species called a springtail live there. No vertebrate animals sustain life on the Antarctic continent, but large numbers of whales, seals, penguins, and birds such as petrels and skuas live in the neighboring seas and along the coasts. The Arctic tern is a regular visitor. It makes the flight of 11,000 miles (17,700 kilometers) each year from the North to the South Pole, always traveling with the Sun.

Although increasing numbers of scientists from around the world study at bases in Antarctica, no humans make permanent homes on this vast wasteland. The continent's barrenness pro-

tects it from human pollution from ships and settlements. For many years, Antarctica's remoteness and extreme cold made it a dumping place for dangerous nuclear waste, but the 1959 Antarctic Treaty forbade this practice. Any disturbance to the interaction between plants and animals on this highly isolated continent could spell disaster.

Ecological balance

There is a delicate balance of nature in all habitats, and the polar regions are no exception. The search for oil and minerals, hunting of sea mammals, and threats to lower forms of life that support the food chain are degrading the once pristine environments of the Arctic and Antarctic. Ozone, a form of oxygen in Earth's upper atmosphere that protects the planet from the Sun's rays, is thinning. This means that more ultraviolet light could reach Earth's surface, increasing harm to all life. In 1987 the nations of the world took steps to reduce chemical emissions causing ozone breakdown; this action is known as the Montreal Protocol on Substances that Deplete the Ozone Layer. In the 1990s scientific research added to the knowledge and understanding of the processes that led to the depletion of the ozone layer. However, early in the 21st century it is still not possible to determine if the steps are working. The ozone layer continues to show signs of depletion in the Antarctic and Arctic.

Polar hunters

More than a century ago, American and European whalers and sealers decimated populations of whales and seals. These mammals were harvested for their valuable pelts and oil. Many species of animals have been hunted to extinction, such as the Steller's sea cow and the auk, a flightless bird. Some whales nearly met the same fate, including the narwhal, an Arctic whale whose ivory tusks were once prized. Hundreds of thousands of adult and young fur seals were clubbed to death, and not enough of them survived to reproduce. The polar bear was hunted nearly into oblivion, although its numbers are now increasing due to strict controls.

Huge ships called vacuum trawlers moor for months at a time in Arctic waters, scooping up vast quantities of fish.

It was estimated that by the mid-1980s, 90 percent of Antarctic cod was sucked into these cavernous ships. Krill, tiny shrimplike fish, are also harvested for human consumption. This disturbs the balance in the food chain, because the diet of whales, penguins, and other fish is comprised largely of krill.

Many larger animals are dependent on lower members of the food chain, especially a tiny ocean plant called phytoplankton. These small plants absorb energy from the Sun and nutrients from the mineral salts in the ocean; they form the basic food for birds, and fish, and some whales. Larger animals, such as penguins and seals, feed on the fish that feed on phytoplankton. Still larger animals, such as polar bears and killer whales, eat seals, so it is important that the phytoplankton remains plentiful. This is another reason scientists are concerned about the loss of ozone in Earth's atmosphere. Natural disasters, such as the eruption of volcanos, spew particles into the air that break up ozone molecules over Antarctica. These ozone holes allow ultraviolet light to penetrate to the marine-rich waters of Antarctica, and destroy some phytoplankton.

These are not the only dangers to the food chain. The world's reliance on oil is keenly felt in the Arctic as the search for it continues. Already the huge Alaskan oil pipeline cuts a swath across the tundra, interrupting the migration routes of caribou. A great risk is a huge spill from the pipeline or an oil well that could poison rivers, lakes, and the ocean. Thousands of caribou, birds, fish, and delicate tundra vegetation could die, drastically affecting the future of the Arctic.

There were two serious accidents in the 20th century. In January 1989, an Argentine ship leaked diesel fuel into the waters off the Antarctic Peninsula, killing thousands of krill, penguins, and other wildlife. The long-term effects of the spill reduced animal populations for years to come. Two months later, in March 1989, in the pristine waters of Prince William Sound in Alaska (south of the Arctic Circle), the tanker *Exxon Valdez* went off course and hit a reef, spilling 10 million gallons (about 38 million liters) of oil and spreading an oil slick that covered 1,600 square miles (4,144 square kilometers) of water and 800 miles (1,290 kilometers) of shoreline. This disaster killed thousands of otters, deer, ducks, and eagles outright, but posed a far greater risk for future generations of animals. The poisons in the crude oil continued to contaminate marine microorganisms that feed mollusks and salmon, and the poison was passed on to birds, deer, and brown bears.

Hundreds of thousands of tourists travel by plane, ship, rail, and ferry through the Alaskan and Canadian tundra yearly. This lucrative industry has taken a toll on the breeding grounds of many birds. Large snow vehicles that transport tourists to view polar bears at close range scar the fragile Arctic ground. Garbage idly thrown overboard from tourist ships pollutes Arctic waters.

Vested interest
Yet the debate between environmentalists, oil excavators, and lawmakers continues. United States senators decided in February 1992 to amend a bill to protect the environment in Alaska's Arctic National Wildlife Refuge. They believe that

Alaska's economy would be bolstered by as many as 10,000 jobs if the coastal plain were opened for oil and gas drilling. Environmentalists believe the wildlife will suffer from this energy policy.

Strides have been made to save the polar wilderness, however, despite the international debate. Individuals, companies, and conservation organizations have recognized the danger in unlimited plunder and exploration of the polar regions and have begun to work in unison to save them.

A plan instigated by oil companies raised parts of the Alaska pipeline onto bridges, permitting caribou to walk under it unhindered. Quotas for threatened fish and mammals have been set that restrict the number of animals that can be killed yearly.

Polar bears and endangered whales—blue, right, and humpback—are no longer hunted.

Many European countries have stopped buying sealskin and as a result, the killing of seals has dramatically declined.

Vital treaty
Twenty-six nations signed a 1991 treaty to protect the icy continent of Antarctica. The treaty bans mining, oil exploration, and nuclear explosions; regulates waste disposal; conserves marine resources; and protects native plants and animals on the continent for the next 50 years.

The signing of this treaty is important not only to Antarctica, but to the whole world. It reflects a growing awareness that all types of habitats are interconnected, and that all creatures—from blue whales to humans to phytoplankton—should be protected, nourished and sustained by their interdependence on one another.

Cecilia Fannon

Wetlands

THEY GO BY THE names fen, wet meadow, bog, marsh, swamp, slough, prairie pothole, creek, river, pond, reservoir, lake, beach, and estuary. Collectively, these natural wonderlands are called wetlands.

Water and life
The common thread around which life revolves in all wetlands is water—the most abundant chemical compound on our planet's surface. With two-thirds of Earth being covered by this precious liquid, it is no wonder that all life, whether it is animal,

plant, or bacteria, depends upon water for its survival. Without the existence of water, life as we know it would be impossible. Only oxygen is more important in terms of sustaining our existence. People can survive several weeks without food, but without water, death is measured in days.

As the dominant species on the planet, human beings have almost always placed their interests and need for water above those of other animals and plants. Partially because of necessity as well as lack of knowledge about the environment, people

have often used water with little regard for ecological consequences. Not surprisingly, water supplies—including wetlands—were once thought of as too vast and plentiful to be seriously affected by our activities. However, in the past two or three thousand years (a short period in all of human existence), as our population and demand for resources rapidly increased, people have made a significant impact on water systems and the organisms these systems support.

The diversity of life in wetlands ranges from single-celled

An American alligator (*Alligator mississipiensis*) watched by a white heron, basks in the Everglades, Florida.

creatures to large carnivores, and the web of life that has evolved around wetlands is formidable. Wetlands support freshwater and saltwater fish of all kinds; crustaceans and mollusks such as crayfish and oysters; microscopic crustaceans called plankton; amphibians, including frogs and salamanders; reptiles such as alligators and turtles; birds such as ducks and herons; mammals such as beavers and otters; and a variety of unusual creatures such as Australia's duck-billed platypus and the muskratlike nutria of the South American rain forest. Then there is the most diverse group: insects.

Different wetlands

The range in wetland types is enormous. Three criteria are used to define wetland areas: veg-etation type, soil type, and the degree to which the soil is saturated or covered with water. Wetlands support plants such as cattail and algae, which grow best in water or saturated soil. These regions contain soils that are unique to wetlands such as peat; they are saturated or flooded with water for at least part of the year. This classification system is not restricted to freshwater environments; it includes brackish water (diluted saltwater) as well as coastal marine (saltwater) areas. These wetland regions are defined below.

• *Marine systems.*
Marine wetlands include shoreline areas, bays, coastal salt marshes, mangrove thickets, and other coastal zones that receive insignificant amounts of fresh water. They are strongly affected by tides, waves, and currents. Some of these areas become completely exposed at low tide or as waves ebb after breaking on shore. But they remain saturated with water, more or less, on a continual basis.

• *Estuarine systems.*
An estuary is the boundary region between a freshwater stream and the saltwater marine system into which it flows. These brackish-water areas experience tidal activity like the marine systems. They are partially drained and exposed on a regular basis. Runoff from surrounding land as well as flow from the stream can contribute to dilution of the seawater in an estuary (especially in

the periodically exposed tidal regions).

• *Riverine systems.*

Riverine systems include natural or human-made open channels that usually carry flowing water from one standing-water body to another. These freshwater systems can be dry during certain times of the year, but as with all wetland systems, they are dominated by wetland plants and soils. There is some debate as to whether all floodplains adjacent to rivers should be included as part of riverine systems. Those areas that are flooded regularly (seasonally) can be included.

• *Lacustrine systems.*

Lacustrine wetland systems are formed as water collects in depressions or when a stream channel is dammed. More commonly called lakes, ponds, and reservoirs, lacustrine systems are deep and are generally greater than 20 acres (8 hectares) in total surface area. They can also be smaller water bodies with a minimum water depth of no less than about 7 feet (2 meters). These wetlands usually have a well-defined shoreline that is significantly influenced by wave action. Intermittent or so-called playa lakes (usually found in desert areas) are in this category; so are coastal plain tidal lakes (those with water levels that are influenced by ocean tides but contain very low-salinity water).

• *Palustrine systems.*

Palustrine systems include all wetlands not influenced by tides but rather are dominated by water-loving trees, shrubs, and other wetland vegetation. Many marshes, bogs, fens, wet meadows, and swamps are classified as palustrine systems.

The role of wetlands

The benefits derived from wetlands are many. Wetlands contribute not only to plant and animal populations but to human life as well. Wetlands, particularly marshes and swamps, reduce or totally eliminate the threat of flooding in many areas by absorbing floodwaters and releasing them slowly into lakes and rivers. The abundant plants in many wetlands hold and stabilize soil and prevent harmful erosion caused by floodwaters, ocean storms and tides, and heavy rains.

Wetlands offer recreational and educational opportunities unparalleled in other environments. Fishers, duck hunters, birders, researchers, and educators spend billions of dollars and millions of hours each year visiting wetlands and enjoying the diversity of plant and animal life there. Because of their diverse range of animal life, both above and below the water surface, these unique ecosystems have contributed greatly to our understanding of nature and its dynamics.

As natural water filters, wetlands have no equal. They have the ability to cleanse water of pollutants, a quality put to use in unique ways. For example, urban water and sanitation districts are using wetlands as part of their treatment and filtration process. This is an efficient and cost-effective way to reduce pollution.

Formerly seen as barriers to agricultural development, wetlands are now being maintained instead of drained to make room for row crops. They provide water storage for irrigation and for cattle and can be modified to raise valuable aquatic crops such as catfish, shrimp, rice, seaweed, and even algae. Algae are used to provide specialized food products, lubricants, and other valuable commercial and industrial goods. Arguably, the most important benefit of wetlands is the food, habitat, and water they provide to plants and animals. Not surprisingly, given the value and importance of wetlands to the planet, almost 35 percent of all threatened and endangered plants and animals in the United States depend upon these areas for their survival.

Their changing faces

The pressures put on wetlands by an exploding human population have been enormous. Rather than treating wetlands with care, shortsighted landowners as well as government institutions have been systematically altering these vital living systems. This has been done in the name of progress, but the end result is often to the detriment of the local human population. North America's Great Lakes serve as a prime example of what can occur.

For millennia, wetlands have served as the waste dump for human refuse, including some of the most toxic chemicals ever formulated. For decades, some commonly used industrial compounds called polychlorinated biphenyls (PCBs) were allowed to enter the Great Lakes system. Through a process called bioaccumulation, high levels of PCBs were reaching the diets of people eating Great Lakes salmon. Rather than being diluted in the lakes, the compounds were being incorporated into small organisms at the bottom of the food chain. The poisons became concentrated on their way up the chain. At the top of this aquatic ecosystem sat the salmon, which, when consumed by unsuspecting salmon lovers, exposed them to alarming levels of a known cancer-causing agent. The same chain of events can happen in other wetland environments.

Altered wetlands

Water diversion, stream damming, and stream channelization are three of the most destructive forms of alteration that can occur to wetlands. Diversion of water for agricultural purposes is a common practice that would at first seem entirely beneficial. Water from the Colorado River has been used for decades to irrigate crops in dry desert regions of the United States. However, large dams across the Colorado River, such as the Glen Canyon and Hoover Dams in Arizona, have forever altered the river's habitat for valuable native fish. Once free-flowing with warm, murky water, the Colorado now offers long stretches of cold and clear-water environments for which native fish are not suited. Additionally, water diversion totally eliminated flow at the mouth of the river. Once a productive estuary, the Colorado River delta is now a dried-up wasteland.

In central Florida, water diversions and pollution threaten the very existence of the Everglades. In Louisiana, channelization and diking of the Mississippi River may help reduce flooding in populated areas, but reduction in fresh water flow to the state's southern coastal marshes has caused the salinity of the water to rise. This has significantly reduced overall productivity of the region, to the detriment of those who harvest fish, oysters, and shrimp. And while dams on the Columbia River in Washington and Oregon produce cheap electricity, they have also had a severe impact on salmon runs, which are tourist attractions and economic mainstays of the area.

Finally, even activities outside wetlands can have devastating effects within these systems. Deforestation by lumber or agriculture in areas adjacent to wetlands can turn clear and productive streams and estuaries into muddy and relatively sterile channels. Soil erosion and sedimentation—the by-products of timber cutting and farming—slowly smother wetland inhabitants.

Additionally, sedimentation hastens the aging of lakes and marshes that receive runoff and can cause biological havoc in what is an otherwise stable and balanced system.

What have we learned?

Clearly, some hard lessons have been learned through the processes of studying and observing wetlands. We now know that poorly planned human development and disregard for natural systems lead to decreased diversity. The trickle-down effect is profound and far-reaching.

These systems are not infinite, nor are they capable of absorbing whatever blows people might inflict upon them. Rather, they are finite and a true barometer of our planet's health.

Manipulation of wetlands and ecosystems can have damaging long-term effects. The interconnection between land, water, and air is more complex than we yet fully understand. As a species at the top of the food chain, we need to understand and appreciate these relationships as much as possible.

There is a popular saying, "waste flows downhill." For the most part this saying is true, but in many ways it is misleading. Just as in the case of the Great Lakes salmon, wastes such as PCBs that flow downhill to wetland environments like Lake Michigan do not necessarily stay there. By passing through the food chain they can eventually make their way back up to humans. Appreciation of this unbroken chain is vital. It is necessary for people to care for the health and well-being of wetlands and the plants and animals that inhabit them, because just like those plants and animals, humans are inextricably linked to all living creatures through a common thread—water.

Working with nature

While it is technically impossible and politically unrealistic to turn the clock back on many of the changes people have imposed on wetlands, we can begin to act differently. Rather than dominating, destroying, or controlling wetlands, we can develop imaginative ways to work with natural wetland systems to the benefit of all of their inhabitants and users.

In the process, we will not only ensure that other plants and animals will survive and thrive, but we will create a sustainable and stable environment for ourselves as well.

William E. Manci

GLOSSARY

achene: a small dry, one-seeded fruit

actinopterygii: the Latin scientific name for fish

albino: any organism lacking color in the skin or fur; albino species have pink eyes, while albino fish often have no functioning eyes

amphibia: the Latin scientific name for amphibians

apically: relating to, or situated at the apex

arboreal: living in or adapted for living in trees; arboreal animals seldom, if ever, descend to the ground (see terrestrial)

aves: the Latin scientific name for birds

barbels: a slender growth on the mouths or nostrils of certain fishes, used as a sensory organ for touch

bipedal: any organism that walks on two feet

bract: a leaf at the base of a flower stalk in plants

buff: in bird species, a yellow-white color used to describe the plumage

calyx: the green outer whorl of a flower made up of sepals

captive breeding: any method of bringing several animals of the same species into a zoo or other closed environment for the purpose of mating; if successful, these methods can increase the population of that species

carnivore: any flesh-eating animal

carnivorous: flesh eating

carpel: known as the pistil, it is the female reproductive organ, made up of an ovary, stigma, and style

clutch, clutch size: the number of eggs laid during one nesting cycle

corolla: the separate petals, or the fused petals of a flower

cotyledon: the first leaf developed by the embryo of a seed plant

deciduous: dropping off, falling off during a certain season or at a regular stage of growth; deciduous trees shed their leaves annually

decurved: curving downward; a bird's beak is decurved if it points toward the ground

defoliate: to strip trees and bushes of their leaves

deforestation: the process of removing trees from a particular area

diurnal: active during the day; some animals are diurnal, while others are active at night (see nocturnal)

dominance: the ability to overpower the behavior of other individuals; an animal is dominant if it affects others of its own species in a way that benefits itself; also, the trait of abundance that determines the character of a plant community:

grasses dominate a prairie, and trees dominate a forest

dorsal: pertaining to or situated on the back of an organism; a dorsal fin is on the back of a fish

ecology: the study of the interrelationship between a living organism and its environment

ecosystem: a community of animals, plants, and bacteria and its interrelated physical and chemical environment

endemic: native to a particular geographic region

estrous: the time period when female mammals can become pregnant

exotic species: a plant or animal species that is not native to its habitat

feral: a wild animal that is descended from tame or domesticated species

filament: the stalk of a stamen with an anther at the tip

forest: a plant community in which trees grow closely enough together that their crowns interlock to form a continuous overhead canopy

fry: young fish

gene pool: the total hereditary traits available within a group; when isolated from other members of their species, individual organisms may produce healthy offspring if there is enough variety in the genes available

through mating

gestation: the period of active embryonic growth inside a mammal's body between the time the embryo attaches to the uterus and the time of birth; some mammals carry dormant embryos for several weeks or months before the embryo attaches to the uterus and begins to develop actively, and this dormancy period is not part of the gestation period; gestation period is the length of a pregnancy

granivore: any seed-feeding animal

granivorous: seed feeding

guano: manure, especially of sea birds and bats

habitat: the environment where a species is normally found; habitat degradation is the decline in quality of a species' home until it can no longer survive there

herbivore: any plant-eating animal

herbivorous: plant eating

hibernate: to spend the winter season in a dormant or inactive state; some species hibernate to save energy during months when food is scarce

hybrid: the offspring of two different species who mate; see interbreed

hybridization: the gradual decline of a species through continued breeding with another species; see interbreed

immature(s): a young bird that has not yet reached breeding maturity; it usually has plumage differing from an adult bird of the same species

in captivity: a species that exists in zoos, captive breeding programs, or in private collections, perhaps because the species can no longer be found in the wild

incubation: the period when an egg is kept warm until the embryo develops and hatches

indigenous species: any species native to its habitat

inflorescence: a group of flowers that grow from one point

insecta: the Latin scientific name for insects

insular species: a species isolated on an island or islands

interbreed: when two separate species mate and produce offspring; see hybrid

invertebrate(s): any organism without a backbone (spinal column)

juvenal: a bird with an intermediate set of feathers after its young downy plumage molts and before growing hard, adult feathers

juvenile(s): a young bird or other animal not yet mature

litter: the animals born to a species that normally produces several young at birth

lore(s): the irregularly shaped facial area of a bird between the eye and the base of the beak

migrate, migratory: to move from one range to another, particularly with the change of seasons; many species are migratory

montane forest: a forest found in mountainous regions

natural selection: the process named by Charles Darwin (1809-1882) to describe how species evolve by such methods as adapting to their environment and evading predators

nocturnal: active at night; some animals are nocturnal, while others are active by day (see diurnal)

nomadic species: a species with no permanent range or territory; nomadic species wander for food and water

offal: waste products or leftovers; usually the internal organs of a slain animal

old growth forest: forest that has not experienced extensive deforestation

omnivore: any species that eats both plants and animals

ornithologist(s): a scientist who studies birds

panicle: compound cluster of flowers

pelage: the hairy covering of a mammal

pelagic: related to the oceans or open sea; pelagic birds rarely roost on land

perennial: persisting for several years

plumage: the feathers that cover a bird

prairie: a plant community without trees and dominated by grasses; a grassland; often incorrectly used synonymously with plain or plains, which is a landform feature and not a plant community

predation: the act of one species hunting another

predator: a species that preys upon other species

primary forest: a forest of native trees that results from natural processes, often called virgin forest

primate(s): a biological ranking of species in the same order, including gorillas, chimpanzees, monkeys, and human beings (Homo sapiens)

range: the geographic area where a species roams

recovery plan(s): any document that outlines a public or private program for assisting an endangered or threatened species

relict: an isolated habitat or population that was once widespread

reptilia: the Latin scientific name for reptiles

riffle(s): a shallow rapid stretch of water caused by a rocky outcropping or

obstruction in a stream

riparian: relating to plants and animals close to and influenced by rivers

roe: fish eggs

rosulate: in a rosette formation

rufous: in bird species, plumage that is orange-brown and pink

secondary forest: a forest that has grown back after cutting, forest fire, or other deforestation; secondary forests may or may not contain exotic tree species, but they almost always differ in character from primary forests

sedentary species: one that does not migrate

sepals: leaflike structures around a bud

terrestrial: living in or adapted for living principally on the ground; some birds are terrestrial and seldom, if ever, ascend into trees (see arboreal)

territory: the area occupied more or less exclusively by an organism or group, usually defended by aggressive displays and physical combat

veld: a grassland region with some scattered bushes and virtually no trees; other terms are *steppe*, *pampas*, and *prairie*

ventral: on or near the belly; the ventral fin is located on the underside of a fish and corresponds with the hind limbs of other vertebrates

vertebrates: any organism that has a backbone (spinal column)

water column: the zone of

a pond, lake, or ocean below the surface and above the bottom that holds free-swimming or free-floating fish and other animals and plants

woodland: a plant community in which trees grow abundantly but far enough apart that their crowns do not intermingle, so no overhead canopy is formed

INDEX

The scientific name of a plant or animal is entered in *italics*; its common name is in roman type. Page numbers in *italics* refer to picture captions.